THE VICE PRESIDENT
AS POLICY MAKER

Recent titles in Contributions in Political Science
Series Editor: Bernard K. Johnpoll

The American Governorship
Coleman B. Ransone, Jr.

Strategic Studies: A Critical Assessment
Colin S. Gray

Keeping a Finger on the Public Pulse: Private Polling and Presidential Elections
Bruce E. Altschuler

The Quest for Nuclear Stability: John F. Kennedy and the Soviet Union
Bernard J. Firestone

The Solzhenitsyn-Sakharov Dialogue: Politics, Society, and the Future
Donald R. Kelley

Governor Rockefeller in New York: The Apex of Pragmatic Liberalism in the
United States
James E. Underwood and William J. Daniels

Neo-Marxism: The Meanings of Modern Radicalism
Robert A. Gorman

The Politics of Pressure: American Arms and Israeli Policy Since the Six Day War
David Pollock

Congress, the Executive Branch, and Special Interests: The American Response to
the Arab Boycott of Israel
Kennan Lee Teslik

Third World Policies of Industrialized Nations
Phillip Taylor and Gregory A. Raymond, editors

''For Immediate Release'': Candidate Press Releases in American Political
Campaigns
Jan Pons Vermeer

THE VICE PRESIDENT AS POLICY MAKER

Rockefeller in the Ford White House

• MICHAEL TURNER •

CONTRIBUTIONS IN POLITICAL SCIENCE, NUMBER 78

GREENWOOD PRESS
WESTPORT, CONNECTICUT • LONDON, ENGLAND

Library of Congress Cataloging in Publication Data

Turner, Michael, 1942–
  The vice president as policy maker.

  (Contributions in political science, ISSN 0147-1066 ;
no. 78)
  Bibliography: p.
  Includes index.
  1. Vice-Presidents—United States. 2. Rockefeller,
Nelson A. (Nelson Aldrich), 1908-1979. 3. United States—
Politics and government—1974-1977. I. Title.
II. Series.
JK609.5.T87 1982   353.03'18'0924   81-20301
ISBN 0-313-23229-6 (lib. bdg.)

Library of Congress Catalog Card Number: 81-20301
ISBN: 0-313-23229-6
ISSN: 0147-1066

First published in 1982

Greenwood Press
A division of Congressional Information Service, Inc.
88 Post Road West
Westport, Connecticut 06881

Printed in the United States of America

10 9 8 7 6 5 4 3 2 1

FOR WENDY

CONTENTS

FIGURES

ACKNOWLEDGMENTS

In completing this study I was assisted and encouraged by the contributions of experience and insight given by many of the political actors involved with Nelson Rockefeller at various levels of the Ford administration. While these are too numerous to list individually here, my thanks is given to all of those listed on pages 242-43.

Special thanks must be given to two individuals without whom this study would not have been possible. First, I would like to record my appreciation of the assistance of the subject of this study, the late Nelson Rockefeller. He not only met with me to discuss his various endeavors and experiences as vice president, but also made available to me his vice presidential papers. Second, I wish to thank Hugh Morrow, former assistant to Nelson A. Rockefeller, for his invaluable help in facilitating access to the former vice president and his vice presidential papers.

My understanding of American politics was assisted greatly by various members of the Department of Political Science at the State University of New York at Binghamton, in particular, Harold Nieburg, Richard Young, and Edward Weisband. I am especially grateful to James P. Young for his sustained encouragement over the years since we were first introduced as professor and undergraduate at the University of Keele, England. Finally, the manuscript benefited greatly from the perceptive eye of Charles Forcey.

In addition, my warm appreciation is expressed to my friends and former colleagues in the Washington Semester Program of the State University of New York: Michael Weaver, Anne Weaver, and Walter Oleszek. My years in Washington, D.C., provided me with the most valuable learning experience of my life, and this was due in large measure to the Weavers.

To my typists, Mrs. Betty Farley, Washington, D.C., who typed an earlier version of this study, and Mrs. Margaret Bright of the Department of Politics and Sociology, Paisley College of Technology, who typed the final draft, goes special appreciation for their capacity to remain calm in the face of crisis.

Finally, to my family goes my warmest appreciation for their support and consideration in the course of this study. My children are probably now among the best informed on the subject of the vice presidency! In thanking my wife, Wendy, for the support, understanding, comfort, and assistance she has provided over the years, I should declare that none of my efforts would have succeeded without her.

INTRODUCTION

The office of Vice President of the United States has long been the butt of music hall humor concerning how little there has been for the vice president to do after his election and inauguration. Sadly, but not without justification, past vice presidents have enlivened the burlesque treatment of this office with their own pithy comments. Thus, Thomas Marshall, discussing the vice president's ex officio position as regent of the Smithsonian Institution, was moved to observe, "There if anything he has an opportunity to compare his fossilized life with the fossils of all ages."[1] While, in 1960, John Nance Garner summed up his experience in the office in counseling Lyndon Johnson at the Democratic Convention: "I'll tell you, Lyndon, the vice presidency isn't worth a pitcher of warm spit."[2]

At bottom, of course, the problem with the office lay in the very evident fact that the Constitution had prescribed no executive branch duties for the vice president. Although the vice president was designated by the framers as the constitutional successor to the president in the event of his death, resignation, or impeachment, all executive power had been vested in the office of the president. The sole constitutionally ordained function assigned to the vice president was to preside over the Senate, with a vote only in the case of a tie. Thus, the constitutional lacuna concerning vice presidential involvement with the executive branch, cojoined with the prescribed Senate role of presiding officer, established the prevailing nineteenth-century view that the vice president was wholly a creature of the legislature. However, because his legislative role was exceedingly minor in nature (and anomalous, since he presides over but is not a member of the Senate), it was of little wonder that the office of vice president failed to achieve distinction or importance.

While there were no sudden shifts away from the prevailing view of the nineteenth century, the twentieth century saw a gradual gravitation of the vice president toward the executive branch. Interaction with the president and his cabinet became established by convention, and vice presidents acquired some presidential duties of modest proportions. Some statutory recognition of the vice president's place within the executive branch came with congressional approval of his membership in the National Security Council under the terms of the National Security Act, 1947.

However, the gradual incorporation of the vice president into the executive branch was not accompanied by substantive involvement in the policy work of the president. Such an absence of policy involvement has been, for some twenty or thirty years, the subject of some discussion and debate among scholarly observers of executive branch institutions and politics. While there was general disquiet about the continued absence of vice presidential policy involvement, two distinct schools of thought developed concerning the conclusions to be drawn from that situation. On the one hand, those skeptical of the utility of the office concluded that because there is so little to justify the continued existence of the office it ought to be abolished, with the provision for presidential succession by means of a special election.[3] On the other hand, proponents of the office, while recognizing its inherent weaknesses, have called for its upgrading, arguing that "the rapid march of events demands a twentieth-century kind of vice president; trained, capable, and informed, to assist the president."[4]

Both schools, while divergent on the resolution of the problem of the vice presidency, have been convergent on the source of the problem: that, as Lord Bryce so aptly put it, the vice president is *"aut nullus aut Caesar."*[5] The vice president's dependency on the president for his role in the administration is the vital point to grasp in understanding the past failure of the office of vice president. The fact is that presidential candidates tend to select running mates for reasons principally concerned with electoral necessities and only minimally (if at all) with vice presidential competence or the dimensions of the vice president's role in the administration. Arthur M. Schlesinger, Jr., has expressed this point well in declaring, "[Presidents] pick a running mate not because he is the second citizen of the republic but because of intricate and generally mistaken calculations about the contribution he will make at the polls."[6]

Therefore, it has followed that even in cases where presidents have declared their intentions to employ their vice president substantively in the mainstream of the administration (and most recent presidents have to be included in this category), the record sadly has evidenced that this has been a pledge honored mainly in the breach.[7]

Until the adoption and implementation of the Twenty-fifth Amendment to the Constitution, scholars could only speculate on the possibilities inherent in the proposition: What if the vice president were to be selected on the basis of the role he might play in, and of the substantive contribution he could make to, the policy work of the administration?[8] With dramatic suddenness, the implementation of Section 2 of the Twenty-fifth Amendment, twice in the space of less than twelve months, elevated that proposition from the level of academic speculation to the concrete.[9]

In October, 1973, Gerald R. Ford was selected as President Richard Nixon's vice presidential nominee to succeed Spiro Agnew, who had resigned the vice presidency in the wake of criminal corruption charges against him. Within a year, Ford succeeded to the presidency on the resignation of Richard Nixon and was thus faced with the task of naming his own successor. On August 20, 1974, Ford announced the selection of former New York Governor Nelson Aldrich Rockefeller as his vice presidential nominee.

The selection of Rockefeller was based on some hard realities concerning Ford's personal situation. Chief among these was the very evident fact that Ford brought with him no executive experience to the office of the president. As the representative from Grand Rapids, Michigan, he had established no notable record of legislative achievement in twenty-five years in the House and consequently entered the White House with no significant policy background to draw upon. However, one of Ford's strengths had been an honest ability to perceive and acknowledge his own weaknesses, and this ability led to the recruitment of talented individuals to the Ford cabinet whose positions owed much to a "compensation effect" as the new president attempted to compensate for his own deficiencies by harnessing the talents and experience of others.[10]

The case of Rockefeller's vice presidential nomination bore every appearance of a "compensation effect." With his unprecedented four, four-year terms as governor of New York State, together with a notable personal interest in and involvement with public policy planning, Rockefeller clearly brought to the fledgling Ford administration expertise, experience, and interest that were conspicuously absent from the president's own background.

The president's private and public statements concerning Rockefeller's role in the administration gave a firm and clear indication of his commitment to provide a substantive policy role for the vice president. In a private telephone conversation with Rockefeller on August 17 to discuss the vice presidential nomination, Ford outlined a domestic-policy role and indicated that he wanted Rockefeller to take responsibility for the development of domestic-policy programs.[11] This conversation received public confirmation at Ford's first press conference on August 28, 1974, eight days after he announced the vice presidential nomination. In response to a question about the Rockefeller role, the president declared, "I think Governor Rockefeller can be extremely important as my teammate in doing effective work in the area of the Domestic Council."[12]

The Rockefeller vice presidency presented intriguing possibilities. It extended the promise that Ford and Rockefeller might succeed where past presidents and vice presidents had failed in establishing a substantive policy role for the vice president. So enthralled at this prospect was everyone that even as staunch an abolitionist as Arthur M. Schlesinger, Jr., was moved to observe of the Ford-Rockefeller effort, ". . . it may be that President Ford and Vice President Rockefeller are going to reverse the course of history and demonstrate that the vice presidency can be more than a nonjob. But this should be regarded as the final experiment, as the last chance for what has always been up to now a meaningless and futile office."[13]

The focus of this study is on the effort to invest the vice presidency of Nelson A. Rockefeller with a substantive policy role in Gerald R. Ford's administration. Unlike previous studies of past vice presidencies, it is not concerned with providing a comprehensive examination of all aspects of Rockefeller's incumbency and does not treat, for example, the interesting role played by Vice President Rockefeller in dealing with the revision of Senate Rule 22 in his capacity as the Senate president in the spring of 1975. Rather, the study is concerned with the extent to which he was able, as vice president, to play an active role as a developer and shaper of policy proposals and policy initiatives within the Ford administration.

It is acknowledged at the outset that the Rockefeller vice presidency presents a special case, that it was peculiarly the unique product of the operation of the Twenty-fifth Amendment. Accordingly, the study may well be circumscribed in its ability to provide an understanding of the wider possibilities and prospects of vice presidents within the policy processes of future administrations. With such a circumscription in mind, it is hoped nonetheless that examination of what Arthur M. Schlesinger, Jr., regarded as the "final experiment" will yield some broader observations that will provide an improved appreciation of the potential and limitations inherent in investing the vice president with a substantive policy role.

While this study primarily provides an examination of Vice President Rockefeller's endeavors to function as part of the policy structure of the Ford administration, such an exercise necessarily demands consideration of the elements of that policy structure and the dynamics of its operation. Moreover, the locus of the president at the "vital center" of decision making in the White House requires consideration of the leadership style of Gerald Ford. Accordingly, to provide a meaningful discussion of Rockefeller's role as a participating member of the administration, it is a secondary task of the study to examine the organizational structure of the Ford White House and the policy operations of the president and his senior staff within that structure.

Schematically, the study commences with an assessment of the historical development of the vice presidency (Chapter 1). This assessment provides a useful backdrop against which the subsequent examination of the Rockefeller vice presidency can be viewed. Chapter 2 considers the selection and confirmation of Rockefeller as vice president. The following three chapters (3, 4, and 5) document Rockefeller's vice presidential role in the policy work of the Ford administration. Chapter 6 provides an assessment of the institutional and personal factors that combined to shape the particular contours of Rockefeller's experience. Finally, the concluding chapter (8) assesses the outcome of what Arthur M. Schlesinger, Jr., termed "the final experiment" and presents considerations for future vice presidents.

ABBREVIATIONS

CEA	Council of Economic Advisers
EFC	Energy Finance Corporation
EIA	Energy Independence Authority
EPB	Economic Policy Board
ERC	Energy Resources Council
ERDA	Energy Research and Development Administration
ERFCO	Energy Resources Finance Corporation
FEA	Federal Energy Administration
NSC	National Security Council
OMB	Office of Management and Budget
OSTP	Office of Science and Technology Policy
OTS	Office of Technology and Science
RFC	Reconstruction Finance Corporation
RPFC	Resources Policy Finance Corporation

THE VICE PRESIDENT
AS POLICY MAKER

· 1 · THE VICE PRESIDENTIAL OFFICE: AN HISTORICAL ASSESSMENT

When the Founding Fathers created the office of vice president in the course of deliberating the drafting of a new Constitution at Philadelphia in 1787, they outlined two basic functions to be performed by vice presidents:

i. The vice president of the United States shall be president of the Senate, but shall have no vote, unless they be equally divided.

ii. In the case of the removal of the president from office, or of his death, resignation, or inability to discharge the powers and duties of the said office, the same shall devolve on the vice president.

Thus provision was made for a constitutional heir to the president, as well as for a presiding officer in the Senate (with power to break tied votes) who was not a legislator representing the interests of a particular state.

However, despite the prima facia importance of the two vice presidential functions ordained by the founders, the work of creating the position of vice president at the Philadelphia convention was neither extensive nor anticipated. Indeed, it is symptomatic of the problems of neglect and obscurity that were to plague holders of the vice presidential office that it should emerge at the Constitutional Convention, in the resolution of matters of unfinished business, from a set of committee deliberations that have remained essentially undocumented.

The initial drafting of the office of vice president came in the proceedings of the Committee of Eleven, which comprised eleven delegates (one for each of the states at the convention) chosen by ballot on August 31, 1787, and charged by the convention with the task of resolving outstanding matters.[1] Having reported out sundry matters on September 1, the Committee of Eleven reported back to the convention on September 4 a proposal to establish an electoral college system for the election of the president. However, included in the "additions and alterations" recommended to the convention, the committee proposed without explanation or supporting argument the creation of a vice presidential office:

4. After the word 'Excellency' in sect. 1 art. 10 to be inserted. 'He [the president] shall hold his office during the term of four years, and together with the vice-president, chosen for the same term, be elected in the following manner. . . . And in every case after the choice of the president, the person having the greatest number of votes shall be vice president. . . .'

6. 'Sect. 3. The vice-president shall be ex officio president of the Senate, except when they sit to try the impeachment of the president. . . . The vice president when acting as president of the Senate shall not have a vote unless the House be equally divided.'

9. 'He [the president] shall be removed from his office on impeachment by the House of Representatives, and conviction by the Senate, for treason, or bribery, and in case of his removal as aforesaid, death, absence, resignation, or inability to discharge the powers or duties of his office, the vice-president shall exercise those powers and duties until another president be chosen, or until the inability of the president be removed.'[2]

Because no notes were kept of the work of the Committee of Eleven, the authorship of the provision of a vice presidency is shrouded in mystery. There had been no mention of creating a vice presidential office prior to September 4. However, there had been some preliminary discussion of the question of presidential succession. In mid-June, Alexander Hamilton had sketched in the constitutional heir function of the office. During general debate on June 18, in the course of a lengthy speech on a desirable framework for a national government, he had called for:

The supreme executive authority of the United States to be vested in a governor to be elected to serve during good behavior—the election to be made by electors chosen by the people in the election districts. . . . On the death, resignation or removal of the governor his authorities to be exercised by the president of the Senate till a successor be appointed.[3]

In embryonic form, this approximates a similar proposal for provision of a constitutional succession in case of presidential disability to that recommended by the Committee of Eleven on September 4. The difference lies in the nature of the presiding officer of the Senate: in the committee's proposal, that officer is the vice president.

Despite the lack of any direct preliminary discussion about the creation of a vice presidency, the committee's recommendation failed to generate much immediate debate in the convention. What discussion there was on September 4 centered around the mechanism for the selection of the vice president. However, Nathaniel Gorham of Massachusetts raised a prophetic point about the selection mechanism with the observation that "as the regulation stands a very obscure man with very few votes may arrive at that appointment."[4]

On September 7, the convention took up the recommendation that "The vice president shall be ex officio president of the Senate." Much of the reported debate was in opposition to the proposal. Elbridge Gerry of Massachusetts objected to the propriety of having a vice president who would have a "close intimacy" with the president at the head of the Senate. In his view, there should be no such creation.[5] Edmund Randolph of Virginia generally associated himself with the opposition to the vice presidential office, while Hugh Williamson of North Carolina dismissed it totally as "not wanted."[6] George Mason raised a principled objection that ". . . the office of vice-president [was] an encroachment on the rights of the Senate; and that it mixed too much the legislative and executive, which as well as the judiciary departments, ought to be kept as separate as possible."[7] On the other side, in support of the proposal, Gouverneur Morris of New York tartly observed (of Gerry's presumption of a "close intimacy" between president and vice president), "The vice president then will be the first heir apparent that ever loved his father." Turning to more substantive argument, Morris went on to state that in the absence of a vice president the president of the Senate would be the constitutional heir, and this would be little different from the committee's proposal.[8] Roger Sherman of Connecticut joined with Morris in support, putting a practical point: "If the vice-president were not to be president of the Senate, he would be without employment, and some member by being made president must be deprived of his vote, unless when an equal division of votes might happen in the Senate, which would be but seldom."[9]

When the question was put to the vote, "Shall the vice president be ex officio president of the Senate," eight states voted affirmatively, two were opposed, and one abstained. The vice presidency was established.[10]

At first glance, it would appear that the vice presidential office was entirely a novel creation of the framers at Philadelphia. However, some of the appearance of novelty vanishes when it is realized that it had a direct counterpart at the state level: the office of lieutenant-governor. Alexander Hamilton, who, as we noted earlier, had called for a national chief executive patterned on the state office of governor, makes this point explicit in *Federalist* No. 68. There, Hamilton countered objections to the office as superfluous with the observation:

that as the vice-president may occasionally become a substitute for the president, in the supreme executive magistracy, all the reasons which recommend the mode of election prescribed for the one apply with great if not equal force to the manner of appointing the other. It is remarkable that in this, as in most other instances, the objection which is made would lie against the constitution of this state [i.e., New

York]. We have a lieutenant-governor, chosen by the people at large, who presides in the Senate, and is the constitutional substitute for the governor, in casualties similar to those which would authorize the vice-president to exercise the authorities and discharge the duties of the president.[11]

In the process of gaining ratification of the Constitution in the state conventions, the proposal to have a vice presidency was readily accepted. Not one state convention put forward an amendment to alter or remove the vice presidency as a constitutional provision, which suggests that the office gained a ready acceptance due to its similarity to the established state-level office of lieutenant-governor.

THE STAGNANT YEARS

The long period extending from the inaugural administration of George Washington up to the New Deal administration of Franklin D. Roosevelt was a time of stagnation for the office of vice president. John Adams, the first vice president, set the tone for his successors when he confided in a letter to his wife, Abigail: "My country has in its wisdom contrived for me the most insignificant office that ever the invention of man contrived or his imagination conceived."[12] And, when Woodrow Wilson leveled his scholar's gaze at the vice presidency almost one hundred years later, he concurred with John Adams's assessment: "The chief embarrassment in discussing his office is, that in explaining how little there is to be said about it one has evidently said all there is to say."[13]

Clearly a major part of the explanation for the stagnation and obscurity in which vice presidents have found themselves (at least until the emergence of the modern presidency with the New Deal) lies in the nature of the office created at Philadelphia in 1787. The only employment given vice presidents by the framers was the task of presiding over the Senate and voting only in cases of tied votes. Beyond this less than demanding role, the vice president was simply an understudy waiting in the stage wings in case some adversity should strike the principal player. As John Adams acutely observed of his occupation: "I am possessed of two separate powers, the one in esse and the other in posse. I am vice-president. In this I am nothing, but I may be everything."[14]

The real problem with the office was that the framers had prescribed no executive duties for it. The vice president was to exercise executive power only as an acting president in the case of presidential disability or as the successor to a president removed from office by death, resignation, or impeachment. As an actual working member of the executive branch, the vice president simply was a fiction. As for his legislative duties, these did not amount to much. As presiding officer, the vice president's principal responsibility in the Senate is the constitutionally mandated casting of a tie-breaking vote. However, in practice this duty has proved to be underwhelming: since 1789, vice presidents have voted on approximately 200 occasions.[15] Beyond the tie-breaking vote, the legislative duties that devolve upon the vice president principally center on his power of preserving order. However, this power has been largely delegated to a designated senator acting as president pro tempore in the absence of the vice president.[16]

As designed by the Constitutional Convention, the office of vice president put its occupants in a wretched situation. As the presidential candidate with the second highest number of votes in the electoral college, the vice president was a self-declared rival of the president who had obtained a majority of the electoral college votes (or, in cases where there was no such majority, was chosen in a runoff contest in the House of Representatives). Even if the vice president had desired executive duties, these were vested in the hands of his political rival, the president. Thus in crafting a selection process that would insure that the vice presidency was occupied by candidates of presidential quality, and in providing no executive duties for the office, the convention of 1787 put the vice president beyond the pale regarding the executive branch of government.[17]

However, the selection process that put political rivals together in the presidency and vice presidency did not remain long in place. The electoral college did not anticipate the effects of party politics in the election of the president and vice president. Each elector in the electoral college was given two votes to cast for the office of president, the vice presidency being filled by default by the candidate who was runner-up to the victorious presidential candidate. Thus the development of political parties in legislative and executive politics could result in situations where two candidates of the same party might receive identical majority votes from electors voting along party lines. Because no candidate would have a leading majority, the selection of the president would proceed to the House of Representatives where the possibility could exist of a majority opposition party choosing between the candidates. The election of 1796 followed this pattern exactly, and the runoff between the two Republican candidates (Jefferson and Burr, who had run as a team for the presidency and vice presidency, respectively) lay in the hands of a Federalist-dominated House. After thirty-six ballots, Jefferson won election as president. However, the eventual outcome was the Twelfth Amendment to the Constitution to insure that the electoral college process of presidential and vice presidential selection reflect the realities of party politics. The amendment, ratified in September, 1804, provided that each elector cast one vote for president and another vote for vice president, thus removing the possibility of more than one candidate receiving a majority of the electoral college votes.

The effect of the Twelfth Amendment on the office of vice president was distinctly harmful: it all but assured the selection of "obscure men" prophetically denounced by Nathaniel Gorham at the convention in 1787.[18] The problem was, of course, that the remedy against "obscure" candidates had been removed: no longer would the vice presidency be filled by the *presidential* candidate who received the second-highest vote in the electoral college or who was runner-up in a runoff contest in the House of Representatives. Henceforth, all candidates for the office would be *vice presidential* candidates from the outset.

Yet, it does a considerable disservice to associate a second-tier status with vice presidents in the stagnant years of the office in the nineteenth century. Many of these men were after all successful public figures when viewed in the context of their own social milieus.[19] We should more properly consider the limited nature of their vice presidential role in association with the role assigned to the president for the greater part of the century.

Apart from the demands of foreign affairs and the domestic exigencies of national security (notably the Civil War), the role of the president throughout the nineteenth century was a limited one.[20] The fabric of American society in this period was permeated with the laissez-faire principles of a liberal tradition, which embraced the Jeffersonian doctrine of government "that government governs best when it governs least." With a night-watchman role assigned to the state, the opportunities for a vigorous and assertive presidential role were considerably limited. Therefore, it should surprise no one that many of the century's presidents have remained relatively unknown figures.

In keeping with a limited executive role, the office of the president remained small. Indeed, between Washington and McKinley it changed in size hardly at all. The presidential office throughout much of the nineteenth century was not one that required much staff assistance and certainly not one that could provide much employment for an underemployed vice president.

Therefore, left with only the limited and dull constitutional task of presiding over the Senate, it is unremarkable that the vice presidency languished. Moreover, the effect of the Twelfth Amendment was to realize the prophecy of Nathaniel Gorham at the Constitutional Convention that the office would be filled with "obscure men." As Lord Bryce observed in *The American Commonwealth*, confirming Gorham's prediction:

The place [the vice presidency] being in itself unimportant, the choice of a candidate for it excites little interest and is chiefly used by the party managers as a means of conciliating a section of their party. It becomes what is called a "complimentary nomination." The man elected vice president is therefore rarely, if ever, a man in the front rank. But when the president dies during his term of office . . . this possibly second-class man steps into a great office for which he was never intended.[21]

THE DEVELOPMENT YEARS

With the twentieth century came some development of a vice presidential role within the executive branch of government. The underlying reason for this development lay in the changing nature of the presidential office, as the institutions of government were adapted to the demands of an industrialized and urbanized society.

A major by-product of the developing industrial economy in the late nineteenth century in the United States was the "trust"—the giant vertically or horizontally integrated corporation that was able to undercut free-market assumptions about economic regulation by competition. Giant corporations such as Standard Oil and United States Steel (in 1901) possessed the capability of setting rates and prices as monopolists or in concert with other "trusts" as oligopolists. To compensate for the absence of regulation by competition, the U.S. Congress enacted regulatory legislation establishing antitrust provisions and creating regulatory agencies to safeguard the public interest.[22]

A consequence of these regulatory measures was the enlargement of the federal role and, with this, a more activist presidency involved directly in the business economy. Presidential activism was advanced conceptually by Theodore Roosevelt, who propounded a "stewardship" theory of the presidency. Roosevelt held that, as steward of the people, "it was not only [the president's] right but his duty to do anything that the needs of the nation demanded unless such action was forbidden by the Constitution or by the laws."[23] And while Roosevelt's immediate successor, William Howard Taft, rejected this "stewardship" concept, his actions as president proved to be no less activist.[24]

The expanding role of the federal government in the domestic affairs of the nation quickened considerably in the 1930s with the myriad creation of regulatory, economic, and social-welfare support agencies of Franklin D. Roosevelt's New Deal. Yet, despite the consequential expansion of the presidential role, the office of the president remained relatively unchanged. This state of affairs produced the somewhat dramatic conclusion of the Brownlow Committee in 1937 that "the president needs help!" The underlying premise of Brownlow's report was that the job of president was simply too large and complex to be handled by a single individual. Accordingly, the report recommended the creation of an executive office of the president to provide much needed staff assistance, and this was established under the terms of the Reorganization Act of 1939.[25]

After Brownlow, the effort to meet the growing staff needs of the president proceeded apace:

- In 1946, the Council of Economic Advisers was established by the Employment Act, 1946.

- In 1947, the National Security Council was created (imposed on a reluctant president by the National Security Act, 1947).

- In 1949, the Hoover Commission recommended the delegation of some presidential powers to cabinet appointees, and this was enacted by the McCormack Act, 1950.

- In the 1950s, the White House developed a formalized staff structure under the Eisenhower presidency.

- In the 1960s came the creation of presidential task forces and ad hoc White House study groups in the Kennedy and Johnson administrations.

- In 1969, the Ash Council made recommendations that led to establishment of the Domestic Council and the reorganization of the Bureau of the Budget as the Office of Management and Budget.

Thus the presidency in the modern era became a highly differentiated institution actively involved in almost every facet of domestic as well as foreign affairs.[26]

With this enlargement of the size and scope of the office of president has come some development of executive duties for the vice president. Initially, these were of an extremely modest nature. Woodrow Wilson began the process by having his vice president, Thomas R. Marshall, meet with the cabinet (a practice that had earlier begun and ended with John Adams's tenure as vice president) and even arranged for Marshall to preside over several cabinet meetings while he attended the Paris Peace Conference.[27] Calvin Coolidge continued this practice, sitting in on cabinet meetings on an occasional basis; but his successor, Charles Dawes, refused to participate on the grounds that it might set what he termed an "injurious precedent." However, since John N. Garner, all vice presidents have regularly attended cabinet meetings—a practice that has had the effect of denting the notion that the vice president is wholly a creature of the legislature.

Unquestionably, the most significant development in establishing the vice president as a member of the presidential family came with the administrations of Franklin D. Roosevelt. Not only were his vice presidents brought into cabinet meetings, but each was given various special assignments. John N. Garner, Speaker of the House of Representatives until his election as vice president, was given an active role in congressional liaison, a role that employed his considerable legislative skills and influence to good use in pushing through Roosevelt's New Deal legislative proposals. Moreover, Garner represented the United States abroad when, as vice president, he attended the inauguration of President Manuel Quezon of the Philippines in 1935. Unfortunately, the prospects of further development of Garner's role were dashed in the second Roosevelt administration, when Garner became estranged from Roosevelt over the president's plan to reorganize the Supreme Court and his call for increased liberal legislation.[28]

Garner's successor, Henry Wallace, was given administrative duties by Roosevelt that significantly widened the scope of the vice presidency. In July, 1941, the president issued an executive order establishing the Economic Defense Board, with the vice president named as board chairman. Wallace was put in command of a staff of some 3,000 and charged with oversight responsibilities concerning the import, export, and stockpiling of strategic materials. Chairmanship of this board (which became the Board of Economic Warfare after entry of the United States into World War II) gave to the vice presidency a substantive executive role as an administrator and policy maker for the first time.[29]

Roosevelt widened the vice president's role still further in September, 1941, when he made Wallace chairman of the Priorities and Allocations Board, a coordinating panel of the nation's major defense agencies. Wallace additionally served as a member of a five-man Advisory Committee on Atomic Energy, which ultimately recommended that the United States should build an atomic bomb.

Besides these novel executive duties, Wallace expanded considerably the role of goodwill ambassador begun by Garner. His first mission abroad was to represent the United States at the inauguration of President Camacho of Mexico. As a member of the Commission on Inter-American Affairs, Wallace sought to establish better U.S. relations with Latin America. Other foreign assignments took him to China, Siberia, Russia, and India.

However, following this extraordinary development of the role of vice president, presidents moved slowly to utilize their vice presidents in any substantive executive role within the administration. Indeed, beyond his membership in the National Security Council (a membership insisted on by an adamant President Truman in 1949), and the chairmanship of such bodies as the National Aeronautics and Space Council and the Office of Intergovernmental Relations, little was done in the postwar period to provide the vice president with much of a substantive role. The experience of Vice President Richard Nixon is instructive here.

Apart from his attendance at meetings of the Eisenhower cabinet and the sessions of the National Security Council, Nixon's principal activities as vice president centered on extensive travel around the world on promotional tours that were all but devoid of substance and on campaign trips around the nation as a surrogate for a president who saw himself as being above politics. Nixon often has been cited as an example of an effective vice president who had an "important" as opposed to an essentially ceremonial role in the administration. However, this view is severely undercut by a response made by Eisenhower at a press conference in August, 1960, at a time when the vice president was gearing up his presidential election campaign. A newsman asked Eisenhower, "What major decisions of your administration has the vice president participated in?" Ike's reply was: "If you give me a week, I might think of one. I don't remember."[30]

Similarly, the vice presidencies of Lyndon Johnson and Hubert Humphrey produced little development of the vice presidential role. Both men were considered to be presidential timber in their own right, but neither man was given the opportunity to employ his talents in the number-two spot. In Johnson's case, the vice president's acknowledged legislative genius lay fallow as President Kennedy relied on his own staffers (particularly Larry O'Brien) for promotion of his legislative program on Capitol Hill.[31] Likewise, Hubert Humphrey was denied any kind of an opening to develop his creative abilities as Johnson's vice president.[32] Humphrey became so submerged, in fact, that he became the butt of humorist Tom Lehrer, who sang: "Whatever became of Hubert?"

Like Lyndon Johnson, Richard Nixon as president showed no real interest in providing a substantive role for the vice president, despite his own acknowledged frustration while in that office. Vice President Spiro Agnew was effectively excluded from the inner circle of the Nixon administration, an exclusion that worked to his direct advantage as the "White House horrors" became revealed. Having had no role within the Nixon White House, Agnew was regarded as a major contender for the 1976 Republican presidential nomination, until his own dark past caught up with him with his corruption trial and resignation in 1973.[33] His successor, Gerald R. Ford, the first vice president appointed under the provisions of the Twenty-fifth Amendment, was given little to do besides sitting out the unfolding saga of Watergate until Nixon's resignation from the presidency in August, 1974.[34]

In sum, while the vice presidency has advanced in becoming a part of the executive branch in the twentieth century, the greatest gains (the administrative duties of the Wallace vice presidency) were fleeting and can be viewed as part of the extraordinary measures resorted to by Roosevelt during the war. The period of "normalcy" that followed in the postwar vice presidencies highlights an office that is long on appearance but short on substance. The life of the postwar vice president has been largely ceremonial and shadowy—a life filled out by attendance at meetings of the cabinet, the National Security Council, the Domestic Council (which met only rarely as a formal body), and the chairmanship of presidential commissions on an occasional basis. The twentieth-century vice president, in other words, has found himself in the administration but not of it.

THE NEED TO DEVELOP A VICE PRESIDENTIAL
POLICY ROLE

It might be possible to dismiss the absence of a substantive role for the vice president as little more than a minor irritant. However, such a dismissal requires that we ignore the events of recent history that show that the vice presidency is the most direct route to the presidency.

In the twentieth century, six out of sixteen American presidents have first been vice presidents, including three of the five most recent presidents: Lyndon Johnson, Richard Nixon, and Gerald Ford.[35] Moreover, since the respective offices of president and vice president were written into the Constitution at Philadelphia in 1787, some thirteen of the forty presidents (approximately one-third) had served first as vice president. Analyzing the prospects of vice presidential advancement to the presidency, a study done by the Institute of Politics, Harvard University, suggested that "the odds are now about one to two that the vice president will one day become president."[36]

What is surprising is that, despite the apparent odds in favor of vice presidential advancement to the presidency, little attention is paid to the role of the office of vice president as a preparation or an apprenticeship for the office of president. Some attention was given in 1976 (a presidential election year) to the wisdom of selecting vice presidential candidates who could demonstrate competence as potential presidents. This was the focus of the Harvard study, which concerned itself with the process by which the vice presidential nominees of the two major parties are selected, as well as the selection criteria employed by presidential nominees in choosing running mates. However, omitted from the Harvard study was any consideration of the use to which an elected vice presidential running mate could be put after the election.

The relative absence of discussion about the *content* of the vice presidential role is disturbing, to say the least. The events of the past two decades reveal the folly of treating the vice president as nothing more than "standby equipment." The assassination of John F. Kennedy and the forced resignation of Richard M. Nixon demanded the sudden accession to the presidency of two men who were not prepared to assume with immediacy the reins of power. Given the odds suggested by the Harvard study that one in two vice presidents will become presidents, a solid prima facie case exists for involving the vice president in a substantive way in the president's administration.

It can be argued, of course, that the absence of such a vice presidential role has not harmed the interests of the United States, that in modern instances of sudden vice presidential succession to the presidency the lack of a "vice presidential apprenticeship" has not been disastrous. It must be conceded that the record bears out this argument. However, this may well be due to the workings of *fortuna* (one of Machiavelli's indispensable ingredients for successful statecraft). In the case of the Truman succession, the war was in its final stages, V-E Day was a month away, and only the war in the Pacific remained. However, the fact was that the new president had no knowledge whatsoever about the weapon that would subsequently hasten the surrender of the Japanese: the atomic bomb. Although Vice President Wallace had been part of the group that recommended building the atomic bomb, Vice President Truman was unaware of the bomb's development much less its potential as a weapon.[37]

In the case of the Johnson succession, the United States fortunately was not caught up in any kind of national security crisis—the days of the Cuban

Missile Crisis had preceded the Dallas assassination by a sufficient margin to pose no dramatic East-West confrontation for the new president. Moreover, as in the case of Truman, Johnson was able to draw upon the support and understanding of a nation numbed by the death of a president, and this (with much-needed assistance from the staff of the dead president) made the transition from the vice presidency relatively smooth.

However, we should not have to adduce actual past disasters to suggest problems inherent in the folly of excluding the vice president from the policy processes of the administration. The plain fact is that the Constitution requires the availability of "standby equipment," personified in the being of the vice president, in the event of the death, resignation, or disability of the president. Common sense, in the national interest, requires that the vice president be actively involved in the affairs of the administration to maintain a desirable state of readiness as a "standby president."

Some consideration has been given over the years to the matter of investing the vice presidency with responsibilities and duties that would make him a credible successor. One early proposal came from Theodore Roosevelt in September, 1896, who argued that:

One way to secure this desired result would undoubtedly be to increase the power of the vice-president. He should always be a man who would be consulted by the president on every great party question. It would be very well if he were given a seat in the cabinet. It might be well if in addition to his vote in the Senate in the event of a tie he should be given a vote, on ordinary occasions, and perchance on occasions a voice in the debates. A man of . . . character . . . is sure to make his weight felt in an administration, but the power of thus exercising influence should be made official rather than personal.[38]

A proposal that sought to achieve the goal of investing the vice presidency with an official influence came in October, 1896, in the suggestion of Walter Clark, who proposed that a Department of Interstate Commerce be created with the vice president as its ex officio head. In this way, Clark argued, the office would provide its incumbents with a useful role.[39]

Analyzing the office in December, 1909, in an article significantly entitled "The Fifth Wheel in Our Government," Albert Beveridge considered the possibilities of enlarging the vice president's powers in the executive branch:

Why not make him a sitting, voting member of the cabinet? It is a logical arrangement in the case of the death, disability, or removal of the president, whom he is to succeed. Why, then, should he not be kept intimately familiar with the whole course of the administration which he may be called upon to direct? It would as perfectly equip him for the duties of the succession as any conceivable method could equip him. He would no longer be a fifth wheel, but one of the four wheels of government. He would have at his fingers' ends the operations of the administration, both foreign and domestic, both public and private; for of course everybody knows that much of the information and many of the operations of government in foreign affairs cannot be made public. In the case of the death of the president he would have become accustomed to his shoes in advance; he would walk in those shoes with ease; and he would walk right forward, instead of taking the back track, as is inevitable under the present arrangements.[40]

In the fall of 1920, Franklin D. Roosevelt, then a candidate for the Democratic Party's vice presidential nomination, posed the question, "Can the vice president be useful?" Commenting that the presence of the vice president at cabinet meetings would not, by itself, accomplish much, Roosevelt went on to conclude:

There is hardly any limitation upon the ways in which the vice president might be of service to the president. He might serve as an executive aid to the president, and in that capacity could easily enough, even if he did not possess such executive authority as might without a constitutional amendment be granted him, exercise considerable influence through his close relationship with the president. He could, at the request of the president, serve in relation to the determination of large matters of policy that do not belong in the province of a member of the president's cabinet. He might serve as a kind of liaison officer to Congress and aid perhaps in carrying the large burden of interpreting administration policies to Congress and to the public.[41]

The 1948 presidential election produced further discussion of the need to provide a substantive vice presidential role. Homer Durham considered the possibilities that election of Thomas Dewey and Earl Warren might open up for the vice presidency. As Durham envisaged this future, he saw great utility in a

legislative council which might be developed in national affairs. The president, the vice president, the Speaker of the House of Representatives, and the majority leader of the Senate could constitute its core. Occasionally, prominent chairmen of important committees could be included as time and occasion required. A "team-man" president, as Mr. Dewey is alleged to be, could well develop such a council as the legislative policy counterpart to some of the existing mechanisms in the executive office of the president. The need for coordinating policy between the executive and legislative branches is constant. . . . In times when either house or both may fall to the opposition party, the legislative skills and political skills of a vice president might be significant in perfecting another aspect of the "living Constitution."

If such a legislative council could be established, either formally or informally, the president should, of course, be chairman. But the vice president would be that familiar figure, known as the "executive chairman."[42]

In that same election year of 1948, Clinton Rossiter advanced his own proposals, declaring firmly: "The time has come for a strengthening of the vice presidency." In Rossiter's view, statutory changes needed to be undertaken that would have the effect of designating the vice president as "the president's chief assistant in the overall direction of the administrative branch." It was important for Rossiter that the enabling legislation be carefully drafted, but equally important that "no doubt be left in anyone's mind that the purpose of the act is to shift almost the entire administrative burden from the one to the other."[43]

Rossiter's proposal was based largely on a constitutional amendment proposed by Congressman Monroney of Oklahoma in 1946, which had sought to revive the vice presidency by transferring administrative responsibilities from the president to the vice president. However, Rossiter went further with his own proposals. He argued that it was the responsibility of the vice president to set precedents (limiting, for example, his duties in the Senate as presiding officer to major occasions only). Moreover, the vice president should be established by the president as a permanent and active member of the cabinet, underlining his status as a working member of the administration. Finally, Rossiter argued that the party conventions had the responsibility of nominating candidates for the vice presidency who possessed "known executive ability."[44]

Echoing Rossiter's judgment that the vice presidency "needed strengthening," Joseph Menez observed in June, 1955, that

The presidency must be strengthened. . . . The responsibilities are at once too many and too great. The president is overworked and any device to lessen his burden and streamline the executive should be seriously considered. In meeting his problems, the president could quite readily delegate some responsibility to the vice president. Perhaps the latter could be given the statutory job of planning the annual budget and sending it to the Congress. Or he might be designated an "assistant president" and be concerned with the overall direction of the administrative branch. . . . First rate vice presidents are desperately needed. They should definitely be considered potential presidents.

The rapid march of events demands a twentieth-century kind of a vice president; trained, capable, and informed, to assist the president in faithfully executing the laws with continuity, dispatch, knowledge, and confidence.[45]

In a *New York Times Magazine* article in October, 1955, James McGregor Burns put forward a package of proposals designed to prevent the vice presidency from reverting to the "Throttlebottoms" of the stagnant years of the office. His proposals were modest, but of a highly practicable nature. Essentially, Burns called for:

1. The provision of more staff assistance for the vice president.

2. The provision of an official residence for the vice president, together with an adequate entertainment allowance.

3. The provision of a vice presidential airplane, more office space, and other facilities commonly needed by modern executives.

4. The clarification of the confused provisions regarding presidential disability.

Burns based his belief in the need to strengthen the office of vice president on the straightforward grounds that: "The vice presidency is here to stay. President and people, working together, have it in their power to make the incumbent a strong left arm for the man in the White House, and a trained and worthy successor if the office falls vacant."[46]

In January, 1956, former President Herbert Hoover proposed to the Senate Subcommittee on Reorganization that the Congress create a statutory position of administrative vice president in the executive office.[47] Hoover recommended that the president be authorized to delegate to this official "such administrative and coordination duties" as the president saw fit within existing law. This would not impinge on the constitutional duties of the president: the proposal was addressed to the purely administrative side of the presidential burden. Among the duties that Hoover envisaged an administrative vice president discharging were such responsibilities as:

• Supervision of independent agencies;

• Appointment of certain officials (e.g., postmasters of first-, second-, and third-class post offices, and others);

• Coordination of interdepartmental committees;

• Supervision of reorganization within the executive branch;

• Resolving conflicts among executive agencies;

• Supervision of closing down abolished executive agencies.

Herbert Hoover's proposal to create an appointive post of administrative vice president, while at the same time retaining the elected vice president (or constitutional vice president as Hoover termed him), also was taken up in a study carried out in March, 1956, for President Eisenhower by Nelson Rockefeller as chairman of the President's Advisory Committee on Government Organization. Essentially, the Rockefeller study came to similar conclusions as former President Hoover concerning the utility of the post of administrative vice president. While acknowledging that "an appointed vice president might make the position of the elected vice president more difficult than it now is" (something critics of the Hoover proposal were also quick to point out), Rockefeller advised Eisenhower that it would be advantageous for the president to delegate administrative functions to an appointed administrative vice president. His advice on this point related to the question of compatibility between the major principals: elected vice presidents historically had not always enjoyed full compatibility with presidents because of the nature of the running-mate selection process, whereas appointees could be selected with compatibility (and executive ability) specifically in mind.

Recommending presidential endorsement of the administrative vice president proposal, the Rockefeller study advised that:

1. The president consider requesting the elected vice president to undertake on his behalf more extensive activities of a ceremonial and public relations nature to lighten the president's burden as chief of state and chief of his political party.

2. The president approve the development of legislation to authorize the establishment of the position of administrative vice president to be appointed by the president with Senate confirmation. The legislation . . . should authorize the president, with absolute discretion, to delegate and withdraw delegations of authority to act in his behalf with respect to executive branch administration.

3. The assistant to the president, who now serves as "chief of staff," also acts in the same capacity for the elected vice president in his White House activities and for the administrative vice president. The two vice presidents should also utilize the White House staff and facilities.[48]

Perhaps because of the absence of enthusiasm from the Senate Subcommittee in response to the Hoover proposal, Eisenhower took no action on the recommendations of the Rockefeller Committee. Certainly, from the standpoint of the constitutionally ordained vice presidency, the Hoover-Rockefeller proposals would have had the effect of perpetuating the consignment of vice presidential incumbents to the oblivion of ceremony, presiding over the Senate, and functioning as constitutional heir to the president in case of death, impeachment, or resignation.

While the hearings on Hoover's proposal failed to advance the concept of administrative vice president, at the same time the subcommittee did elicit a further reform proposal on the vice presidency advanced by Clark Clifford, former special assistant to President Truman.

The essence of Clifford's proposal was to transfer the vice presidency, by constitutional amendment, from the legislative to the executive branch. If that were done, Clifford told the subcommittee,

the vice presidency could be built up into the important position that it should be. I think the vice president could be the second officer in the executive branch of the government. He could take over from the president a vast amount of administrative detail. And it would help the president immensely if you had that kind of arrangement. I believe, too, you would get the sort of man that you wanted for the job, because when the great parties met in convention they would know that they were then nominating the two men who were to guide the destinies of the nation. I believe that the presidential nominee would be sure that the vice presidential nominee would be one with whom he could work.

Also, you would be in the process of preparing a man for succession to the presidency. No matter what committees you put the present vice president on, no matter what functions you give him in attending cabinet meetings and National Security Council meetings, I do not believe he is prepared to the degree that he would be if he were the day-to-day working assistant to the President of the United States.[49]

Concerning these various proposals to reform and strengthen the office of vice president, several points are in order. First, the advocates of a substantive role for the vice president may well have been influenced in some cases by two related sets of events involving the death and disability of the president. The former event concerns Roosevelt's death in 1945. This almost certainly influenced the proposal for a constitutional amendment put forward by Congressman Monroney in 1946, and this, in turn, influenced Rossiter's proposals in 1948. The latter event concerns Eisenhower's first heart attack in September, 1955 (he suffered a second stroke in November, 1957). Eisenhower's periods of disability can be said to have influenced Burns's proposals of October, 1955, and the various proposals discussed in the hearings held in January, 1956. Both sets of events served well in underlining the reality that the vice president *is* the constitutional heir in cases of presidential death, resignation, removal, or disability. As a constitutional successor, he ought to be thoroughly prepared and equipped to assume the presidency at a moment's notice. As almost every advocate of reform was to note, no such state of vice presidential readiness did in fact exist.

A second point to be noted about the reform proposals is that the case for investing the vice presidency with executive duties stems largely from the evident realization that the president is grossly overburdened. The advocates of reform generally endorse the view that the vice president should be viewed as a member of the executive branch and, as such, is therefore a logical choice for the role of principal assistant to the president. In some cases, this role was seen as primarily one that could be initiated personally by the president by administrative transfer of duties, while other advocates envisaged the need for a statutory or constitutional basis for transfer of duties from the president to his vice president.

Finally, a measure of the actual development of the vice presidential role can be obtained from consideration of the reform proposals. The first proposal outlined above, the suggestion of Theodore Roosevelt that a vice president sit in on cabinet meetings (a proposal echoed in 1909 by Beveridge), is modest in the extreme. When this is contrasted with Clifford's outright dismissal of *actual* vice presidential attendance at cabinet meetings (and other modern extensions, e.g., the NSC meetings) as inadequate preparation for succession to the presidency, it indicates that some progress has been made in developing the argument that the vice presidency is deserving of a substantive policy role.

THE PROBLEMS OF A VICE PRESIDENTIAL ROLE

The first and most important point that should be established concerning development of a substantive policy role for the vice president is that we are talking about a role that, of necessity, cannot be formally institutionalized without a constitutional amendment. In the absence of such an amendment, the provision of a vice presidential role within the executive branch lies where it has always lain—within the discretion of the president.

However, this does not mean that such a role for the vice president is unlikely to be forthcoming, despite the daunting historical precedents. Although American history is replete with the unfulfilled pledges of presidential candidates who indicated their firm resolve to provide their running mates with a significant role when elected,[50] the fact is that there are sufficient payoffs to justify presidential power-sharing with the vice president. Such action could, for example, free presidential resources of time and energy for priority areas demanding the exclusive attention of the president and, at the same time, insure that other important areas of concern receive adequate coverage and attention. Moreover, there may well be a political advantage in directing the vice president to field troublesome areas of concern in which successful outcomes are by no means guaranteed. Finally, there would appear to be considerable advantage in having an experienced political figure, the only nationally elected public official besides the president, to deal with cabinet and agency heads, state and local government officials, the senators and congressmen on the president's behalf; in recent years, all of these sets of officials have shown great disdain for the relatively young, inexperienced, and unelected staff surrounding the president in the modern White House.

However, it should be recognized at the outset that there are some problems associated with investing the vice presidency with a substantive policy role. First, should the vice president be given a cabinet-level appointment as administrator, executive director, or chairman, there would exist a potential problem should the vice president and the president become involved in a disagreement of such magnitude that it would normally result in the appointee's dismissal. Opponents of such a vice presidential role contend that such a situation would produce an embarrassing standoff, since the elective nature of the vice president's office would preclude his dismissal from the administration. Even worse, it is contended, such a situation poses enormous potential for a divided government. Second, there is too much political risk involved in the president giving to his vice president the position of chief administrative officer as envisaged by Rossiter and Clifford.

The risk comes in presidential power-sharing with the only other nationally elected official in the administration: the vice president is, after all, a politician in his own right with his own constituency of support. To give such a figure a portion of the president's power, it is contended, poses a real risk of building a rival center of power to the president himself. Third, the real problem of creating a substantive role for the vice president lies in the essentially ephemeral nature of the role. Without a constitutional amendment or enabling statute, the role would vanish with the administration because each president is free to shape the contours of his own administration. Accordingly, it is not possible to institutionalize vice presidential roles and functions of one administration for automatic transfer to the next without some constitutional or statutory provisions to that effect.

Turning to the first of the three problem areas briefly outlined, what may be called the dismissal problem, we need to consider more fully the dimensions of the alleged problem. Basically, what is being argued is that the vice president is wholly dissimilar to other political appointees of the president. Whereas the president can demand and get the immediate resignations of his political appointees in the executive branch, the vice president (because of his elected status) is beyond his power of dismissal. Thus, in cases of major disagreement between the president and his vice president, or between the vice president and other senior members of the administration, the president is portrayed as powerless to apply the normal sanction of removal.

The apparent problem of presidential inability to effect removal of the vice president deserves much closer examination. Precisely what is the problem? Most certainly it is true that a vice president may not be removed from his constitutionally ordained vice presidential office, except under the impeachment process provided by Article II, Section 4, of the Constitution. But such a removal is not the basic problem. The problem arises in the case of a position to which the vice president was *appointed* by the president pursuant to his discretionary appointment powers. To such an appointive position, the constitutional process of removal from the vice presidential office is inapplicable. The fact is that, in the case of an appointive position, the tenure and removal status of the vice president is the same as that of any other presidential appointee: he can be removed at will by the president.

Of course, it would be disingenuous to pretend that the position of the vice president is exactly the same as that of any other presidential appointee concerning removal from a presidential appointment: his constitutional status sets him apart politically from other appointed officers. After removal from appointed office, the vice president would remain in his constitutional office as presiding officer of the Senate and successor to the presidency.

Although such a turn of events might well be controversial (presidential firings of major appointees are, almost without exception, fraught with controversy), this does not necessarily signify disaster for a president. He is, after all, the president, and he commands the position of real power in the administration. The vice president is still the vice president and commands an office historically and constitutionally weak and devoid of power. Moreover, removal of a vice president from an appointive position does not necessarily entail for the president the loss of political support from an aggrieved vice president. The case of Henry Wallace is instructive here because it provides the only recorded case of presidential dismissal of a vice president from an appointive administrative office.[51]

In September, 1941, President Roosevelt appointed Vice President Wallace to the chairmanship of the Economic Defense Board, thus giving the vice president a cabinet-level administrative position that had policy-making powers. Wallace's position as chairman of the board (renamed the Board of Economic Warfare [BEW] on U.S. entry into World War II) quickly brought him into conflict with Jesse Jones, who headed the Reconstruction Finance Corporation (RFC). The basis of the conflict lay in the overlapping jurisdictions of the BEW and the RFC, respectively, an overlap common in the Roosevelt administration.

The turf dispute between Jones and Wallace grew bitter and was ended only when Roosevelt abolished the BEW and with it Wallace's position as chairman. At the same time, the president transferred from Jones's control the various RFC operations disputed by Wallace, placing them in a newly created Office of Economic Warfare. Jones hailed Roosevelt's actions as a personal triumph over the vice president, who had in effect been fired by the president.

Although Vice President Wallace was understandably hurt and angry, it is important to note that he continued his political support for Roosevelt policies and programs. His personal feelings toward the president were revealed in a statement Wallace made to some of his close staff aides, when he quoted the Bible: "Though he may slay me, yet will I trust Him."[52]

The Wallace case provides a useful precedent, one that is frequently cited in discussing the problem of the tenure and removal of the vice president from administrative positions. However, the precedent usually is employed as a justification for withholding from the vice president an administrative role in an administration.[53] The deportment of Vice President Wallace after the abolition of the BEW seriously undermines such a view. On the contrary, the precedent strongly supports the contention that presidents may have little to fear from their vice presidents.

Turning now to the second of the three problem areas outlined earlier, the question is raised of political risk involved in a president transferring to his vice president much of the administrative burden of the presidential office. The risk here would arise in sharing power with a potential rival politician, thus creating the basis for a disloyal vice president to challenge the president politically. Two points deserve consideration here: first, the nature of the relationship between presidents and vice presidents, and, second, what the element of risk actually comprises.

On the matter of the relationship between a president and his vice president, this is an area of concern that ought to be thoroughly explored in the selection process governing the vice presidential nomination. It is in this process that the dimensions of compatibility and potential for conflict between a presidential candidate and his potential running mates need to be considered exhaustively.

However, a major problem concerning the consideration of compatibility presents itself at the outset if the presidential nominee is not in a position to control the selection process regarding choice of his running mate. When this is the case (and there are ample historical examples),[54] the relationship between the two nominees must proceed on the basis of trial and error, hardly a solid foundation for insuring compatibility between a president and a vice president.

In other cases, where the presidential nominee can be said to have had an element of choice in selection of the vice presidential nominee, it has often turned out that the freedom of choice was more apparent than real. Traditionally, the criteria of political and geographical balancing have outweighed other selection criteria in the choice of a running mate. Again, this produces a trial-and-error basis for developing a relationship between the two candidates.

The problems inherent in vice presidential nominee selection have been addressed fully by the Institute of Politics study and need not be repeated here. However, it is important to note that the study concluded that the traditional selection criteria of political and geographic balances should be secondary to the criterion of competence to assume the office of president. As the study emphasized, the standards of presidential competence and political and geographic balances

are neither naturally exclusive nor naturally contradictory. . . . It is implausible that the dictates of short-term political balance are so compelling, and that the available set of high-quality political figures so limited, that a presidential nominee need be forced to sacrifice competency to campaign victory in a possible successor.[55]

Assuming that competence to assume the presidency was the primary selection criterion employed by a candidate who controlled the choice of his running mate, it is evident that the compatibility question could be explored with potential vice presidential nominees. It is in the course of these explorations that a presidential nominee should determine the risks involved in sharing administrative duties with the vice president. Such an effort would provide a solid basis for developing a harmonious working relationship between the two nominees after Election Day.[56]

As for the actual risk involved in the transfer to the vice president of some of the administrative duties of the presidential office, this cannot be rated as at all high. Rossiter provided a useful assessment of the risks in such a transfer when he considered the matter in 1955. It was his view that

Whatever duties and leadership [the president] may renounce in the field of public administration, he remains the undisputed leader in military affairs, foreign relations, ceremony, public opinion, and politics. Moreover, he will sharpen his command in these important fields in direct proportion to the added hours and freshened mental powers he will bring to his briefings and decisions. . . . A weak president might give too much authority to a strong vice president, but he might give it to a secretary of state or an entire cabinet, too. . . . Furthermore, the vice president could gain nothing by a challenge to the president but a loss of the customary power that a friendly president would willingly grant him . . . .[57]

As Rossiter explained the situation, the vice president has more to lose than to gain from mounting a challenge to the president. The fact remains that the vice presidential office is weak and dependent upon presidential patronage in the absence of constitutional or statutory changes affecting his status. Therefore, the element of risk inherent in presidential power-sharing would appear to be low.

Turning to the last of the three problem areas outlined, it would appear to be self-evident that no institutionalization of a substantive vice presidential role can be achieved in the absence of constitutional amendments or statutory changes. Since the last legislative attempt to alter the nature of the vice presidency in 1956 (which, in any case, failed to move beyond initial Senate hearings), no efforts have been made to pursue changes via constitutional amendment or statute. Accordingly, any change in the role of the office must come at the discretion of the incumbent president. Here the hard reality is that the power to create is also the power to destroy: no incoming president is obligated to retain the administrative configurations of the outgoing White House office.

However, having said that, there is a sense in which an ongoing institutionalization of vice presidential roles is taking place. For example, it would be inconceivable for a president today to exclude the vice president from meetings of the cabinet; yet Vice President Marshall was breaking essentially new ground by meeting with the cabinet in December, 1918. Similarly, it is now unquestionably accepted that the vice president is a part of the executive branch; he has enjoyed an office within the Old Executive Office building and, more recently in the cases of Mondale and Bush, has enjoyed an office in the west wing of the White House. In contrast, the prevailing nineteenth-century conception of the vice presidency essentially was that of

Jefferson: as presiding officer in the Senate, the vice president was wholly a creature of the legislature.

Therefore, there are some vice presidential roles that have been institutionalized by convention. This would appear to suggest that once new duties and responsibilities are invested in the vice president and are accepted as valid by the political community, it becomes increasingly difficult for a president to withdraw them, so that even in the absence of statutory or constitutional change, institutionalization of new vice presidential roles has been, and continues to be, possible. The only limits to institutionalized expansion of the vice presidency would seem to be those imposed by the willingness of presidents and vice presidents to set and accept precedents.

· 2 · ROCKEFELLER AS VICE PRESIDENT: HIS SELECTION AND CONFIRMATION

SELECTION OF FORD'S VICE PRESIDENTIAL NOMINEE

On August 9, 1974, Richard M. Nixon became the first President of the United States to resign from office. At the same time, Vice President Gerald R. Ford was sworn in as president, thus creating a vacancy in the office of vice president. After serving a mere eight months in the vice presidency, Ford found himself with the critical task of selecting his own successor.

Speculation about selection of the vice presidential nominee began even before Nixon's resignation. It started when Melvin Laird, a close confidant of Ford, had flatly predicted in a news story published on August 7 that Nelson Rockefeller would be Ford's choice.[1] Questioned about Laird's prediction, a somewhat embarrassed Vice President Ford emphasized that it was premature to discuss selection of a successor.[2] However, speculation about the likely choice continued, and it intensified with Nixon's resignation.

In the days following August 9, rival lists of likely candidates for the vice presidency were compiled by political commentators. Most of these lists contained, in addition to that of Nelson Rockefeller, the names of George Bush (Republican National Committee chairman), Melvin Laird, Elliot Richardson (who had been fired as attorney general in Nixon's infamous "Saturday Night Massacre"), and Senators Howard Baker, Hugh Scott, and Barry Goldwater.[3]

Following his swearing in as president on August 9, Ford informed the congressional leadership that he hoped to name his choice for the vice presidential nomination within ten days. This period of time would allow the new president to sound out the various components of the Republican Party about their own particular preferences. In addition, this small delay in naming a successor would allay fears of a hasty selection: in 1973, Nixon had been severely criticized by the press for naming a successor to Agnew in only two days.

Although speculation in the media was focused on Rockefeller as the leading contender, Ford's own preference for the nomination was Melvin Laird.[4] As a representative from Wisconsin, Laird had enjoyed a long and close congressional association with Ford and had helped to install him as minority leader in the House following the ouster of Charles Halleck in January, 1965. Moreover, Laird had furthered his reputation as secretary of defense in Nixon's first administration. More recently, he had left government service for a lucrative position as senior counselor on international and domestic affairs with *Reader's Digest*.

Ford, in fact, offered Laird the nomination in preliminary discussions prior to Nixon's resignation. However, Laird turned down the offer. He told Ford that it would be a bad appointment because both men were from the same geographic location, from the same conservative wing of the party, and, besides, he could do more for the president outside the administration.[5] As he confided later to the *Milwaukee Journal*, Laird believed, "A president needs a few friends he can bounce things off. The president understands that. He knows I want nothing in this administration."[6]

In turning down Ford's offer of the nomination, Laird suggested that Ford consider the merits of selecting Rockefeller: "I told [Ford] exactly who would help him the most, that Rockefeller would be the best man. . . . I made as strong a plea for Rockefeller as I could. I felt that it would be the best ticket for 1976. I figured it was a winner."[7]

In his efforts to advance Rockefeller's candidacy with the vice president, Laird indicated to Ford that it would be useful to gauge conservative reaction to a Rockefeller nomination by means of a trial balloon in the press. Laird's opinion was that it would be best to get the possibility of a Rockefeller selection out in the open as soon as possible. Although Ford did not actively direct Laird in this effort, according to Laird: "Ford knew I was going to do it; he did not discourage me. I felt it was in his best interest that I test it."[8] Accordingly, on August 7 Laird came out with his prediction of a Rockefeller nomination.

At about the same time that Laird was floating his trial balloon, he contacted Rockefeller directly to make certain that he would accept such a nomination if it were offered. He told Rockefeller that Ford was considering selecting him as his nominee for the vice presidency and that he (Laird) had recommended the selection. Rockefeller's immediate response was to demur. He told Laird, "Mel, you really ought to take on that job." Laird replied firmly, "No. I've got to wait four years, I've got to make some money in the meantime." He then pressed Rockefeller: "I think you're ideal. Ford needs you."[9]

Laird has indicated that he did not have to be very persuasive in getting a positive response from Rockefeller.[10] In his view, Rockefeller "was ready to go." However, on Rockefeller's side, there was skepticism about the possibility raised by Laird. The problem for Rockefeller was that Laird had a considerable reputation for deviousness; consequently, Rockefeller was uncertain as to whether he should take the proposition seriously.[11]

Besides the signals about Rockefeller that the press was picking up, there were signs in the days following Ford's assumption of the presidency that George Bush was also under active consideration. This came as no great surprise for, like Melvin Laird, Bush had worked with Ford while a member of Congress. Moreover, as GOP chairman, Bush had worked closely with Vice President Ford in a valiant effort to steer the Republican Party away from entanglement with Watergate problems without, at the same time, alienating Richard Nixon. However, damaging reports began to circulate in Washington, D.C., that linked Bush to the "slush fund" operations of the Nixon White House. Specifically, it was alleged that about $100,000 of White House money had been injected into Bush's abortive 1970 Senate campaign in Texas against Lloyd Bentsen. It also was charged that some $40,000 of these funds had not been properly reported as required by election law.

The effect of these reports was widely regarded as damaging and possibly fatal to Bush's candidacy for the nomination. When directly questioned about this, White House sources confirmed a real potential for embarrassment in the event of a Bush nomination.[12]

However, Bush was not the only target of apparent smear stories directed at contenders for the nomination. Columnist Jack Anderson reported that some of E. Howard Hunt's White House files indicated that Rockefeller had been involved in financing a group paid to disrupt the 1972 Democratic Convention in Miami. No evidence was adduced to link Rockefeller with such an activity, but the report had the effect of throwing the White House into a state of confusion about the situation.

At first, White House spokesmen indicated that the president had received similar information about Rockefeller and that he had referred the matter to the Office of the Special Prosecutor. Later that same day, August 17, it was announced that the investigation of this alleged involvement had been completed and had turned up "nothing whatsoever" to link Rockefeller to it. In an effort to affirm that Rockefeller's candidacy was still very much alive, presidential press secretary Jerry ter Horst observed that, in his view, Rockefeller had been the victim of a smear campaign which he characterized as "the work of extremists who wished for reasons of their own to discredit Governor Rockefeller." Significantly, ter Horst added:

President Ford has advised me that former Governor Rockefeller has been and remains under consideration for the vice presidential nomination.

The president regards the inaccurate information given to Mr. Buchen [White House legal counsel] as a deplorable example of the lengths to which certain persons will go to discredit Mr. Rockefeller and thereby remove him from consideration.[13]

On President Ford's own short list of candidates, in addition to Rockefeller and Bush, was Donald Rumsfeld, ambassador to the North Atlantic Treaty Organization in Brussels. As a former congressman from Illinois, Rumsfeld was a close associate of the new president, who had already brought him into the White House as a member of the Ford transition team.[14] Rumsfeld's credentials were fairly impressive: in the Nixon administration he had served as director of the Office of Economic Opportunity, then as director of the Cost of Living Council, and, finally, had become counselor to the president before his appointment as ambassador to NATO. Although Rumsfeld had enjoyed a close association with the Nixon White House, he was totally untarnished by the Watergate scandals, having been far away at NATO when what came to be known as the "White House horrors" took place. Moreover, Rumsfeld was reported to be anxious to achieve high public office. He had intimated at times that he had been mistaken in giving up his congressional seat to serve as director of the OEO.[15] Publicly, reports that Rumsfeld was under investigation by the FBI intensified speculation among political commentators that he might well be edging out Rockefeller and Bush as the leading candidate for the nomination.[16]

However, the reality was altogether different. Rockefeller was, after Melvin Laird had removed himself from consideration, the president's candidate. Despite all the indications to the contrary in the period of public deliberation over selection of a nominee, Ford had his mind made up within two days of his swearing in as president. This is confirmed by Laird, who has disclosed: "I had a personal meeting with Ford on Sunday, August 11. I had no question after the meeting that his first choice was going to be Rockefeller. Ford had pretty well made up his mind on the eleventh of August."[17] Ford kept his discussions with Laird to himself and had his senior White House staff proceed with the process of consulting with party members on Capitol Hill and in the various states. Robert Hartmann, who had been Ford's key assistant as House minority leader, was given the task of devising a procedure for tabulating nomination suggestions received on a "point system" basis. Fortunately, as it turned out, Rockefeller led all other candidates in the rank ordering of Republican preferences.[18]

By August 16, Ford was ready to communicate his intentions on the nomination directly to Rockefeller. He had Alexander Haig, Nixon's chief-of-staff who had remained to assist the new administration, contact Rockefeller to indicate that the president would be calling the following day. Rockefeller confirmed to Haig that he would await the president's call.

Rockefeller was, at this time, still skeptical about his prospects of having the nomination offered to him. However, his staff advised him that the early soundings by Laird and the expected call from the president indicated that such an offer was indeed on the cards and that he should have his mind made up to respond definitively when Ford called the next day. Although skeptical, Rockefeller was not resisting the idea of becoming vice president under Ford. He felt that there was such a crisis of confidence in the country because of Watergate and the Nixon resignation that it was essential that anyone who was asked to help out should respond affirmatively. Moreover, he strongly believed that the vice president should be someone who clearly had the background and experience to step into the presidency should something happen to the president.[19] And Nelson Rockefeller was such a candidate.

Accordingly, Rockefeller was relaxed and composed as he waited in his living room at Seal Harbor to take the president's call on the afternoon of August 17. When Ford called, he told Rockefeller, "We are seriously thinking of offering you the vice presidency." Therefore, it would be necessary to have the FBI run a check on him. Then, perhaps with the Eagleton affair in mind, Rockefeller was asked whether there was anything in his past that could be a bar to his nomination. Rockefeller responded that he could think of nothing. Meanwhile, the president reassured Rockefeller that the smear story about alleged involvement with campaign dirty tricks had been totally discounted. Although Ford did not explicitly tell Rockefeller that he was the nominee, the discussion implicitly confirmed that. The two men discussed in general terms, for example, the kind of role that Rockefeller might have in the administration.[20]

After he had finished talking with the president, Rockefeller went for a long walk in the woods with his wife, Happy, to talk over the whole thing. His chief concern was for his family. When he resigned the governorship of New York State in 1973, he had, for the first time, enough hours each week to spend with his wife and children. He was enjoying, as were Happy and the children, the absence of the frequent interruptions that public service had imposed on his family life.[21] Happy's response to Nelson's news about the vice presidential offer was supportive. Both agreed that the vice presidency would be essentially for just two years. Therefore, they would not move the family down to Washington; this would avoid disrupting the children's schooling. Instead, they decided that Nelson would commute to Washington, returning each weekend to the family home at Pocantico Hills, New York.[22]

After the FBI had completed its check into Rockefeller's background and given him clearance, Ford instructed Haig on the evening of August 19 to contact Rockefeller in New York to request him to come down to Washington for a ten o'clock meeting at the president's oval office the following morning. Ford had decided to announce to the nation his selection of Rockefeller as his nominee for the vice presidency.

On August 20, Ford first broke the news of Rockefeller's nomination to the congressional leadership and then to the various members of his cabinet. He then joined Rockefeller in a sitting room off the oval office. There, a few moments before the announcement was to be made on national television, he told Rockefeller: "Well, I guess you've guessed by now that you're my choice, and I think I've made a good one." He replied, "Mr. President, I'm gonna do whatever I can to help you and the country."[23]

The decision on Ford's part to offer Rockefeller the nomination had hinged on two basic concerns about which Ford had to satisfy himself: first, whether Rockefeller would be acceptable to the conservative wing of the Republican Party, and, second, whether he might be overshadowed as president by having a Rockefeller in the vice presidency.

On the first of these concerns, Ford had been reassured by the reaction to Laird's trial balloon in the media on August 7. The absence of an outcry signaled to him that the old distrust (which at times had bordered on hatred) of Rockefeller on the party's right wing had abated. Senator Goldwater indicated that the wounds of the 1964 battle between himself and Rockefeller for the Republican nomination had healed, and he stated that he would not object to a Rockefeller vice presidential nomination.[24] Two other conservative Republican senators, Strom Thurmond and John Tower, also indicated that they would not oppose selection of Rockefeller, though neither regarded him as his first choice.[25]

As for the second concern, Ford was able to overcome his own personal misgivings that, even from a historically weak office, as vice president Rockefeller might upstage him. Ford had shown himself in the past to be essentially comfortable and confident within himself, conscious of his own weaknesses and failings but able to live with them. Concerning the prospective problems that might accompany selection of Rockefeller, Ford had his own sense of self-confidence reinforced by a close associate who pointed to the case of Kennedy and Johnson. As Senate majority leader, Johnson had dominated the Senate, but when he became vice president he had been totally overshadowed by President Kennedy who, as Senator Kennedy, had been a mere backbencher during Johnson's Senate leadership years. Furthermore, Ford's associate had counseled, "I have an idea that Nixon picked Spiro Agnew because he was insecure and didn't want anyone who would overshadow him. Don't *you* do anything like that! When you're president, you don't have to worry about being overshadowed by anyone."[26]

If Ford had initial apprehensions about offering the nomination to Rockefeller, in turn Rockefeller might well have been expected to have misgivings of his own about accepting the nomination. Indeed, Laird's preliminary inquiry before Nixon's resignation was designed to find out whether Rockefeller might harbor any such misgivings. After all, Rockefeller had rejected twice before entreaties to accept the vice presidential nomination. First, during the 1960 campaign for the Republican presidential nomination, he had been urged by his main rival, Richard Nixon, to accept the number-two position on a Nixon-Rockefeller ticket. Then, however, Rockefeller had dismissed the idea out of hand, declaring that he refused to regard himself merely as "standby equipment." The second offer had come in 1968, when Rockefeller was approached by Hubert Humphrey. Faced with a splintered Democratic Party, Humphrey sounded out Rockefeller on the possibility of having him as a running mate. Politely, but firmly, Rockefeller had rejected this approach, pointing out that his lifelong Republican ties made a Humphrey-Rockefeller ticket improbable at best.[27] Having passed up vice presidential nominations twice, why did Rockefeller accept at the third asking?

Contemplating the prospects of the vice presidency in the fall of 1974, Rockefeller had to consider the very different circumstances of both the nation and himself. The national situation following the long months of Watergate and a presidential resignation was troubled, despite Ford's declaration following his swearing in as president that "Our long national nightmare is over." Not only did the new president lack an electoral mandate, but also he had taken over an office that was under unremitting attack as the Nixon administration crumbled in the face of revelations about Watergate. Facing the new president were economic problems of crisis magnitude, as the economy continued on a downward path toward recession. The national atmosphere of crisis brought out in Rockefeller the traits of duty and responsibility inculcated in him by a father whose credo was: "Every right implies a responsibility; every opportunity, an obligation; every possession, a duty."[28] As he pondered the state of the nation in August, 1974, Rockefeller's responsibilities, obligations, and duties were clear: they indicated acceptance of the vice presidential nomination.

Rockefeller's own political circumstances were also considerably different in 1974. Whereas in 1960 and 1968 he had ongoing presidential aspirations that precluded consideration of the vice presidency, he had abandoned such aspirations by 1974. It is true that he had reignited his presidential hopes in 1973 when he resigned the governorship of New York, ostensibly to devote himself to two national commissions. Most commentators saw this resignation as a prelude to a campaign for the 1976 Republican presidential nomination. Rockefeller himself had lent credence to such speculation by declaring, "I should like to keep my options open."[29] However, the virtual certainty of an open Republican nomination in 1976 vanished abruptly with the resignation of Nixon in August, 1974. The accession of Ford to the presidency immediately gave to the Republican Party an incumbent eligible to run for election in 1976.

Therefore, like other Republican presidential aspirants, Nelson Rockefeller was left with little or no prospects for 1976.[30] Worse still for Rockefeller was his age: he would be seventy-two in 1980 and too old to mount a serious challenge to other candidates.[31] Accordingly, the offer of the vice presidential nomination by Ford in the fall of 1974 presented

Rockefeller with his last available option to achieve national office. And he accepted it.

NELSON ALDRICH ROCKEFELLER:
THE VICE PRESIDENTIAL NOMINEE

As Jacob Javits, the senior senator from Rockefeller's home state of New York, was to observe as he introduced the nominee on the opening day of his confirmation hearings on September 23, 1974: "If you gave a civil service examination for President of the United States, the head of the class would be Nelson Rockefeller."[32] While such a comment might be dismissed as mere hyperbole normally delivered in support of a "favorite son" nominee, in the case of Rockefeller such a dismissal would be mistaken. Nelson Rockefeller was by background and experience superbly qualified to occupy an office that he might well be called upon to assume.

Born on July 8, 1908, at Bar Harbor, Maine, Nelson Aldrich Rockefeller was the third of six children (a daughter and five sons) of John D. Rockefeller, Jr., and Abby Aldrich Rockefeller.[33] In 1926, he graduated from Lincoln School in New York City. He then entered Dartmouth College where he majored in economics and was elected to Phi Beta Kappa. On graduation from Dartmouth in 1930, he married Mary Todhunter Clark and quickly became a director of the newly built Rockefeller Center in New York City. He remained an officer and board member of Rockefeller Center until he was elected governor of New York State in 1958.

Rockefeller's government career began in 1940, when President Roosevelt named him coordinator of Inter-American Affairs. In this post, he had responsibility for coordinating defense activities and commercial and cultural programs in the American hemisphere. In 1944, Roosevelt named him assistant secretary of state for American Republic Affairs, a post that involved him in formulating a mutual defense pact among the nations of the American hemisphere as well as involving him in the founding of the United Nations at San Francisco.

Although he left government several months after the death of Roosevelt in 1945, Rockefeller returned at President Truman's request to chair the newly created International Development Advisory Board. This board was established by Truman to review his "Point Four" program for international economic and social development in the postwar period.

In 1953, President Eisenhower asked Rockefeller to chair the President's Advisory Committee on Government Organization.[34] Under Rockefeller's direction, this committee produced some fourteen reorganization plans, including a recommendation for the creation of a cabinet-level Department of Health, Education, and Welfare. Other reorganization plans recommended changes in the Departments of Agriculture, Defense, and Justice. When

HEW was established in 1953, Rockefeller became under secretary with operational responsibility for managing the new department. As under secretary, he also was involved in developing rehabilitation programs, as well as widening the scope of Social Security coverage.

In 1954, Eisenhower shifted Rockefeller from HEW and brought him into the White House as special assistant to the president for foreign affairs. This new assignment centered on advising the president on cold-war strategy and involved Rockefeller with the National Security Council as the de facto presidential coordinator for the Central Intelligence Agency. However, this appointment brought with it considerable frustrations. Although he was actively immersed in policy planning and development at the highest levels, as a presidential assistant Rockefeller lacked the decision-making capabilities of the cabinet members with whom he began to clash.[35] His growing concern was with long-range planning, and he became increasingly disaffected by the reactive approach of dealing with each crisis as it arose. In December, 1955, Rockefeller resigned over dissatisfaction with what he regarded as a wholly inadequate response on the part of the Eisenhower administration to the Soviet lead in missile development following the launch of *Sputnik I*.[36]

His concern about the lack of long-range planning in the federal government led Rockefeller to establish a massive study project to review America's domestic and international position and prospects. Financed by the Rockefeller Brothers' Fund at an ultimate cost of $1 million, the "Prospect for America" study was organized under the direction of Dr. Henry A. Kissinger, Harvard University, into a series of six panels. Membership of these panels involved a varied and influential group of individuals including: General Lucius D. Clay; Lester B. Granger, National Urban League; Jacob S. Potofsky, Amalgamated Clothing Workers of America; Edward Teller, University of California; Frazer B. Wilde, Connecticut General Life Insurance Company; and Chester Bowles, former U.S. ambassador to India.

Although Kissinger was the official study director, the driving force behind the study panels and the reports that they produced was Rockefeller. The scope of these reports was wide: they ranged from national-security and foreign-policy concerns to education and "the power of the democratic idea."[37] Issued during the latter part of the 1950s, at a time when many Americans were concerned about Soviet advances in education, technology, and military preparedness,[38] the study's reports received favorable national attention. The reports did much more than spotlight some possible national deficiencies in planning and preparedness; they also had the effect of providing an issues base from which Rockefeller could launch himself into political office—first, in his successful 1958 gubernatorial race in New York State, and then in his abortive attempt to gain the Republican presidential nomination in 1960.

In his first election for public office, Rockefeller scored a spectacular success, defeating incumbent Averell Harriman for the governorship of New York. This 1958 victory was the first in a series of successful gubernatorial campaigns as Rockefeller went on to win election in three successive campaigns: in 1962, over Robert M. Morgenthau; in 1966, over Frank O'Connor; and in 1970, over former Supreme Court Justice Arthur Goldberg.

At bottom, Rockefeller was a New Dealer, and, like Roosevelt, he was convinced that government had a positive role to play in responding to the social and economic needs of the people. Accordingly, as governor of New York over an unprecedented four, four-year terms he worked actively to expand state services. His record of achievement was impressive,[39] and included the following:

- Legislation to prohibit discrimination in private housing;
- Extension of state health and welfare programs;
- Establishment of the largest public university system in the world, which grew to seventy-two campuses and 232,000 full-time students;
- Development of a state revenue-sharing system which ultimately distributed 62 percent of state tax revenues to city and town governments;
- Adoption of statewide air and water pollution control provisions;
- Creation of a large interstate highway system, much of which was built with federal funding.

The major drawback to Rockefeller's active liberal approach, when translated into state programs, was that the programs cost money. The annual budget of New York State during his four-term administration rose from $2 billion in 1959-1960 to more than $10 billion by 1973. In addition to the on-budget costs, there were off-budget expenditures such as the massive state building program, which raised the state debt by an additional $6 billion. The inevitable outcome of rapidly rising state spending was that it raised the tax level of state taxpayers, who became the highest taxed of any state in the union. All of which earned for Rockefeller the reputation of being a spender, a reputation he strenuously resisted.

Like other governors of New York State, Nelson Rockefeller harbored presidential ambitions. In three successive presidential election campaigns, he made abortive attempts to win the Republican presidential nomination. In 1960, he lost to Richard Nixon after a campaign best described as "on-again, off-again." His problems in this race against Nixon were twofold: first, he was indecisive due to a basic uncertainty about the true extent of Nixon's possible delegate strength at the convention; second, he alienated the conservative wing of the Republican Party by insisting that Nixon run on a liberal platform that appeared to repudiate the Eisenhower years.[40]

In 1964, Rockefeller ran a distinctly liberal campaign against the conservative challenge of Senator Barry Goldwater. However, it was a time when the Republican right wing was in the ascendancy and able to dominate the party's convention. Furthermore, Rockefeller's own national constituency of liberals and moderates diminished in size in reaction to his 1963 divorce and remarriage. The contest with Goldwater was bitterly fought and climaxed with Rockefeller being drowned out by a chorus of conservative boos while addressing the convention on national television.[41]

In 1968, Rockefeller again displayed the indecisiveness he had demonstrated in 1960, when he ran for the presidential nomination in a rematch against Nixon. At first, he threw his support behind the campaign of Governor George Romney of Michigan. Romney's withdrawal before the New Hampshire primary prompted speculation that Rockefeller would declare his own candidacy. However, on March 21, Rockefeller announced that he had decided against running. This decision was reversed on April 30, in the wake of Lyndon Johnson's stunning announcement declining to run for a second term. Again the Rockefeller campaign had been activated too late: Nixon won the nomination easily at the Miami Convention.[42]

When Rockefeller left elective office on December 11, 1973, with his resignation as governor of New York State, he announced that he would devote himself to the work of two bipartisan study commissions: the National Commission on Water Quality and the Commission on Critical Choices for Americans. The former commission was one that had been established by the Congress to study pollution and water-quality problems on a nationwide basis. The latter commission broadly resembled the 1955 "Prospect for America" project. Like the 1955 study, the Commission on Critical Choices organized its work into six panels, as follows:

1. Energy and Its Relationship to Ecology, Economics, and World Stability;
2. Food, Health, World Population, and Quality of Life;
3. Raw Materials, Industrial Development, Capital Formation, Employment, and World Trade;
4. International Trade and Monetary Systems, Inflation, and the Relationships among Differing Economic Systems;
5. Change, National Security, and Peace;
6. Quality of Life of Individuals and Communities in the U.S.A.

Here again, the panelists were drawn from the worlds of business, labor, academe, and public life. Included as members of the commission were Robert O. Anderson, chairman, Atlantic Richfield Company; Daniel Boorstin, Smithsonian Institution; Lane Kirkland, AFL-CIO; Sol Linowitz, Coudert Brothers; Clare Booth Luce; Russell Peterson, chairman, Council on Environmental Quality; George Schultz, Bechtel Corporation; Edward Teller, Hoover Institution on War, Revolution, and Peace; Arthur K. Watson, IBM; and George Woods, former president, World Bank. Also serving as a commission member was Gerald R. Ford, Vice President of the United States.

The task of the commission was to formulate long-range proposals for the resolution of the problems that lay ahead as America entered its third century.[43] Echoing his dissatisfactions with the Eisenhower era, Rockefeller observed in his prefatory remarks to the commission:

We can no longer continue to operate on the basis of reacting to crises, counting on crash programs and the expenditure of huge sums of money to solve our problems. We have got to understand and project present trends, to take command of the forces that are emerging, to extend our freedom and well-being as citizens and the future of other nations and peoples in the world.

Accordingly, when the nominee for the office of Vice President of the United States presented himself for confirmation by the Congress in the fall of 1974, the record of achievement, wealth of executive experience, and concern for long-range problem solving that he possessed was one that was virtually matchless. Senator Javits was almost certainly correct: in any civil-service examination for the office of president, Rockefeller would be head of the class.

THE VICE PRESIDENTIAL CONFIRMATION PROCESS

Asked at a press conference at his Seal Harbor vacation home on August 23 about the amount of time that it would take to be confirmed by the Congress, Rockefeller responded:

As long as they want. I have to say this is a tremendously interesting and exciting historic period we are living in and this is the first time that a president and a vice president [have been chosen], whether myself or someone else, who have not been elected by the people of this country. Therefore the Congress has a tremendous responsibility because they're the surrogates for the people of the United States, and their approval will be tantamount to election, so that they have to go back to their own constituents and . . . say we have examined the situation, we went over all this, and he should be confirmed or he shouldn't be confirmed.[44]

At the time, what Rockefeller did not foresee (and, like everyone else, had no means of foreseeing) was that it would take almost four months to gain confirmation in the House and Senate. He would wait for four long months, preoccupied for much of the time with defending his personal financial affairs and those of his family and, at the same time, excluded from the administration he was impatient to join.

The Rockefeller confirmation hearings provided Washington, D.C., with an eagerly awaited spectacle in the fall of 1974. The hearings appeared to hold the promise of revealing to a curious nation hitherto undisclosed details of the wealth and power of a family that had become legendary in its own time. As William V. Shannon wryly observed in the *New York Times*: "Not since Lady Godiva rode naked through the streets of Coventry have the inhabitants of any town itched to see something usually hidden as people here [in Washington] now desire to see the extent of the Rockefeller fortune."[45]

On Capitol Hill, the concern that had to be satisfied was whether there was an inherent conflict of interest posed by the nominee's supposed vast holdings (as well as those of the Rockefeller family) of stocks and shares in major corporations that dealt almost daily with the executive branch he shortly hoped to join. The conflict-of-interest concern sprang from the reality that, although the vice presidency was by itself historically a weak and uninfluential office, the vice president could at any moment succeed to the office of president. It was the possibility of having the power of the presidency wedded to the wealth of the Rockefellers that gave cause for concern.

In his testimony to the Senate Rules and Administration Committee on the first day of hearings on September 23, Rockefeller directly addressed what he termed "the myth or misconception about the extent of the family's control of the economic life of the country." He declared to the committee:

About my holdings, both outright and in trusts for my benefit, my total holdings in any oil company, the highest percentage I own is two-tenths of 1 percent, and the list of the companies and the percentage of stock owned in each is in the material before you.

Now, no member of our family is on the board of any Standard Oil Co. nor do we have representation upon any Standard Oil Co. board, nor do we have any control over the management or the policies of these companies.

I would like to say now about the family, as a whole, and the oil companies, that the total family holdings outright and in trust, all living members of my father's family, that is all of us, the maximum we have in any one company is 2.06 percent of the outstanding stock.[46]

Having laid out the extent of his own personal holdings, as well as those from which he derived any benefits, Rockefeller went on to propose a means of precluding any possible conflicts of interest that might arise should he receive confirmation as vice president:

Now, I have created a blind trust with Morgan Guaranty Trust Co., and should I be confirmed and should Congress request it, I will be glad to put all of my securities that I own outright in a blind trust for the duration. . . . And I will only keep in my own name family real estate in the United States and art.

Now, I will also request the trustees of the two trusts created by my father, of which I am a lifetime beneficiary, I will request them to treat me as if they were a blind trust during the duration.[47]

The personal fortune detailed by Rockefeller, though large by any normal standards, was actually much less than had been anticipated. He had calculated his personal net worth at $62 million, of which more than half (some $33 million) comprised the estimated value of his huge art collection. In addition to these personal assets, he disclosed that he was a lifetime beneficiary in a trust fund established by his father, John D. Rockefeller, Jr., and estimated to be worth $116 million. Thus the total worth of Nelson Rockefeller was put at around $178 million.

For two and one-half days Rockefeller testified before the committee, providing the senators with assurances that the national interest would be of higher concern than Rockefeller family interests. In this effort, he was able to point to his record in New York State to evidence the fact that as a public servant he had never allowed his private affairs to influence executive decisions made in the public's interest. On questions concerning actions taken by President Ford, he was less forthcoming. He was pressed about the wisdom of Ford's issuance of a presidential pardon for ex-President Nixon on September 8, as well as Ford's handling of the Nixon tapes agreement, but he refused to be drawn into passing any kind of judgment about either action.

At the end of the second day of the hearings, prospects for confirmation looked bright. Senator Robert Byrd, who had provided the most vigorous questioning of the nominee, agreed with Committee Chairman Howard Cannon that nothing had arisen that might become a barrier to confirmation.[48] On September 26 the hearings were recessed, with a vote on the confirmation awaiting only the completion of an audit of Rockefeller's taxes.

Meanwhile, no action had been taken on Rockefeller's nomination by the House of Representatives. Although some criticism was voiced about the delay on the House side, Speaker Carl Albert told news reporters: "We want to expedite it, but I don't want to dictate to the Judiciary Committee how much investigation is necessary."[49]

However, all hopes of an easy and early confirmation were abruptly shattered with a series of embarrassing disclosures in successive weeks in October. The first embarrassment came on October 5, when Rockefeller revealed that he had made sizable gifts to several key associates who had held New York State positions under him as staff assistants or as public officials. As this disclosure developed, the total amount of such gifts was calculated to be almost $2 million, not including gift taxes paid by Rockefeller amounting to an additional $840,000. Then, on October 9, Chairman Cannon of the Senate Committee on Rules and Administration, cognizant that the gift disclosures had raised potential problems for the nomination, indicated that there would be no decision on reconvening the committee until after the November 5 elections (by which time the tax audit would be completed). Five days later, on October 10, it was disclosed that the House Judiciary Committee was investigating FBI reports that Rockefeller had financed a derogatory book by Victor Lasky on former Supreme Court Justice Arthur Goldberg. The damaging aspect of this allegation lay in the fact that the book had been financed and published during Rockefeller's reelection race against Goldberg for the governorship in 1970. Finally, on October 18, the results of the tax audit of Rockefeller's taxes were released, and it was disclosed that the Internal Revenue Service was demanding payment of $1 million in back taxes.

Of the problems with which the Rockefeller nomination was now confronted, the easiest to dispose of for Rockefeller was the IRS audit. When the Senate hearings resumed on November 13, Rockefeller made much of the significant fact that the IRS had imposed no interest or penalty on the sum of $1 million now assessed as due. Accordingly, Rockefeller argued, this demonstrated that there had been no improprieties in the handling of his tax affairs.[50]

The problem regarding the Lasky book on Goldberg presented a more difficult concern to deal with because it raised in people's minds aspects of the "dirty tricks" associated with the Watergate scandal. Rockefeller's response to the committee on this issue was to say that he had referred backers of the Lasky book project to his brother Laurance for financial support, without realizing at the time the nature of Lasky's treatment of Goldberg. Laurance had then invested $60,000 to finance publication of the book. Rockefeller was straightforward in admitting to the committee:

Let us face it—I made a mistake. I made a hasty ill-considered decision in the middle of a hectic campaign in 1970.

I . . . want to apologize to Mr. Goldberg . . . I want to apologize to my brother. . . . I want to say that the concept was out of character with the family. I feel very badly, and I made a mistake.[51]

Although the senators pressed Rockefeller and his brother Laurance closely about the Lasky book, nothing was developed in the testimony that demonstrated anything more disturbing than the exercise of "poor judgment."

On the issue of gifts to his staff associates, Rockefeller had no apologies to make whatsoever. On the contrary, he declared to the senators on the committee:

Throughout my life, I have been fortunate to have a relationship of mutual respect, confidence and affection with those . . . men and women of outstanding ability and heritage.

Almost invariably, these have been long time associations—some for over forty years.

Whatever successes I may have had, in both public and private life, have been due to the character, brilliance and continuing sense of common purpose of those with whom I have been associated.

Therefore it was the most natural thing in the world for me to make loans when individual members of this group had personal or family problems, or serious concerns
as to their future ability to meet the needs of their family in their later years.

I know that every one of you has helped friends in need.

And I don't think there is a man or woman in this country who would not have done
the same.

The American tradition has been to share—to help one's neighbor in time of trouble,
to share one's blessings with friends and family.[52]

The concerns of the senators focused on the propriety of giving large
loans and gifts to state officials who were on the state payroll. In particular,
Rockefeller was questioned about his largesse to Dr. William Ronan, chairman of the Port Authority of New York and New Jersey, and a close adviser to the Rockefeller family.

Rockefeller's gifts to Ronan had begun in 1958, when Ronan joined him
in Albany, New York, as secretary to the governor, and had received a gift
of $75,000 prior to taking up his Albany appointment. Subsequently, in a
series of loans ranging in amount from $50,000 to $150,000, Rockefeller
had advanced Ronan some $105,000 between 1962 and 1969. These loans
were made, Rockefeller explained to the committee, to help Ronan "meet
pressing family responsibilities and problems." Then, in 1973, after
Rockefeller's resignation from the governorship, Ronan left his post as
chairman of the Metropolitan Transit Authority to become Port Authority
chairman. During the two weeks' interregnum between Ronan's departure
from the MTA and his appointment at the Port Authority, Rockefeller
forgave him the $510,000 in outstanding loans and made Ronan an addi-
tional gift of $40,000.[53]

Although the senators pressed hard to uncover possible benefits that
Rockefeller family interests might have reaped from decisions made by
Ronan while MTA chairman, nothing was developed to undercut
Rockefeller's claim that no such ulterior motives lay behind his financial
assistance. The plain fact was, Rockefeller declared to the committee, that
Ronan had been (like all of the other staff associates who had received
assistance) responsible and answerable to himself as governor. Since each
was already in the service of Rockefeller in a state capacity, there could be
no question that the financial assistance was a form of bribery.

The committee clearly disliked the pattern of gifts and loans that
Rockefeller had disclosed to it but concluded that there was "no evidence of
any ulterior motive, personal or economic gain, or wrongdoing for any purpose."[54] On his part, Rockefeller bowed to the concerns expressed by the
various senators and agreed to limit his staff gift giving if confirmed as vice
president.[55]

Just before the Senate concluded its second set of hearings, the House Judiciary Committee began its own hearings on the nomination. These hearings were spread over nine days in late November and early December. However, the House traveled over ground already covered by the Senate, and nothing new of any significance was developed.

When the Senate Committee on Rules and Administration voted on Rockefeller's nomination on November 22, the vote was unanimous to recommend confirmation to the full Senate. Formal debate on the Senate floor was held up until the House Judiciary Committee had completed its hearings. The full Senate voted on the nomination on December 10, after a debate spread over two days, and Rockefeller was overwhelmingly confirmed by a vote of ninety to seven.

Later that same week, on December 12, the House Judiciary Committee voted in favor of recommending confirmation to the full House by a vote of twenty-six to twelve. After six hours' debate on the House floor on December 19, Rockefeller was easily confirmed on a 287 to 128 vote.

Shortly after the House confirmation vote, Rockefeller was sworn in as Vice President of the United States by Chief Justice Warren Burger in a special ceremony in the Senate chamber that was carried live on national television. In a brief swearing-in address, Rockefeller looked back on his confirmation experiences and observed:

The thoroughness with which the Congress exercised its responsibility on behalf of the American people under the Twenty-fifth Amendment has been another dramatic evidence of the enduring strength and vitality of our Constitution and our unique American system.

I've learned a great deal from this experience of the past four months. And I've come out of it with an even greater respect for the Congress of the United States, a more profound appreciation of the collective wisdom of the American people as expressed through the Congress, and a deeper understanding of the breadth of the responsibility to the people of this great free land that falls upon those of us in positions of public trust.[56]

Nelson Aldrich Rockefeller had now become the forty-first Vice President of the United States. He was eager to become the first vice president with a substantive policy role to perform.

THE VICE PRESIDENT'S ASSIGNMENTS

The question of Nelson Rockefeller's vice presidential role was raised during the first day of his confirmation hearings before the Senate Rules and Administration Committee. In response to Chairman Cannon, Rockefeller indicated that President Ford was awaiting the conclusion of the confirmation process before he "crystallize[d] the nature of the relationship.'' When Senator Marlow Cook of Kentucky pressed Rockefeller about his possible role in foreign policy and, in particular, about his future relationship with Secretary of State Henry Kissinger, he received a much fuller response:

In the very broad conversations which I have had with the president on this subject, I got the impression, frankly, that what he had in mind was my assistance in the domestic field and not in the foreign field.

I had the impression that he was talking about the domestic field when he and I talked.

I am sure that there will be something that will develop only as and when I do get confirmed.

My relationship with Secretary Kissinger is long-standing. I have been a sort of sounding board for him on various occasions. Everybody has to talk to somebody once in a while that they have known for a long while and known well, and he and I have that relationship.

Whatever the relationship was, it would be prescribed by the president and would be within the framework of the Constitution and his powers and whatever he asked me to do. I would not intervene or interfere in any way, and I think I am sensitive to these questions.[57]

In fact, consideration of a vice presidential role for Rockefeller in the Ford administration had begun prior to his actual selection for the nomination. Melvin Laird has disclosed that it was his recommendation to Ford, when discussing with him the selection of Rockefeller prior to Nixon's resignation on August 9, that Rockefeller would greatly strengthen a Ford administration in domestic affairs. As Laird put it:

My recommendations were that we get him very heavily involved in the domestic problems that faced the United States, particularly as they applied to the cities and as they applied to minority population groups. This could have a tremendous influence on the [1976] campaign and on the acceptancy of the Ford presidency.

I wanted [Rockefeller] to be chairman of the Domestic Council, and *act* as the chairman of the Domestic Council with those [domestic] sections of the cabinet reporting in through him.[58]

Laird's concerns about Ford's anticipated presidency were twofold: first, Ford had to reach outward to begin the process of building a national constituency for the 1976 election; second, Ford had to bring executive talent into his administration to establish distinctly a Ford record of achievement. Involving Nelson Rockefeller actively in the Ford administration would greatly assist in meeting these goals. That Rockefeller possessed some kind of national constituency was beyond doubt: the earlier overtures of Nixon and Humphrey to have him as a running mate, in 1960 and 1968, respectively, testified eloquently on that score. Moreover, Rockefeller's appeal lay within liberal and moderate groups—groups that a somewhat conservative Ford might have trouble capturing without a liberal running mate. Furthermore, in addition to his own acknowledged executive skills, Rockefeller had a wide reputation for attracting talented people to work for him in government and with his various study panels.

Accordingly, when President Ford called Rockefeller at Seal Harbor to indicate that he was seriously under consideration for the vice presidential nomination, he discussed the kind of role that Laird had recommended. As Rockefeller recalled his conversation with the president:

He . . . talked about this on the phone, the role, the domestic role: he wanted me to take responsibility for the development of the domestic programs.

He wanted me to help him secure people because, he said, "You have a reputation and a record of always getting the best people and you can be very helpful."[59]

Meanwhile, the transition team assembled by Ford to consider the manifold problems of putting together a new administration gave some consideration to a vice presidential role. The team's recommendation indicated that the vice president should have an advisory role in policy areas, a role that went beyond the traditional one of ceremony and symbolic duty. However, the transition team did not devote much time and attention to vice presidential functions because the president had indicated that he wanted to keep "a close hold on that."[60]

During the four months that Rockefeller found himself stranded on Capitol Hill awaiting the outcome of the congressional confirmation process, there was little contact between himself and the White House. As Rockefeller recalled the situation: "I had no contact with the president. I felt badly that I was causing him this delay [and] difficulties. . . . So we didn't do anything."[61]

Two days after Rockefeller had been confirmed and sworn in as vice president, President Ford presented him with an agenda of vice presidential responsibilities. At a White House meeting between the president and the vice president on December 21, with their respective close aides in attendance,[62] Ford gave Rockefeller the following list of assignments:

1. The vice president was to be a member of the National Security Council;[63]

2. The vice president was to be vice chairman of the Domestic Council, with a strong emphasis on working with the White House to find a replacement for Kenneth Cole as executive director of the council;[64]

3. The vice president was to play a role in coordinating Domestic Council activities with the nation's governors and mayors;[65]

4. The vice president was to employ his wide association in and out of government to help recruit top people for the Ford administration;

5. The vice president was to become a member of the Murphy Commission. This commission (formally entitled the Commission for the Conduct of Foreign Policy) had been created to analyze and make recommendations on the implementation and improvement of U.S. foreign policy;[66]
6. The vice president was to study the question of whether a White House science adviser, or board of advisers, should be appointed and to produce recommendations for the president within a month;
7. The vice president was to assist in presenting and explaining the president's domestic and foreign policy programs (the SALT agreement was specifically mentioned) throughout the country;
8. The vice president was asked to consider some new, or more clearly defined direction for the American Revolutionary Bicentennial Administration;
9. The vice president's staff was to attend all regular White House staff meetings.

At first sight, the list of vice presidential assignments appears to signal little change in the standard role played by modern vice presidents. Since 1949, all vice presidents had enjoyed membership in the National Security Council, and, since 1970, they had also participated as members of the Domestic Council. Moreover, the coordination role with the nation's governors and mayors was fairly traditional, one that Agnew, for example, had undertaken in the Nixon administration. Similarly, the assignment of recruiting people for the administration had less than a novel appearance. As for Rockefeller's membership in the Murphy Commission, this was clearly in the best tradition of vice presidential assignment to past presidential commissions. Likewise, the tasks of providing recommendations on creating a White House science advisory unit and on the shape of the bicentennial celebration typified presidential consultation with the vice president. Finally, all modern vice presidents had been pressed into service as spokesmen for the administration.

However, such surface appearances masked an important underlying reality; Ford *needed* Rockefeller as an active contributing presidential assistant able to provide vision, purpose, and achievement in the fledgling Ford administration. With Rockefeller as the incumbent, the vice president had some thirty-four years of experience and achievement in domestic- and foreign-policy development and implementation at federal and state levels of government, as well as excellent access to the corporate heads of the banking and industrial worlds. Accordingly, when the December 21 assignments are reconsidered in the light of Ford's need for substantive input from Rockefeller, the nature of the vice president's role becomes much clearer.

In the case of the National Security Council assignment, Rockefeller brought to an otherwise mandatory membership considerable depth of background in national-security and foreign-policy affairs. In the Eisenhower White House, as noted, he had been national security adviser to the president, and he enjoyed a close relationship with the current Ford national security adviser, Henry Kissinger, who also held appointment as secretary of state. This background and his long association with Kissinger gave his NSC membership a different coloration from that of previous vice presidents. Similarly, Rockefeller's membership in the Murphy Commission was intended to utilize his vast experience in the national-security/foreign-policy areas. His precise role as a commission member was to lend to a sagging effort an invigorated sense of purpose and direction.[67]

As for the vice president's assignment of assisting with the recruitment of talent for the administration, this again was no mere courtesy extended by the president. Rather, it reflected explicit recognition that the Ford administration had the services of one of the best recruiters of imaginative and creative staff; Rockefeller had a reputation par excellence for attracting the best people in whatever field of endeavor he had pursued. Anxious to secure replacements for Nixon holdovers, the Ford administration had a substantial interest in employing the recruitment services of the vice president.[68]

The assignment regarding the proposal to create a presidential science adviser was an appropriate assignment to be given to Vice President Rockefeller because he had a personal contribution to make on the question. He was an enthusiast on the proposal, having employed the consulting services of a science adviser since the 1950s, when he had begun an association with Edward Teller, nuclear physicist and recipient of the Fermi Award.

Some three of the vice president's assignments of December 21 can safely be viewed as standard vice presidential fare: those involving the Federal Pay Commission, the Bicentennial Administration, and liaison with governors and mayors—although, even here, Rockefeller's considerable background as a federal executive responsible for a vast public service payroll, and as a governor of a major state, related in respective ways to these assignments. Nonetheless, each of these tasks typified the assignments of secondary importance that had become the hallmark of the vice presidency.

The assignment that carried with it the most substantive involvement in the policy work of the administration was unquestionably the vice president's role with the Domestic Council. With a formal membership that spanned the domestic cabinet departments and several key domestic agencies, the Domestic Council occupied a strategic policy-making position, one that brought with it extraordinary potential for influence in an administration.[69] Previous vice presidents had held membership in the Domestic Council, but, since the work of the council was done at the staff level under the direction of the executive director, formal vice presidential membership had been a hollow assignment. In Rockefeller's case, his Domestic Council assignment involved him as vice chairman of the council, a newly created position that seemed to presage greater direct vice presidential involvement with the work of the council. More significantly, Rockefeller had been assigned the task of finding a new executive director to replace Kenneth Cole.[70]

President Ford's intentions regarding Rockefeller's involvement with the Domestic Council were straightforward at the outset. His preliminary discussions with Rockefeller during the August 17 telephone conversation had essentially accorded to him the principal administration role in the development of domestic policy, a role that was to be the domestic counterpart to Henry Kissinger's in the areas of national security and foreign policy. Rockefeller, of course, was admirably equipped for such a domestic-policy role. Not only had he served as under secretary of the Department of Health, Education, and Welfare, and as chairman of President Eisenhower's reorganization committee, but he had also been an activist chief executive of the state with the most developed social programs in the nation. As the principal actor in the domestic-policy area, Rockefeller's assumption of the vice presidency held high promise that the vice presidential office would become elevated to a much higher stature and status.

When President Ford and Vice President Rockefeller concluded their meeting on December 21, Ford appeared to be enraptured by the prospect of working closely with Rockefeller. He declared to his new vice president: "I am excited about it." He then remarked to those around him: "In looking forward to the future with the vice president now in place, we have a great opportunity."[71]

Meanwhile, Rockefeller arranged to fly off for a much-needed vacation at a Rockefeller-owned resort in the Caribbean to recover from the rigors of his lengthy confirmation hearings. He would report back to begin work as vice president on Saturday, January 4, 1975.

· 3 · ROCKEFELLER AS DOMESTIC-POLICY MAKER: VICE CHAIRMAN OF THE DOMESTIC COUNCIL

THE DOMESTIC COUNCIL

The Domestic Council, upon which President Ford had placed a special emphasis when discussing Vice President Rockefeller's role in the administration, had enjoyed a brief but checkered history. Originally it was conceived by the Ash Council as a small White House unit staffed by professionals, "where major domestic programs may be evaluated against each other and against available resources, and integrated for maximum effectiveness."[1]

As it was operated under the direction of its first executive director, John Ehrlichman, the Domestic Council rose to such a position of power in the Nixon administration that it completely dominated the domestic cabinet secretaries and began to involve itself directly in departmental program activities. After Ehrlichman's departure from the Nixon administration in the wake of Watergate revelations, the council's role was severely cut back, and under the direction of Kenneth Cole the council operated principally as a service mechanism linking the White House with the domestic departments and agencies.

The proposal of the Ash Council in 1969 to reorganize the Bureau of the Budget as the Office of Management and Budget and to create the Domestic Council was a response to the enormous expansion of the federal role, particularly in domestic-policy areas, during the 1960s. Incorporating the Ash Council's proposals in Reorganization Plan No. 2 of 1970, President Nixon outlined to Congress in March, 1970, the functions of the proposed domestic-policy and budget units:

Essentially, the plan recognizes that two closely connected but basically separate functions both center in the president's office: policy determination and executive management. This involves (1) what government should do, and (2) how it goes about doing it.

My proposed reorganization creates a new entity to deal with each of these functions:

1. It establishes a Domestic Council to coordinate policy formulation in the domestic area. This cabinet group would be provided with an institutional staff, and to a considerable degree would be a domestic counterpart to the National Security Council.

2. It establishes an Office of Management and Budget, which would be the president's principal arm for the exercise of managerial functions.

   The Domestic Council will be primarily concerned with what we do; the Office of Management and Budget will be primarily concerned with how we do it and how well we do it.[2]

Like the National Security Council, the Domestic Council had a formal membership: this comprised the president (as chairman); the vice president; the secretaries of treasury, interior, agriculture, commerce, labor, health, education, and welfare, housing and urban development, and transportation; the attorney general; and the heads of several domestic federal agencies. However, the basic work of the council would be done by its professional staff, operating under the council's executive director.

As outlined by Nixon, the role of the Domestic Council was to advise the president on the entire range of domestic concerns and to integrate the various domestic-policy components into a coherent whole. Specifically, the council was assigned five basic functions:

1. Assessing national needs, collecting information, and developing forecasts for the purpose of defining national goals and objectives.

2. Identifying alternative ways of achieving these objectives and recommending consistent, integrated sets of policy choices.

3. Providing rapid response to presidential needs for policy advice on pressing domestic issues.

4. Coordinating the establishment of national priorities for the allocation of available resources.

5. Maintaining a continuous review of the conduct of ongoing programs from a policy standpoint, and proposing reforms as needed.[3]

Under the direction of John Ehrlichman, the functions of the Domestic Council staff were extremely varied and dealt with policy considerations on both a long-term and a short-term basis.[4] Overall, the staff provided a mechanism for processing domestic-policy proposals that came to the White House from a variety of sources, including departments and agencies, units of the executive office of the president (in particular, OMB), the Congress, and public- and private-interest groups. The staff worked to clarify and articulate presidential options on policy proposals, insuring that all arguments for and against were presented and that all necessary recommendations had been obtained from department and agency staff and from staff assistants within the executive office. On the long-range side, the primary responsibility of the staff was developing the domestic-policy component of the annual State of the Union Message, setting out the president's legislative agenda for the year ahead. However, the consideration of long-range planning concerns was subjected to constant interruption as the attentions of the staff were diverted to day-to-day work or firefighting activities.

Organizationally, the Domestic Council staff was differentiated on the basis of subject matter specialization. The various subject matter areas concerning the staff were dealt with singly or in clusters under the direction of associate or assistant directors, as the following set of six divisions indicates:

- Welfare, labor, school desegregation
- Revenue sharing, budget procedures
- Administration, staff management
- Environment, agriculture, national-growth policy
- Law enforcement, housing, transportation, government reorganization, drugs
- Minority groups[5]

Although the Ash Council's recommendations for the establishment of the Domestic Council had been concerned with the policy needs of an overworked presidency, the reasons underlying President Nixon's acceptance of the recommendations went further than considerations of policy development. While Nixon was concerned about the policy needs of the presidency, from the standpoint of getting better developed policy, he was at the same time much more interested in establishing for the president central control of policy throughout the entire executive branch. The inevitable result of this approach was the downgrading of the cabinet secretaries, who were frequently cut off from direct contact with the president, having to deal instead with Ehrlichman or a member of his Domestic Council staff. The relative standings of council staffers and cabinet officers were made clear in a revealing account of Domestic Council operations provided by John Ehrlichman. As he described the situation when he served as executive director:

One of the most persistent and difficult aspects of staff management was the refusal of a few cabinet officers to believe that the president actually did not want to hear their oral arguments on policy disputes. Occasionally, these unrequited debaters would publicly charge that an opportunity to present their views had been denied them by an overprotective staff. In point of fact, the staff had a converse problem: frequently, it was hard to meet congressional and other deadlines because work was bottlenecked in the office of some cabinet secretary.

At times, the staff would persuade the president, against his desire and judgment, to see a cabinet officer and listen to his oral presentation. Now that we know that these sessions were tape-recorded, historians will be in a position to judge whether they were worth the time of the president, the secretary, and countless bureaucrats who prepared the secretary's briefing papers. Obviously, I did not attend all such sessions, but I do not recall any in which a new fact or argument was offered.[6]

Under the pressures of Watergate revelations, Nixon felt compelled to restore some authority and prestige to the cabinet. He established four "super-secretary" positions with Agriculture Secretary Earl Butz given overall supervision of natural resources, HEW Secretary Caspar Weinberger assigned oversight of human resources, HUD Secretary James Lynn assigned to cover community development, and Treasury Secretary George Schultz given oversight of economic affairs. These four super-secretaries were expected to function both as cabinet department heads and as counselors to the president for their oversight areas. Although this did not totally return power to the cabinet as a whole, the effect of the arrangement was to reduce some of the authority and influence of the Domestic Council staff who had to deal somewhat circumspectly with the new counselor-cabinet officers.[7]

Following the resignations of Haldeman and Ehrlichman in 1973, Nixon implemented further reorganization of his administration. First, he abandoned his experiment with the super-secretaries and thus appeared to enlarge the overall status of the cabinet.[8] Second, he divided White House domestic-policy responsibilities between Melvin Laird and Kenneth Cole: Laird was given the position of counselor to the president for domestic affairs while Cole became executive director of the Domestic Council. Since Ehrlichman had held both positions simultaneously, this represented a further cutback in the power and influence of the Domestic Council: for the first time, its executive director reported to a presidential adviser and not directly to the president himself.[9]

Under Cole's direction, the council's staff was involved largely in operational work, providing scheduling services for the president as well as monitoring and analysis functions and the normal firefighting chores demanded by the White House. Cole was sensitive to charges that the Domestic Council's role had been downgraded and insisted:

Our functions are basically the same. We were never intended to be a decision-making or policy-making body. Our function is to insure that the president has the information to make the best possible judgment.

Our job is the same: the mechanism is different. We are less self-contained. We are trying to accomplish more of our work through the counselors and people in the departments.[10]

However, the fact was that the role of the Domestic Council had been reduced, a fact underscored by the cutback in staff levels from a high of seventy under Ehrlichman to some thirty under Cole's direction.

When Ford assumed the presidency following Nixon's resignation in August, 1974, his transition team examined the Domestic Council's role and functions from the standpoint of the needs of a Ford White House. The major recommendation of the Ford team was to stress the need for a decentralized White House establishment, a recommendation considered virtually obligatory in the wake of the discredited Nixon administration. However, some merit was recognized in advocating retention of the Domestic Council, but at the level it had assumed under Cole's tenure.

When the president sought Cole's recommendations on the retention of the Domestic Council, Cole put the case strongly to Ford: "You need a domestic-policy staff which is responsible for sorting out and presenting in an unbiased fashion conflicting or differing domestic-policy advice from the departments and agencies, the OMB, the Congress, outside interests, including state and local government, and others." Although he conceded to the president that the long-range policy development work of the council's staff had been overwhelmed by the day-to-day responsibilities, this did not suggest to him that these should be abandoned. Rather, he advised: "If you elect to keep the Domestic Council structure, we should strengthen our capacity for development of a 'think tank' to generate new ideas. I'd like to say that all the new ideas come from the cabinet, but that has not been the experience of the last four years."[11]

VICE PRESIDENT ROCKEFELLER AND HIS
DOMESTIC-POLICY ROLE

When Gerald Ford first discussed with Nelson Rockefeller the vice presidential nomination in August, 1974, he had indicated that he intended Rockefeller to play a substantive role in the domestic-policy area, telling him: "I want you on the domestic, and Henry [Kissinger] on the foreign, and then we can move these things."[12] Accordingly, Rockefeller regarded the Domestic Council assignment given to him as vice president on December 21 as the means of effecting the major domestic-policy role envisioned by Ford earlier in August. In the vice president's view, the vice chairmanship of the Domestic Council, cojoined with the task of securing a replacement for Kenneth Cole as executive director, indicated his responsibility "to pull the Domestic Council together and to come up with a program on that, and to take over that."[13]

In fact, Rockefeller had begun preparations for his domestic-policy role just prior to his confirmation as vice president. In early December, he was briefed on the nature and functions of the Domestic Council by Peter Wallison, who was serving as counsel to the Commission on Critical Choices. Wallison was well equipped for this briefing task since he had served as a staff member of the Ash Council during the development of the Domestic Council concept. In a memorandum to Rockefeller on December 9, Wallison advised:

The Domestic Council . . . has extremely broad powers to gather, analyze, and project data, and can (with the president's support) convene interagency meetings for the purpose of formulating policy. It appears to have a preeminent claim to review, alter, or reject policy initiatives coming out of any executive agency before they reach the president's desk.

Since the departure of John Ehrlichman, the council has been without substantial presidential patronage. As a result, it has lost its mandate and much of its staff resources.[14]

However, within the new Ford administration the position of the Domestic Council had been further weakened by the emergence of two new executive office units: the Economic Policy Board (EPB) and the Energy Resources Council (ERC). Both had been established in accordance with the broad recommendation of Ford's transition team that the White House structure be decentralized; therefore, both had roles and functions that overlapped those of the Domestic Council. Moreover, both the EPB and the ERC were headed by close associates of the president, indicating perhaps that they might be strong challengers to any claim of preeminence asserted by the Domestic Council over domestic-policy matters. Directed by William Seidman, the EPB had been established by executive order on September 30, 1974, with a mandate "to oversee the formulation, coordination, and implementation of all economic policy, and to serve as the focal point for economic decision making."[15] The ERC also had been created by executive order, on October 11, 1974, in order "to provide a means for the coordination of energy-policy matters at the presidential level."[16] Ford had appointed Commerce Secretary Rogers Morton as ERC chairman, with Frank Zarb, FEA administrator, serving as ERC executive director.

Accordingly, as Rockefeller examined the situation, the difficulties inherent in asserting preeminence for the Domestic Council in domestic policy were immediately apparent. It was, for him, "a very difficult thing to visualize how you could get a composite Domestic Council approach to the problems of this country: economic, financial, and social. And you can't separate them with these groups which had independent status."[17]

Therefore, when Vice President Rockefeller was given his Domestic Council assignments, he had given considerable thought to the council's possible role and functions in the Ford administration. Building on this preparatory thinking, he developed a proposal to incorporate both the ERC and the EPB into the sphere of the Domestic Council. However, he did much more than merely formulate an institutional leadership role for the council; by proposing that he personally replace Kenneth Cole as executive director, the vice president sought to obtain a personal leadership role for himself.[18]

The Domestic Council proposals that he submitted to the president encountered immediate and serious opposition from senior members of Ford's White House staff. These objections were grounded on several arguments, most of which focused on the proposal that the vice president personally would assume the executive director's position.

When Ford asked his legal counsel, Philip Buchen, for his opinion about Rockefeller's proposals, Buchen adduced two sets of arguments to advise rejection of them. First, Buchen argued, it was probably not legally possible for the vice president to hold two Domestic Council positions—vice chairman and executive director. In Buchen's opinion, "This could no more be done than to have the vice president as a cabinet officer." Buchen objected to appointment of the vice president as executive director because the position would be limiting and demeaning for a vice president. As he explained, the executive director's position was essentially "a paper-pushing job and a tough administrative job." In Buchen's view, a vice president ought not to be confined to the daily operations of coordinating the White House domestic-policy paper flow. Furthermore, he argued strongly that it was vital that the White House staff function on the basis of equality. With the vice president in a staff position as director, this situation would not remain possible. As Buchen explained:

I just couldn't envision him, and I don't think anyone else could, doing the kind of interchange between equal advisers to hash out a position of what you'd recommend to the president.

You couldn't operate if there was someone across the Executive Drive who could second-guess what we were doing.[19]

Donald Rumsfeld, who had replaced Alexander Haig as White House coordinator, also had strong objections to Rockefeller's proposal to assume the position of executive director. Rumsfeld's concerns related directly to his own role as coordinator: all of the paper flow to and from the oval office of the president was routed via the White House coordinator, whose function it was to insure that all papers for the president had been fully circulated to all senior White House staff members for comments and recommendations. Having consolidated his central position as White House coordinator in the months following his appointment on October 1, Rumsfeld was not anxious to see his carefully established coordination process bypassed by a vice president who would want to coordinate domestic-policy matters personally. More altruistically, Rumsfeld objected to the Rockefeller proposal because it would alter the basic nature of the Domestic Council's place in the executive office. From its inception, the council had operated as an arm of the presidency; Rockefeller's assumption of its operational direction would make it an arm of the vice presidency.[20]

Concerned about the opposition being generated to his Domestic Council proposal by the senior White House staff, Rockefeller met with Rumsfeld to discuss the situation. At the outset, he pointed out to Rumsfeld: "Look, obviously I can't be useful here unless I have the enthusiastic cooperation and support of the White House staff. I want to find a way of making this [proposal] something.'' According to Rockefeller, Rumsfeld responded: ''Well, I have a seven-thirty meeting every morning, and I have an eight o'clock meeting . . . where I coordinate all of the problems of the day and take them to the president, and how are you going to fit into that?'' Mulling over this question in his mind, Rockefeller indicated that he was not about to participate personally in these daily staff meetings. Instead, he put forward a counterproposal, telling Rumsfeld:

Frankly, that is not the way I would run the White House, but this is your business.

That is all right. What I will do is . . . instead of being chairman of the Domestic Council myself or the special assistant to the president in charge [of it], I will pick somebody who can go to the seven-thirty meeting and the eight o'clock meeting and who can shuffle these papers for you.[21]

Having abandoned his intention to become the executive director, Rockefeller went off to devise a new proposal that would meet the objections previously raised by the senior Ford staff and that would, at the same time, advance his own intentions to establish a dynamic role for the Domestic Council in the administration. Accordingly, he developed a proposal to have two of his own close associates appointed as executive director and deputy director to direct respectively the staff functions and the planning responsibilities of the council, retaining for himself oversight responsibilities as vice chairman.[22] The virtues of this plan were several: on the one hand, it would meet the objections of Rumsfeld and Buchen to the vice president's personal assumption of the executive director's job; on the other hand, it would insure for Rockefeller the control of the Domestic Council that he considered necessary for his role as principal domestic-policy planner in the administration.

However, Rockefeller's new proposal did nothing to allay the apprehensions of those senior White House staffers opposed to his original proposal. In fact, the plan to install Rockefeller aides to the two principal staff positions on the Domestic Council served to heighten fears that the council would become a distinctly vice presidential unit. And, in the cases of Buchen and Rumsfeld, such a prospect was totally unacceptable.

Therefore, consideration was given by Buchen and Rumsfeld to the development of an amendment to the vice president's new proposal that would have the effect of meeting their own objections and grant to Rockefeller control of the policy-planning area he appeared desirous of directing. Their amendment took the form of a proposal to divide the work of the Domestic Council into two distinct parts: one component would perform the daily operational staff functions and would be directed by the council's executive director;[23] the other component would focus on the long-range planning functions and would come under the supervision of the vice president. Explaining the thinking of the senior staff on the situation, Buchen observed:

The conception was evolved: Let's put the executive director in place [with] a deputy director who would be in charge of the long-range planning. Then let [the deputy director] at least filter everything through the vice president, but also have him report to the executive director as to what he was doing.

So we conceived of the notion that the long-range planner ought to be Rockefeller's nominee, and the man who had the title of executive director, but would be responsible for the day-to-day operations, would be a Ford guy.[24]

As their candidate for the executive director's position, under the terms of this amended version of Rockefeller's proposal, Buchen and Rumsfeld agreed upon Buchen's deputy, Philip Areeda. On the face of it, Areeda's credentials were impressive: he was a Harvard law professor whose specialty was antitrust law, and he possessed White House experience, having served in the counsel's office of the Eisenhower administration with domestic-policy responsibilities.[25] Having selected Areeda as their candidate, Buchen and Rumsfeld arranged to have him meet with the vice president to explain to Rockefeller how he envisioned his role as executive director responsible for the operational work of the council. As might have been expected, the outcome of that meeting was not harmonious. Buchen declared of the outcome: "That's when the whole thing blew, and things got very tense."[26]

Meanwhile, disturbed at the way that Buchen and Rumsfeld were amending and adapting his proposals for the Domestic Council's key positions, Rockefeller sent in a blunt memorandum to the president, setting out his assessment that he needed "enthusiastic support and cooperation" from the White House staff in order to succeed in the role that he and the president had agreed upon in August of 1974. Without such cooperation, Rockefeller declared, "I think I am better off to withdraw." Ford responded that he thought his staff was supportive of the vice president, and he reaffirmed his wish to have Rockefeller play a large domestic-policy role in the administration.[27]

With this show of presidential support, Rockefeller then submitted to Ford his proposal to have two close aides, James Cannon and Richard Dunham, appointed to the respective Domestic Council positions of executive director and deputy director. At this juncture, Buchen and Rumsfeld began pushing Areeda as their rival candidate for the executive directorship, and Rockefeller became very upset. His objection to the Areeda candidacy was that, if successful, it would deprive him of control over the operational functions of the council's work. Although it was true, as Buchen and Rumsfeld asserted, that his own interests lay decidedly with long-range planning and policy-development considerations, Rockefeller possessed sufficient experience of government to know the validity of the Ehrlichman dictum "operations is policy" (sic). Accordingly, the vice president was insistent that he had to have his own man appointed as executive director. With Areeda in control of operations, Rockefeller was certain he would be cut off from the ongoing domestic-policy considerations of the administration. Because such a prospect was unacceptable to him, he took his case to President Ford and declared:

Mr. President . . . I don't want anything to do with this under false pretenses and have you think that I am going to do something if I am not. And I know enough about administration and what I can do. This is as far as I can go. If you want this plan I think I can make it work. If you want less than this, these other schemes: forget it. Just let me out of this and I will go on with these other things you have given me.[28]

Confronted with a difficult decision, which in effect meant choosing between his senior White House staff and his vice president, Ford approved the Rockefeller proposal and agreed to appoint Cannon over Areeda as executive director. In doing so, Ford not only reaffirmed his August understanding about Rockefeller's administration role, but also avoided an extremely damaging rift in the administration that would have been occasioned by the vice president's intended withdrawal from any domestic-policy role.

Meanwhile, Rockefeller was concerned also about the institutional roles of the EPB and the ERC, and the adverse impact that each might have on asserting preeminence for the Domestic Council on domestic-policy matters. Accordingly, he arranged a meeting of all interested parties to attempt to resolve the major problems of overlapping jurisdictions and roles.

Therefore, on February 7, 1975, at a meeting attended by the vice president; his two aides, James Cannon and Richard Dunham; James Lynn, OMB director; Frank Zarb, ERC executive director; and William Seidman, EPB executive director, the following guidelines were discussed and agreed upon by all present:

1. The daily 8:30 A.M. EPB executive committee meeting would serve as the coordinating mechanism for short and intermediate problems, since it was attended by all of the coordinating bodies.
2. The vice president and the Domestic Council would establish a task force, including the EPB, the ERC, the NSC, and the Domestic Council, to undertake the long-range planning project now undertaken by the EPB. The task force would have as its objective presenting the president with options for long-range goals and direction for his administration.
3. The Domestic Council would undertake a review of the social programs as a priority need.[29]

From the standpoint of the vice president and the Domestic Council, these guidelines were of real significance because they established for the council the leading role in long-range planning, with the other units participating as members of a Domestic Council task force. At the time, this was an important achievement because it gave back to the Domestic Council a function assumed by the EPB at a time when the council was bereft of power and patronage. Moreover, the agreement created some impetus for a social programs review by the Domestic Council, a review with which the vice president would become intensely involved.

Finally, after two arduous months of discussions, arguments, and compromises, President Ford was able to announce a revised format and role for the Domestic Council as it would function under the supervision of its vice chairman, the vice president. In a February 13 memorandum to all members of the Domestic Council, Ford declared:

Because of the complexity and interrelationship of domestic policies and programs, I believe the broadest possible perspectives must be brought to bear in the Domestic Council's deliberations. For this reason, I have asked the vice president to serve as vice chairman of the council and to oversee the work of the council.

I am also asking the vice president to review the operations of the council staff and to propose such reorganization of the council as from time to time may be necessary.

To expedite the work of the Domestic Council, the vice president will make recommendations to me for the formation of task forces and review groups of officials at the appropriate levels of departments and agencies involved.

For the Domestic Council to carry out its objectives, it is essential that the council have the full cooperation of your department or agency, including the necessary staff support for the various task forces and review groups which will be established.

I am today announcing my intention to appoint Mr. James M. Cannon executive director of the Domestic Council and assistant to the president for domestic affairs. Richard L. Dunham will be the deputy director of the Domestic Council. I expect them to work closely with the vice president in conducting the operations of the Domestic Council.

To provide full cooperation of the work of the Domestic Council with the work of other policy bodies, the executive director of the Economic Policy Board and the executive director of the Energy Resources Council will be designated as members of the Domestic Council.[30]

THE VICE PRESIDENT AND THE DOMESTIC COUNCIL

The president's announcement of the appointment of two close Rockefeller associates to the leadership positions of the Domestic Council appeared to give the vice president dominion over domestic-policy affairs in the Ford administration. However, that appearance was more shadow than substance. For one thing, it masked the reality that the institutional linkages within the executive office of the president bound the Domestic Council staff to the presidency and not to the vice presidency. For another, the real nature of the vast bulk of the Domestic Council staff's functions virtually insured an absence of vice presidential interest in all but a small portion of council activities.

Rockefeller's selection of Cannon and Dunham for appointment respectively as executive director and deputy director reflected a judgment that the two men would work together as a team, complementing each other with different skills and abilities. Cannon brought to his position considerable staff management skills, which were combined with an acute understanding and knowledge of political affairs at the national level. While working with Rockefeller in New York, Cannon had demonstrated a penchant for "getting along in a very tight situation where your power is ill-defined."[31] As for Dunham, he brought to the Domestic Council experience of the substantive, procedural responsibilities of government. He possessed a good knowledge and understanding of federal programs and how they worked.

Essentially, it was Rockefeller's intention to have Cannon operate as executive director to supervise and direct the operational side of the Domestic Council, handling personally the all-important area of relations with other members of the administration within the White House and the various departments and agencies. Dunham's responsibilities would be concentrated on the substantive policy work, developing the long-range policy capabilities of the council's staff. This was the area that Nelson Rockefeller was personally interested in; therefore, Dunham's role was of special significance. Overall, it was the vice president's purpose to operate as vice chairman of the council, working through his associates, Cannon and Dunham, to supervise the pace and direction of the council's work.

The basic flaw in Rockefeller's design to operate the Domestic Council as a vice presidential vehicle was that it had been designed and developed for a different purpose entirely. The council had been created for the express purpose of serving *presidential* needs: all of its operations were geared to the schedule of the White House. To emphasize this point, executive directors of the council served simultaneously as executive director and assistant to the president for domestic affairs. James Cannon was no exception to this; serving to underscore his presidential advisory role was his physical location, not with the council's staff in the Old Executive Office Building, but in the west wing of the White House.

From the outset, Cannon was faced with considerable problems concerning his credentials and loyalties as a presidential adviser in a Ford White House that looked with undisguised suspicion on his past and ongoing association with the vice president. To offset some of this suspicion, Cannon had a professional and political background that gave him some credibility within the administration. In the case of the president, for example, Cannon had worked closely with Ford as House minority leader in the fight to get revenue sharing passed in the House in the early 1970s. Therefore, Ford knew and respected Cannon as someone who could get things done. Similarly, in the case of Rumsfeld, Cannon had established "a kind of acquaintance and an arm's length association" while a journalist for *Newsweek*.[32]

Cannon's own approach to his difficult situation as a Rockefeller associate now functioning as domestic-affairs adviser to President Ford was straightforward and clear:

I never made any bones [about it]. I said that I work for Ford. I came here to work through Ford for the country. I never made any question about it, my loyalty to Ford. When it came to a choice, though, I would give [Rockefeller] my best advice—but I worked for the president and not the vice president. The vice president was my friend, my close ally, and I hoped it would [so] continue. But my responsibility was to Ford and what I believed was the right thing to recommend to him.[33]

Above all, Cannon was determined that he would succeed in his dual roles as executive director of the Domestic Council and assistant to the president for domestic affairs. To make sure that there would be no misunderstandings with the vice president, Cannon discussed the situation with him:

I was going over physically to the White House [to] undertake a very difficult job. And I told Rockefeller that his interest was my interest, that I not fail. [I explained] that every s.o.b. and his brother over there were looking for me to stumble and fail and not, literally not, be able to keep up with the paperwork.[34]

As Cannon indicates, the overwhelming task performed by the Domestic Council staff was moving mountains of paper to and from the White House. Although the Ash Council had in mind more substantive functions when it conceived of the Domestic Council in 1970 as the principal long-range policy planning unit in the executive office, the fact was that under Ehrlichman and Cole the staff had taken on the responsibility for the president's daily domestic paper flow. Even beyond that responsibility, the Domestic Council staff had assumed other service functions, such as the preparation of presidential messages to the Congress on almost any and every domestic concern.[35] The staff also undertook the task of preparing the president for his meetings on domestic matters with interest groups, state and local officials, and citizen groups. For this last service function, the staff had developed stock briefing forms that indicated to the president who was meeting him, the purpose of the meeting, appropriate presidential responses, and pitfalls to be avoided. Consequently, the demands made on the staff to process and transmit paper were so large that staff members frequently missed vital deadlines. These missed deadlines had an adverse effect on the president, who was unprepared at times for meetings and decisions. When Cannon first met with Ford, this was expressed as a major concern of the president, as Cannon noted:

When I first went in to see Ford . . . I said: "What would you like me to do that is not being done, and what is being done that you would like not to be done?" And the first thing he wanted me to do was to get him . . . papers on time. [He said], "The real problem I have is that I never get to see them in time for them to do me any good."[36]

The problems that the pressures of the paper flow posed for Cannon related directly to decisions about retention of existing Domestic Council staff. At the outset, he could count absolutely on the loyalty and performance of only three people: Dunham and two other Rockefeller appointees, Richard Parsons and Arthur Quern. The staff members inherited from Cole represented an unknown quantity both as to performance and loyalties. However, Cannon's urgent need was for a senior staff assistant who knew how to manage the paperwork correctly and efficiently: as new arrivals, none of the Rockefeller people possessed such expertise and knowledge of Domestic Council operations. Therefore, Cannon decided to retain the services of James Cavanaugh, an Ehrlichman holdover who had run virtually all of the staff operations for the six-week period prior to Cannon's appointment as executive director.[37]

In keeping on Cavanaugh (who was made a co-deputy director of the council), Cannon achieved two objectives: first, he secured the services of a senior staff member who could do the paperwork; second, he sent signals of reassurance to senior White House staff who had previously worked with and trusted Cavanaugh.

However, Cannon's decision to retain Cavanaugh did not sit well with the vice president. Rockefeller, in fact, had approached Cannon to have Cavanaugh and several other Cole staff holdovers fired and replaced on the grounds that "they were not of a caliber to give the president the kind of advice and to do the kind of work that needed to be done."[38] Having made a firm decision on the necessity of retaining Cavanaugh, Cannon told the vice president: "In order to make this thing work I have agreed with Rumsfeld that I will have two deputy directors: one for the paperwork and one for the planning. And I have agreed to keep Cavanaugh."[39] Rockefeller was upset by this news and informed Cannon that such an agreement was "contrary to what we have agreed." However, Cannon stuck by his decision and declared: "If I go back on this, my usefulness is destroyed with the staff."[40]

This exchange between Cannon and Rockefeller was critically important because it brought up at an early point the nature of the division of responsibilities between the Domestic Council's vice chairman and executive director. As Cannon perceived matters, there had been no need to consult Rockefeller beforehand on the retention of Cavanaugh. His position was clear:

I had a responsibility to [the vice president] for a broad aspect of the policy development for the future, but not how I was going to do the day-to-day details. I assessed the situation much more carefully than he did. He did not understand and said to me that he was not interested in the nitty-gritty routine of the operation.[41]

On Rockefeller's part, the refusal of Cannon to fire Cavanaugh prompted consideration of removing Cannon. However, that would then pose further problems, as Rockefeller explained: "I really had a choice there whether to fire Cannon, [but] I didn't think Dunham could do what Cannon could do and I didn't have anyone else."[42] The concern troubling Rockefeller that prompted such an extreme action was the revived specter of losing control over the activities of the Domestic Council. He had successfully resisted attempts by senior White House staff members to deprive him of control of the operations side of the council's staff work. In his eyes, the retention of Cavanaugh to process the paperwork gave to the White House (in particular, to Rumsfeld as coordinator) a measure of supervision and control he had not been prepared previously to concede. Operating on the basis that "operations is policy," the situation appeared to be lost as far as Rockefeller was concerned. As he perceived matters: "Right there, the whole thing was sunk. And I knew it, because Rumsfeld had maintained control of what he called the paperwork, which was the flow of daily business which is where policy is made."[43]

The irony is that the decision on the retention of Cavanaugh was one that was made entirely by Cannon purely on the basis of practical utility in the best interests of the operation he had responsibility for as executive director. His stated considerations make this point clear:

The simple fact is that I inherited a staff of mostly poor mediocre people, some twenty or thirty [of them]. . . . Cavanaugh was one more member that I had inherited, [but] he could move paper . . . and I thought that was useful to me. I had responsibility to do this, and I was determined that I would not fail.[44]

However, Vice President Rockefeller had concluded that his oversight responsibility over the Domestic Council's work had been severely compromised, and, therefore, his prospects for successfully utilizing the Domestic Council for development of domestic-policy initiatives had been destroyed. His response to the situation was decisive:

I told the president that I thought that this instrument was not going to function as I had hoped, that this was what had happened, but I wasn't going to disrupt it. And at that point I started focusing on a project which he and I had discussed, which was to hold a series of hearings around the country through the Domestic Council regarding the attitudes of the American people on labor, business, welfare, etc. . . . I figured I would use this as a vehicle to develop policy and positions on domestic issues.[45]

At the time, Cannon was totally unaware of the impact that his decision would have on the vice president's relationship with the Domestic Council. Nonetheless, he realized that the nature of his relationship with Rockefeller had undergone a change: "I think Rockefeller felt that I was in effect declaring my independence from him to a degree he was not prepared to accept. I think he resented that too. I felt always that he resented that.''[46]

An interesting perspective is provided by Richard Dunham, who saw and understood the points of view of both Cannon and Rockefeller. On the one hand, he accepted the validity of Cannon's reason for retaining Cavanaugh. In Dunham's opinion: "Cavanaugh . . . knew the system, he knew the people. He was the guy who knew how to move a piece of paper from one side of the desk to the other." Yet, on the other hand, Dunham saw merit in Rockefeller's position. As he explained the situation: "It's a perfect illustration of the impossibility of separating the operations from policy formulation and proposals. Cavanaugh's lines of communication were [to] Rumsfeld and the others, Phil Buchen, etc., whom Jim [Cannon] and I were just learning to know.''[47]

As just noted, Rockefeller's decision to abandon the Domestic Council as his primary vehicle for domestic-policy development derived in large measure from his conviction that he had lost the necessary degree of control over operational functions that he considered vital. However, contributing to that decision was his experience in attempting to assert preeminence for the council over cabinet departments, an experience that demonstrated the hard fact that Ford's cabinet was not anxious to concede influence or authority to an institution that had previously come to dominate the domestic arena.

The effort to assert preeminence over domestic departments and agencies took the form of a study-directive exercise initiated by Rockefeller to develop ideas and priorities on policy needs. This exercise had its origins in a meeting that a Rockefeller associate, William Ronan, had with Commerce Secretary Rogers Morton on January 7.[48] At the time, the final shape of Rockefeller's authority concerning the Domestic Council's activities had not been determined, but the vice president was anxious to proceed with a consideration of policy initiatives that might be taken by the Council to meet the policy needs of the Ford administration. Therefore, the point of the Ronan-Morton meeting was to examine how such a consideration might proceed.

As they reviewed the situation, there was a need to develop a program package that would "grasp the initiative for the executive branch under presidential leadership." In order to develop a package of policy proposals, Morton and Ronan proposed a Domestic Council initiative under the vice president's direction that would request department and agency heads to outline their program priorities "with an emphasis on items that could be initiated by the Ford administration." To implement this initiative, Ronan recommended the following approach for Rockefeller's consideration:

1. The vice president would write to each department and agency head for submission of proposals.

2. The full Domestic Council, with agency heads, would meet to discuss priorities.
3. The Domestic Council [staff] would coordinate the effort, with a view to developing a presentation for the president.
4. Presentation to the president for his determination of a program.[49]

Six weeks later, in his first memorandum to the president as vice chairman of the Domestic Council, Rockefeller took up the Morton-Ronan recommendations and proposed to President Ford that "a major priority objective of the council [should] be to develop options that will—when added up—assist you as you continue to formulate the comprehensive, cohesive Ford administration program for 1976." In order to begin this development, Rockefeller recommended that Ford authorize him to issue study directives to the members of the Domestic Council requesting from each of them:

• Assessment of major national needs and policy problems in his area of jurisdiction, stated in order of priority.

• Identification of the alternative ways of handling these needs and problems.

• Identification of other departments and agencies that share a responsibility in dealing with specific areas.

When the responses from the study directive had been received and collated, Rockefeller recommended that a full meeting of the Domestic Council be convened to discuss various needs and proposals with the president. This would be followed up by assigning specific issue areas to review groups to develop policy options. Finally, to underscore the importance to be attached to the study directive, Rockefeller proposed visiting each council member personally in his capacity as vice chairman of the council accompanied by the executive director and the deputy director.[50]

Five days later, on February 25, President Ford approved all of the vice president's recommendations concerning the Domestic Council study directive. Anxious to establish some early momentum, Rockefeller sent out a vice chairman's memorandum on February 27 inviting Domestic Council members to prepare estimates of national domestic needs and requesting identification of major policy programs.

However, responses to this initiative were slow in coming out of the various departments and agencies—so slow, in fact, that it became apparent to Rockefeller's staff that the exercise was being regarded as only of "secondary importance" and that it was complied with (albeit reluctantly) only because the vice president had asked that it be done.[51] The experience suggested clearly that the vice chairmanship of the Domestic Council was not going to become a "bully-pulpit" from which to galvanize the domestic departments and agencies into action.

At this point, Rockefeller had begun to reassess his personal role concerning domestic-policy development work within the framework of the Domestic Council in the light of Cannon's retention of Cavanaugh to direct the council staff's paperwork operations. Although the vice president's decision to develop policy initiatives independently of council staff operations was based on the Cavanaugh retention, it also may have been based on a conclusion that Domestic Council preeminence in domestic-policy formulation was an unattainable objective in the Ford administration. The plain fact was that the president had stressed his desire to have a strong and independent cabinet: Rockefeller's experience in getting responses from the cabinet departments indicated how independent they wished to be.

However, having pushed hard to get approval for the Domestic Council initiative, Rockefeller found it necessary to continue the effort toward some conclusion. On April 30, he proposed to the president the convening of a full meeting of the council to review and assess responses to his study directive. The president approved a meeting for the week of May 12. However, for various reasons it was not possible to schedule a council meeting until early June. When the full council actually did convene on June 10, the exercise was largely a formal and empty one. There was an uneventful discussion covering the spectrum of departmental and agency jurisdictions, at the conclusion of which came a recommendation that the following areas be considered further by review groups for the development of policy recommendations:

- Development of natural resources.
- Quality of life and human environment.
- Interrelationship of government and free enterprise.
- Overall transportation policy.
- Future of American industry.[52]

However, by this time the vice president had organized his own domestic-policy review group for the development of social programs policy options for the 1976 State of the Union Message. Although this group was officially a Domestic Council review group for staff support and legitimacy reasons, it was in fact a vice presidential effort headed up by John Veneman, a vice presidential counselor who directed the review from the vice presidential suite in the Old Executive Office Building.

The only outward intimation of Rockefeller's abandonment of the Domestic Council as a policy development vehicle came with the departure of Deputy Director Richard Dunham from the council in September, 1975. As noted above, Dunham had been appointed to the council's staff to work on long-range planning; a role that became an inevitable casualty of the vice president's decision to develop policy proposals as a vice presidential as opposed to a Domestic Council endeavor. That decision rendered Dunham's future a bleak one. As he described his situation, Dunham explained: "I could not see a role that I could play. . . . I was convinced . . . by June or July that I wasn't going to fly because of all this internecine warfare—that's just not my interest. So I very quickly was thinking of making the change for something else."[53]

When President Ford approached Dunham in September with the offer of the chairmanship of the Federal Power Commission, the offer was quickly accepted. With Dunham's departure, the essentially operational nature of the Domestic Council was affirmed.

THE VICE PRESIDENT'S SOCIAL PROGRAMS POLICY REVIEW

The major domestic-policy development work undertaken by the Ford administration in 1975 comprised a broad review of all federal social programs. Although this review was officially undertaken by a Domestic Council review group, the initiative, impetus, and direction of the review group all came from the office of the vice president. The social programs review was from start to finish a vice presidential endeavor.

Certainly, at the outset, it was not Rockefeller's intention to work on domestic-policy options outside the Domestic Council framework. However, for the reasons discussed above, he decided that his ability to shape and direct the activities of the council's staff had been undermined and that he could not rely on the staff for policy development. Since he possessed a broad mandate as vice chairman of the Domestic Council to review domestic-policy programs, he determined that this could be done under the aegis of his vice presidential office.

Rockefeller's interest in undertaking a broad review of federal social programs sprang from two basic concerns. First, the rapid growth of assistance and income transfer programs to individuals and state and local governments of the 1960s had produced a confusing multiplicity of overlapping, ineffective, and inefficient programs that clearly demanded a general reassessment of objectives, costs, and delivery systems. As governor of New York State, Rockefeller had experienced firsthand the problems of administering many of these programs and had called frequently for reappraisal at the federal level. Moreover, he had begun an independent study of social programs through the study panels of the Commission on Critical Choices established in 1973. Second, Rockefeller was convinced that there was an urgent need to develop distinctive Ford administration proposals that would establish a programmatic base for Gerald Ford in the 1976 campaign. As an unelected president who needed to put some distance between himself and the Nixon administration, it was imperative in Rockefeller's view that Ford build a record of personal achievement to secure election as president in his own right. As Ford's vice president, Rockefeller was determined to do all that he could to promote the aspirations of the president.

To direct his review of social programs, Rockefeller appointed John G. Veneman as a counselor to the vice president.[54] Veneman's credentials were impressive: he had been under secretary of the Department of Health, Education and Welfare from 1969 to 1973. While at HEW, he had played a major role in policy development in the areas of health, public assistance, and social services, and during congressional consideration of welfare reform and social security had acted as the administration's spokesman. In short, he was a figure who lent authority and prestige to the social programs review.

Although Nelson Rockefeller wanted to retain absolute control over the work of the review group, and for that reason operated it out of his vice presidential office, he needed to have it officially legitimated as a Domestic Council enterprise for two basic reasons. First, there was the matter of resources: his vice presidential budget did not provide sufficient funds for the salaries and ancillary costs of a major policy review. By designating the review group as a Domestic Council unit, the council's staff and budgetary resources could be drawn upon, as well as those of the departments and agencies that could provide staff on interagency loan. Second, there was a concern that the review group's activities and products be regarded as administration activities and products: under Domestic Council auspices the review group would be seen as a Ford administration endeavor. Exclusive identification as a Rockefeller operation would diminish the group's standing and credibility and might even guarantee ultimate rejection of its proposals.

Accordingly, at the outset, the proposals to establish the review group and obtain a presidential mandate for its activities were routed to the president as recommendations from James Cannon as executive director of the Domestic Council. The initial set of proposals was made in a memorandum to the president on April 17, 1975, in which Cannon recommended that the following areas be studied to develop new program options:

1. Alternatives for the replacement of current federal programs of all income assistance, including food stamps, AFDC, SSI, and the new 10 percent "earned income credit."
2. Alternatives for health financing and delivery.
3. Practical approaches to the consolidation of existing categorical grant programs into block grants.
4. Proposals for the allocation of functions and fiscal responsibilities of the three levels of government—federal, state, and local.

To carry out this review, Cannon recommended the establishment of a Domestic Council review group, headed by a study director, with the staff work to be performed by the Domestic Council's staff, detailees from agencies, and outside consultants as appropriate. Moreover, the staff work should be supplemented with administrative hearings to be conducted in cooperation with members of Congress and state and local government officials.

To facilitate an orderly process for the development of policy proposals, Cannon proposed the following timetable:

- A major presidential address in April calling for the social programs review initiative.

- Review group plans for the public hearings following the presidential address.

- Public hearings to be conducted throughout the country between May and September.

- Possible report to the Congress in October.

- Formulation of a package of recommendations by December 1, 1975.

- Preparation of legislative proposals by January 1, 1976.

- Announcement of complete program as part of the 1976 State of the Union Message.

Finally, to indicate that the recommended proposals had been widely discussed within the administration, Cannon closed his memorandum by informing the president that: "The vice president, Secretaries Butz and Weinberger, Phil Buchen, Max Friedersdorf, Alan Greenspan, Jim Lynn, Jack Marsh, Bill Seidman, and Paul Theis have reviewed this package and recommend approval."[55]

Despite the impressive array of support cited by Cannon for the review group recommendation, the president's approval was not immediately forthcoming. On May 8, Veneman indicated to the vice president that, in the continued absence of presidential approval, "Progress of a formal nature has been deferred." However, anticipating approval, Veneman had met with cabinet members likely to be involved with the review effort, as well as Rumsfeld, Marsh, Buchen, and Hartmann of the White House staff, for the purpose of discussing the nature of the social programs review "so that they will perceive it as a helpful rather than threatening exercise."[56] In addition, he had held a series of meetings with administration officials "responsible for substantive program development" to insure that there would be coordination on the issues to be dealt with by the review group.

Meanwhile, Veneman was also in the process of developing papers that examined the basic issues in income transfer programs and health insurance and the "substantive, procedural, and political problems" surrounding these issue areas. However, Veneman concluded in his memorandum that the basic priority was getting approval from the president of Cannon's April 17 recommendations, which would allow the development of staff support for the review study.[57]

On May 15, prodded by Veneman's memorandum of May 8, Rockefeller restated Cannon's April 17 recommendations in his own memorandum to the president. In this memorandum, the vice president emphasized the need for a Ford administration social programs review by observing: "It is likely that we will be faced with congressional proposals for a wide variety of unrelated domestic programs that are politically popular but fiscally unsound."[58] Ford returned the vice president's memorandum initialed "Approved."

With presidential approval for the review project now in hand, Veneman took up some pressing logistical problems with Cannon, Dunham, and Cavanaugh, making it clear to them that "we have much to do and little time to do it." He estimated that some twelve to fifteen professional staff assistants would be required for about a six-month period to make the enterprise successful: half of this group would be involved with the proposed public hearings and the remaining half would work on substantive issue matters.[59] In Veneman's judgment, James Lynn, OMB director, expected "major input into the 1976 legislative package" to come from the review group.[60]

By June 16, Veneman had arranged for the production of an overview options memorandum for discussion at the first full meeting of the review group.[61] This overview memorandum examined the need for a Ford administration strategy concerning overall social policy as well as the specific areas authorized for review group study, namely, income transfer programs, national health insurance, and intergovernmental relations. Three program-approach options were taken up by the memorandum on a "pro" and "con" basis that considered the political advantages and disadvantages of each for the Ford administration:

- Retaining a "no new initiative" strategy beyond 1976.

- Moving toward a national health insurance strategy.

- Overhauling the welfare system.

Finally, the overview memorandum suggested a set of guiding themes and principles that might be adopted as a framework for articulating a Ford administration social policy program: "forging a new philosophic consensus; making best use of limited resources; building on America's traditional strengths; insuring governmental accountability; and restoring a sense of fairness."[62]

The overview memorandum was warmly received by the vice president, who thought that similar papers should be developed to cover specific topic areas. Agreeing that this would be a useful step, Veneman proposed a range of topics that might be dealt with, including energy, jobs, regulatory reform, the economy, capital formation, transportation, and housing. However, Veneman stressed: "It is essential that these be developed in cooperation with those persons on the Domestic Council who have been involved in the specific subject areas."[63]

By July 14, Veneman had developed Rockefeller's suggestion of producing policy papers to cover wider domestic issues into a general domestic-policy framework. This framework would assist in the design of a comprehensive program of policy options for the 1976 legislative agenda. Essentially, the framework Veneman proposed to the vice president involved clustering some sixteen issues areas under the rubric of four main themes:

Economic Growth	—	jobs
	—	inflation control
	—	regulatory reform
	—	capital formation
Humane Concern	—	welfare reform
	—	health financing and delivery
	—	social insurance
	—	disability and long-term care
Resource Scarcity	—	energy
	—	food
	—	minerals
	—	environment
Infrastructure	—	education
	—	transportation
	—	housing/land use
	—	intergovernmental relations[64]

With Rockefeller's approval, Veneman outlined his issues framework to James Cannon to propose that the Domestic Council commission a set of domestic-policy papers to be developed from the four basic theme areas of economic growth, humane concern, resource scarcity, and national infrastructure. Explaining his purpose, he detailed the utility such papers would have for the review group:

These papers will knit together into a coherent decision-making framework the major national issues under each heading; the papers will include analytical, programmatic, and political analyses of major policy alternatives; and the papers will provide a conceptual basis for articulating the policies chosen.

Most importantly, *an overview domestic-policy analysis* will be produced which discusses the interrelationships among the four issue areas . . . and suggests a set of principles which can form the basis for coordinated and coherent policy making among the four areas.[65]

Emphasizing to Cannon that it was not his purpose to preempt departmental or council staff decisions in recommending the commission of discussion papers, Veneman proposed that the production of the papers be assigned to the consultant firm of ICF, Inc., which had developed the earlier overview options memorandum in June.[66]

In keeping with his general rule that he obtain written presidential approval for all vice presidential projects and assignments, Rockefeller submitted an approval memorandum to the president to gain clearance for the enlarged focus of the domestic-policy review. This review, he told Ford, "should be completed by mid-September so that we can make decisions on future initiatives by the end of the year."[67] On July 24, the president approved the enlarged review process.

With presidential clearance, Veneman arranged for Cannon to contract with ICF, Inc., for the development of five discussion papers within a period of sixty days. Again Veneman reassured Cannon that "ICF would work with the Domestic Council staff and the agencies in developing the . . . discussion papers."[68]

Having set in motion the production of discussion papers, Veneman turned his attentions in early August to the practical aspects of translating policy options work into hard administration legislative proposals. On August 6, he met with Edward Harper (who had handled policy planning in the Domestic Council under Ehrlichman from 1970 through 1972) to gain insights about the problems of such an effort. The outcome of the discussion with Harper was a Veneman memorandum to the vice president underscoring the need to develop a sequence of products that would emerge from the policy work already underway. It was also necessary, Veneman advised, to give some consideration to the development of resources and personal relationships within the administration to ensure realization of the product goals. It was his view that the following products sequence was realistic: "overview discussion papers on major aspects of domestic policy; decision papers derived from these overviews which outline major policy issues for the president; the State of the Union Message; major new legislative initiatives based upon the president's decisions; and material for the party platform."

However, Veneman cautioned Rockefeller that these product goals were conditional on successfully developing adequate resources and necessary relationships. On the matter of relationships, he considered it vital that all components of the Ford administration be aware that "the president's interest in coordinated program development is serious." In particular, the review group's activities would have to become more interrelated with the

OMB; the reality was that program proposals could not be developed in isolation from the budget process. In addition, Veneman stressed that the review group had to have "access to and a working relationship with the president's key political advisers, Don Rumsfeld, Bob Hartmann, and others when necessary." As for resources, Veneman considered these to be inadequate for the tasks at hand. Therefore, he proposed to Rockefeller that four to six people be assigned to the review group's activities and that a budget be developed for outside consultant assistance. Finally, he observed that "as positions are developed, it is essential that there be a process for expediting presidential decisions."[69]

Meanwhile, press reports about the social programs review had begun to appear. On July 26, *Congressional Quarterly* carried a major piece entitled "Ford Plans Restructuring of Social Programs," which presented a comprehensive examination of the administration's efforts. Although the article discussed the work of the Domestic Council's review group under Veneman's direction, it also considered the program budgeting role of the OMB as well as President Ford's public statements on federal spending.[70] On August 13, the *Washington Post* carried a piece by Stuart Auerbach entitled "Welfare Review Planned: White House Eyes Reform of Programs." Essentially, Auerbach's article provided a vehicle for Veneman to reassure internal administration critics and to build external support for the review group's efforts. On the review's objectives, Veneman was quoted as emphasizing presidential underpinnings: "We're trying to find out what's real and can happen in the real world and what isn't possible. The president has been relatively candid on what government can and cannot do, and he's willing to say that some of the programs aren't working very effectively." Moreover, although he was reported by Auerbach as rejecting the view that the exercise should be seen as a Ford administration attempt to cut social programs spending, Veneman displayed some sensitivity to budget conscious critics in the following quoted remarks:

Some people call reform merely cutting back. I call reform rationalizing the system. Sometimes it has the effect of reducing some benefits. And sometimes it has the effect of increasing others. That's what we are looking at—it's more of an attempt to rationalize. As a residual effect you are going to have some savings on the administrative side.[71]

Following up on his discussion of resource needs and product goals, Veneman produced by August 13 a work plan for the domestic-policy review (see figure 1). The pace was beginning to quicken: some four or five staff assistants had been detailed from various agencies to assist in the work on policy options for the 1976 State of the Union Message and related policy activities. On the proposed public hearings on domestic-policy needs and concerns, Veneman advised Cannon that he would personally handle the necessary arrangements.[72]

FIGURE 1. DOMESTIC POLICY REVIEW—TIMEFRAME

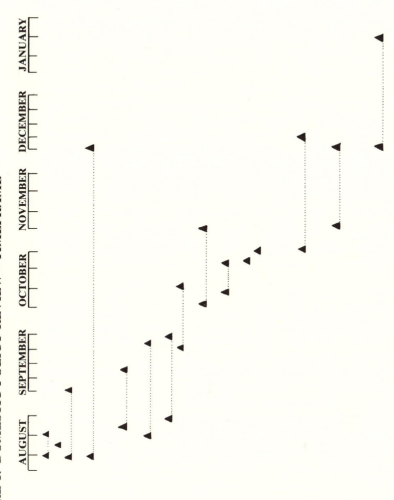

1. Prepare Overview Discussion Paper
2. Forward Work Plan to Vice President
3. Identify Staff
4. Ongoing Review Groups on Specific
   Issues: SSA, Drugs, Food Stamps
5. Individual Domestic Council-Cabinet
   level Meetings on Department
   priorities
6. Prepare and Complete Discussion
   Papers
7. Prepare Materials for Regional
   Hearings
8. Review Discussion Package
9. Hold Regional Hearings and
   Prepare Summaries
10. Prepare Summary and Comments on
    Discussion Package
11. Present Complete Discussion Package
    to President
12. Domestic Council Meeting
13. Domestic Council Review Groups to
    Followup on Any Work Resulting from
    Domestic Council Meeting or from
    President's Comments.
14. Prepare, Clear and Forward Decision
    Memos for President on Specific
    Issues
15. Assist White House Staff and OMB in
    Drafting State of the Union and
    Legislative initiatives in accordance
    with Presidential Decisions.

Source: Memorandum for the vice president from John Veneman, dated August 13, 1975

In mid-August, ICF, Inc., delivered "Domestic-Policy Discussion Memorandum #1: Overview." Essentially, the assessment made by ICF of the political environment likely to be encountered by the 1976 State of the Union Message was that it posed special problems for President Ford's candidacy. Because Ford would have to appeal to a distinctly conservative constituency to gain the Republican nomination, and then to a broad base of independents and moderates to gain election as president, he needed a broad-base strategy that would embrace the right and center groups in the political spectrum. ICF indicated that:

The challenge for the president will be to combine: (a) an appreciation of the traditional virtues and values of America's simpler past—characteristics of openness, forthrightness, unostentatiousness, fairness, and values of private enterprise, free markets, minimal government, dispersed power—with (b) a sophisticated appreciation and positive program for the problems of America's increasingly complex present and future. The first half of this formulation is likely to appeal to both old and new "conservatives"; the second half will gain support among the broad range of sophisticated "independents" and will help in the defense against liberal attacks of "do-nothing-ism." The combined effect would seem to allow the widest possible base of support.

Clearly, the substance of the ICF analysis regarding a Ford strategy for 1976 was such that it provided a basis for proposing positive, programmatic policy initiatives for the 1976 State of the Union Message within a framework of fiscal responsibility—initiatives the review group was working to develop.

ICF, in its overview memorandum, identified and analyzed twelve "fundamental substantive problem areas which would seem to merit presidential attention." Essentially, these were the areas suggested to the vice president by Veneman some four weeks earlier:

1. *Issues of Humane Concern*
   a. reforming low-income support programs
   b. improving health finance and delivery
   c. rationalizing the social insurance system
2. *Issues of Economic Growth* (in addition to fiscal and monetary issues)
   a. increasing the rate of capital formation
   b. rationalizing governmental regulation
   c. reducing unemployment
3. *Issues of Resource Development*
   a. insuring an adequate energy supply
   b. limiting food price inflation while protecting farm income
   c. protecting and improving environmental quality
4. *Issues of Infrastructure Improvement*
   a. advancing comprehensive transportation policy

b. improving housing and land use

c. rationalizing intergovernmental relations

d. insuring a sound educational system

Having set out a discussion of specific areas for policy proposal development, ICF then outlined a framework for a comprehensive domestic-policy strategy for the Ford administration. Here again, ICF built on Veneman's earlier suggestions. The framework proposed comprised a set of guiding principles and themes that could provide the nucleus for a Ford strategy:

• Theme 1: Finding a new philosophic consensus

• Theme 2: Assuring continued American independence

• Theme 3: Building on America's proven strengths

• Theme 4: Fostering sustainable economic growth

• Theme 5: Making best use of limited resources

• Theme 6: Increasing governmental responsiveness and accountability

• Theme 7: Restoring a sense of fairness

Commenting on these themes and principles, ICF noted: "It is perhaps important to make clear that to the extent that Themes 1 to 6 tend to be 'conservative' and to favor the private sector, it is the more important that a degree of counterbalancing emphasis be given to Theme 7—'fairness'—if a wide base of support is sought."

The final section of ICF's overview memorandum examined the strategy choices available for consideration of a Ford administration policy package. As ICF viewed the possibilities, there were three basic strategy options to be considered:

• *Option 1*: A low initiative/strict budget fiscal restraint strategy

• *Option 2*: A mixed emphasis strategy

• *Option 3*: A time-phased comprehensive restructuring strategy

Addressing the first of these options, ICF pointed out that it would continue Ford's "no new programs" approach, therefore possessing strong appeal for traditional conservatives. However, it would not alleviate or solve major national problems and would burden Ford with charges of "failure of leadership" or "lack of vision." As for the second option, this would combine some fiscal conservatism with attention to national problem areas and would thus broaden Ford's appeal to moderate voters. The drawback here was that social problem areas appeared to demand comprehensive rather than selective solutions, and, moreover, Ford might lose some conservative support while still providing "too little" for most liberals. Finally, the third option would indicate an appreciation of the magnitude of social problems, but addressing these on a time-phased basis could provide appeal to a broad center that had both conservative and liberal elements. However, this approach could be outbid by a "fiscally irresponsible" Congress, and, moreover, without some short-term specifics, it could be regarded as simply "electioneering."

Although the third option was the one clearly favored by the vice president, he was not anxious to risk termination of the review effort by pressing Ford for an early decision on option choices. Accordingly, in transmitting the ICF overview memorandum to the president on August 26, Rockefeller observed: "It is not necessary to decide upon the specific strategy questions until after the remainder of the discussion papers are completed, and you have a thorough analysis of the broad issues." Meanwhile, the vice president did want Ford's guidance on the domestic-policy areas and the themes and principles outlined and considered by ICF. He therefore asked the president:

1. Are the domestic issues raised [in the ICF memorandum] the appropriate ones? Should any be excluded and others included?

2. Do the broad themes and principles for a Ford domestic policy appropriately represent your basic philosophy? Should the analyses and strategy development be tied together in this framework?[73]

President Ford affirmed that the issues discussed in the ICF overview were appropriate and that the work of the review group should proceed on the basis broadly outlined above.

While development by ICF, Inc., of the four specific policy area papers proceeded with input from agency and Domestic Council staff, the principal efforts of Veneman and Cannon were directed toward the planning and logistical tasks of scheduling the public hearings on domestic-policy problems and needs. On September 10, in a memorandum to the vice president, Cannon outlined proposals for a series of six Domestic Council Public Forums to: "Outline what the nation is facing with regard to domestic programs; obtain public input in the development of presidential options; and assist the president in formulating his legislative recommendations and initiatives to the Congress in the 1976 State of the Union Message."

The format proposed for each of the forums was to have a one-day meeting split into two types of sessions: a morning plenary session, chaired by the vice president, with participation of cabinet members and other federal officials; and four separate simultaneous afternoon sessions, each chaired by cabinet officers or agency heads and concerned with a particular policy area. The issue areas proposed for consideration at the morning and afternoon sessions were clustered as follows:

- Social programs (welfare, health, etc.)
- Jobs and the economy (manpower programs, inflation, etc.)
- Resources and the environment (raw materials, agriculture, etc.)
- Community development, transportation, and housing

To insure a broad cross section of witnesses to testify at the forums, Cannon proposed that selection be made from recommendations received from state and local officials, labor unions, business groups, consumer groups and other public interest groups, local federal officials, and White House lists. Recommendations from congressmen would also be accepted but not solicited.

The proposed locations for the six forums reflected a concern to achieve a geographic balance. As recommended by Cannon, these were:

- October 21   Denver, Colorado
- October 28   Kansas City, Missouri
- November 11   Austin, Texas
- November 18   Philadelphia, Pennsylvania
- December 1   Nashville, Tennessee
- December 9   Los Angeles or Sacramento, California[74]

Finally, Cannon's proposal on the forums called for an announcement process that recommended presidential briefing of the congressional leadership during the week of September 22. During that same week, there would be a full Domestic Council meeting to unveil the forums program, which would be followed by a joint announcement to the press by the president and the vice president, with a detailed briefing conducted by the vice president.

Approving all of Cannon's recommended proposals, Rockefeller transmitted them intact to the president on September 10 for his approval.[75] Three weeks later, on September 29, the forums program was approved and announced by President Ford.[76] At a cabinet meeting that preceded public announcement, the president discussed the purpose of the forums and emphasized that:

It is essential that we look at domestic policy from a broad perspective and not in isolation. For example, federal programs affecting health and welfare of the American people have a direct impact on employment, the role of state and local governments, and the economy.

Therefore, the Domestic Council [should] neither isolate the issues, nor isolate themselves with only a Washington perspective. They [should] seek out the best and broadest advice possible from throughout the country so that we can use our domestic resources in a way that is responsive to the needs of the people.[77]

Meanwhile, John Veneman, the review group's director, had been working with Arthur Quern of the Domestic Council staff on a further review of the issues and options discussed in the ICF overview memorandum to develop the elements of a State of the Union package. In a memorandum to the vice president on September 25 detailing this effort, Veneman and Quern indicated:

It is our intention to proceed to promptly involve administration staff and agency staff in the analytical process in part for their substantive contribution, but equally for reasons of "due process."

Following this analysis, we will tie together possible State of the Union packages. We are confident that the work already done on the development of themes and principles (which you have reviewed with the president) and the work to be done on specific issues can be readily linked in a coherent, persuasive, and effective whole.

Only after these program items are grouped and developed into conceptual packages would we suggest going forward to the president for specific decisions.[78]

At this juncture, the work on developing the review group's domestic-policy programs component for the 1976 State of the Union Message was proceeding well. Not only were the group's deadlines under control, but shortly the Domestic Council Public Forums would commence and thus provide a vehicle for focusing public attention on policy needs and options on a nationwide basis. It was at this point, when matters were moving smoothly, that the process was jolted abruptly by a presidential decision on the size of the budget for fiscal year 1977. On October 6, President Ford announced to the nation: "I propose that we halt [the] alarming growth [in federal spending] by holding spending in the coming year to $395 billion. That means a cut of $28 billion below what we will spend if we just stand still."[79]

As he outlined it, Ford's budget proposal was certainly novel. Essentially he proposed to trim the projected fiscal year 1977 Current Services Budget estimate from $423 billion to $395 billion, a cut of $28 billion. In return for these cuts in federal spending, the president proposed corresponding cuts in federal income taxes totaling $28 billion.[80]

For the policy proposals work of the social programs review group, Ford's announcements about federal spending cuts were distinctly ominous. Particularly chilling were the president's comments on current and new spending programs:

In January, I will propose to the Congress that many of our current spending programs be revised, consolidated, and held below their projected levels. . . . We have to face hard reality: our financial resources are limited. We must learn to live within our means.

Sometimes when fancy new spending programs reach this desk, promising something for almost nothing and carrying appealing labels, I wonder who the supporters think they are kidding.[81]

In the opinion of Veneman and Cannon, Ford's $395 billion budget ceiling decision destroyed all prospects for having the review group's domestic-policy proposals accepted as a component of the 1976 State of the Union package.[82] Although daunted, Vice President Rockefeller did not share his associates' assessment; in his opinion Ford's budget ceiling was certainly harmful but not necessarily fatal to the domestic-policy review. However, he did agree with Cannon's sentiments that the Domestic Council Public Forums should be aborted. For Cannon, there was no longer any validity to holding the forums. As he explained: "We wanted to get out of the forums, which were going to be a lot of work . . . and Rockefeller didn't particularly want to chair them. We thought it was a great idea when we thought of it six months earlier, but the [new] realities weren't going to get us anywhere."[83] But when the matter was raised with the president, Ford insisted that the forums should proceed as scheduled.

Although there had been disagreements within the vice president's circle about the severity of the impact that the $395 billion decision would have on the domestic-policy programs work, there was complete accord that the work had to be revised to fit the new contours of federal spending in order to have any chance of acceptance. Accordingly, the review group's activities continued under Veneman's direction, with an emphasis on designing options that would stay within the new budget guidelines.

Within three weeks, Veneman and Quern had prepared a draft outline of a prospective State of the Union package that was fashioned to meet the following conditions: "The message would adhere to the $395 billion budgetary ceiling announced by the president, and the message would recognize that fundamental problems exist and would offer creative solutions within the proposed ceilings." Even with these strictures, the revised package would remain true to the original framework developed by the review group. The draft attempted to be consistent with the themes and principles presented to the president in the August overview memorandum: "making best use of limited resources, building on America's traditional strengths, and restoring a sense of fairness." The draft outline also was designed to accommodate "an emphasis on the Bicentennial and on the future of responsible democratic government and on the free enterprise system."

As developed by the review group, the main substance of the draft package comprised nine potential new initiatives, as follows:

- Protecting the environment—early scientific warning

- Increasing efficiency in the food distribution system

- Restructuring income transfer programs

- Reshaping the health system and controlling health costs

- Reviewing federal policy for the disabled

- Consolidating transportation funding

- Reducing the growth of housing costs

- Restructuring student-aid programs

- Revitalizing the federal system

Of these nine initiative areas, the review group's work focused primarily on three: restructuring income transfer programs, reshaping health care, and developing a block-grants proposal. These three areas were of particular interest to the vice president, who had closely identified himself with the movement to effect federal takeover and restructuring of welfare and income-assistance programs, health insurance and health care, and categorical grants to states and cities. The proposals of the review group on income transfer programs called for consolidation of AFDC, SSI, and Food Stamp programs into a single welfare program that would emphasize efficiency and fairness but would include in addition stringent work requirements. The initiatives being developed in this area included a tax-credit approach. It was estimated that the welfare reform package would effect budget savings in the range of $1.5 to $2.0 billion in fiscal 1977. On health care, the proposed initiatives called for health costs controls that would effect budget savings annually of some $700 million, and a time-phased approach to a national health financing system providing universal coverage "only as responsible fiscal policy allows." Finally, on federal grants-in-aid, the initiative called for grant consolidation and development of a system of block grants to assist state and local governments.

With a covering memorandum to the vice president on October 24, Veneman and Quern submitted their draft State of the Union outline proposals to Rockefeller in preparation for a meeting with staff the following week to review options and strategies for getting administration adoption of the review group's initiatives.[84]

However, at this point, a second major blow struck the review group's endeavors. On November 3, Rockefeller hand delivered a letter to President Ford informing him that he would not be, and did not wish to be considered, a candidate for the 1976 Republican vice presidential nomination. The letter came amidst widely publicized criticism of Rockefeller as a liability to Ford's prospects of winning nomination and election in 1976. The fact that the criticism had come from Ford's campaign manager, Howard (Bo) Callaway, gave it a prominence and edge that made it difficult to ignore.[85]

The effect of Rockefeller's withdrawal as an active and vital vice presidential candidate for 1976 on the policy initiatives of the review group was devastating. Basically, the withdrawal certified Rockefeller publicly as a lame-duck member of the Ford administration—a status that virtually insured political impotence. Consequently, the last remaining prospects of getting adoption of positive domestic-policy proposals bearing the vice president's stamp as components of the 1976 State of the Union Message vanished.

However, the vice president was determined that the review group's initiatives should be fully developed and submitted in completed form for the president's consideration in December. Accordingly, with the assistance of the review group staff, he reworked the Veneman-Quern draft of October 24. By November 6, he submitted a package of draft proposals to the president, stressing that these were "consistent with a $395 billion budget in fiscal year 1977."[86]

The theme of Rockefeller's draft package was "America's Third Century: Building on Proven Strengths." Outlining this theme to Ford, the vice president emphasized that the choice confronting the nation was building on these strengths or else backing away from them. He argued:

Our choice must be to build for fiscal stability, for jobs, toward energy independence, a fiscally sound and socially responsible government. If we do not, we will be backing away from economic growth, inflation control and job opportunities, energy independence, meeting human needs, assuring effective government at all levels.

In Rockefeller's assessment, America faced six basic challenges that could be met by building on proven strengths. These challenges were set out for the president in chart form (see figure 2), which indicated under the rubric of each challenge the policy areas for which program proposals were being developed. To develop these proposals to a completed state, some further work was necessary. Accordingly, he outlined for the president some steps that had to be taken to accomplish this: "If you approve of the general structure as proposed for the message, we will develop these concepts in further detail. We will keep the senior White House staff informed as we proceed with further development of these concepts and get their suggestions on these specific initiatives." To sustain the review group's endeavors, the vice president needed the president's clearance for further work. Therefore, he asked the president: "Do you approve of this basic structure?" Next to the space indicated for *approval*, President Ford wrote his initials, "GRF."[87]

FIGURE 2. AMERICA HAS BUILT ON ITS PROVEN STRENGTHS SINCE 1776. AT ITS BICENTENNIAL, AMERICA FACES SIX GREAT CHALLENGES:

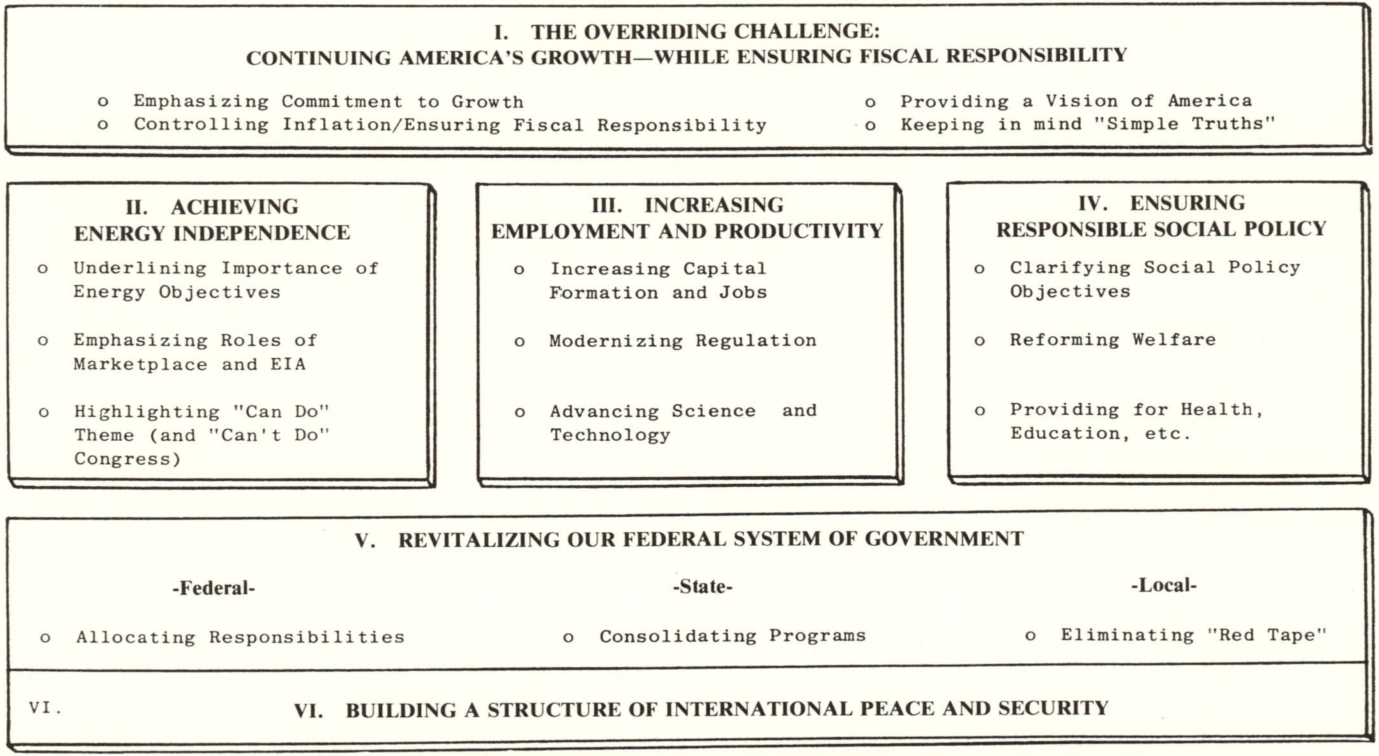

I. THE OVERRIDING CHALLENGE:

CONTINUING AMERICA'S GROWTH—WHILE ENSURING FISCAL RESPONSIBILITY

- o Emphasizing Commitment to Growth
- o Controlling Inflation/Ensuring Fiscal Responsibility
- o Providing a Vision of America
- o Keeping in mind "Simple Truths"

II. ACHIEVING ENERGY INDEPENDENCE

- o Underlining Importance of Energy Objectives
- o Emphasizing Roles of Marketplace and EIA
- o Highlighting "Can Do" Theme (and "Can't Do" Congress)

III. INCREASING EMPLOYMENT AND PRODUCTIVITY

- o Increasing Capital Formation and Jobs
- o Modernizing Regulation
- o Advancing Science and Technology

IV. ENSURING RESPONSIBLE SOCIAL POLICY

- o Clarifying Social Policy Objectives
- o Reforming Welfare
- o Providing for Health, Education, etc.

V. REVITALIZING OUR FEDERAL SYSTEM OF GOVERNMENT

-Federal-

- o Allocating Responsibilities

-State-

- o Consolidating Programs

-Local-

- o Eliminating "Red Tape"

VI. BUILDING A STRUCTURE OF INTERNATIONAL PEACE AND SECURITY

VI.

"AMERICA NEEDS THIS NEW PHILOSOPHIC CONSENSUS ON THE EVE OF ITS THIRD CENTURY."

Source: Enclosure to memorandum for the president from the vice president, dated November 6, 1975

With ongoing approval from Ford for the review group's activities, a revised timetable of Domestic Council "due dates" was drawn up as follows:

- **Domestic Council Forums**

November 18	—	Philadelphia
November 25	—	Indianapolis
December 9	—	Los Angeles
December 20	—	Completion of final report

- **Domestic Council Policy Review**

November 13-14	—	Initial discussion with OMB
November 17-30	—	Discussions with senior White House staff
November 15-December 1	—	Further review of initiatives and cost analysis
December -	—	Submission to the president
December 3 or 4	—	Domestic Council meeting
December 1-10	—	Discussions with the cabinet
December 1-January 6	—	Further Domestic Council staff work on initiatives
December 15	—	Preliminary draft of State of Union
January 10	—	Final draft of State of Union
January 20	—	State of Union Address

Because the OMB was in the process of drafting rival social programs options to the review group's health and welfare proposals, Veneman and Quern arranged to meet with OMB Director James Lynn and his deputy director, Paul O'Neill. From the standpoint of the review group, the outcome of the meeting was distinctly disappointing. In a report of their discussion with Lynn and O'Neill, Veneman and Quern indicated to the vice president:

Their initial response to our health and welfare proposals was negative: welfare because they felt that it would not be attractive to liberals or conservatives; health because they thought that a comprehensive federal health insurance program was not the right direction to move toward at this time. While they generally reacted well to the proposed grant consolidation, they feel they need an explicit decision from the president before redesigning the budget along the lines of our proposal.[88]

Both Veneman and Quern thought that OMB did recognize the need for major reform of the welfare income maintenance program but had concluded that it was "not politically feasible."

Basically, the point of the Veneman-Quern meeting with OMB was to provide information about external reaction to the review group's proposals to help prepare the vice president for a meeting with the president on November 19. Rockefeller's purpose in meeting with Ford was to outline in detail the review group's proposals in the areas of welfare, health care, and grant consolidation. It was hoped that the vice president could secure further and more specific approval of the review group's approaches from the president.

To the extent that the president cleared further development of the vice president's proposals, Rockefeller secured the approval he desired. Accordingly, the review group began to work with the vice president on the final completed versions of domestic-policy recommendations for the 1976 State of the Union Message. After a further month of activity, the recommendations in their final form were ready for the president's consideration.

In his memorandum to the president on December 15, which transmitted his suggestions for the State of the Union Message,[89] Vice President Rockefeller told President Ford: "The purpose of this memorandum is to fulfill the assignment you gave to me and the Domestic Council to review current domestic programs and develop new concepts, policies, and recommendations for your January 1976 State of the Union Message." He then proceeded to outline the various steps that had been taken by the social programs review group in developing themes and principles. Included in this review were the Domestic Council Public Forums, on which Rockefeller indicated he would deliver a separate report. Finally, he referred to the draft proposals he had presented to the president on November 6; these had now been revised and were submitted as "our recommendations for your review."

Rockefeller presented his recommendations as having a twofold purpose: first, the needs of the nation would be addressed but in a manner consistent with budget restraints; second, the needs of Gerald R. Ford would be served by the provision of a programmatic base for asserting positive leadership in the 1976 election year. The positive nature of the recommendations was underscored by Rockefeller's insistence on adoption of a "can-do" approach in confronting the nation's problems, an approach he thought could be developed along the following lines:

We *can* have continued economic growth, more jobs, and greater productivity, while protecting our environment.

We *can* mount the necessary research and development efforts in the private sector to establish energy independence.

We *can* create jobs by continued improvements in labor and management relations, capital formation, science and technology, and regulatory reform.

We *can* help those in need on a basis of equity, human dignity, and sound fiscal policy.

We *can* move immediately to control health cost inflation and expand health insurance protection for all Americans as our national resources permit.

We *can* revitalize the American federal system recognizing that government closest to the people is the best government.

The policy recommendations that Rockefeller proposed were positive "can-do" initiatives that covered a broad swath of domestic concerns. In all, he outlined nineteen sets of initiatives, as follows:

1. Reforming the welfare system
2. Reshaping the health system and controlling health costs
3. Achieving energy independence
4. Citing the improvement of the environment
5. Assuring safety in the removal of nuclear waste
6. Increasing capital formation
7. Utilizing America's proven strength in science and technology
8. Modernizing the regulatory system
9. Highlighting the need for increased productivity
10. Encouraging continued private ownership of small farms and businesses
11. Encouraging small business development
12. Reviewing federal policy affecting the disabled population
13. Restructuring student-aid programs
14. Increasing financing for housing and initiating research to reduce housing costs
15. Generating industrial expansion through targeted tax relief
16. Consolidating transportation funding
17. Developing rural American communities
18. Revitalizing the federal system
19. Conserving urban areas

Summarizing the challenge facing the administration as it made decisions on the shape of its 1976 legislative agenda, the vice president declared to the president:

In our judgment, the American people expect the State of the Union to deal squarely with the country's fundamental domestic issues and to be a statement that can chart a positive, progressive course as we enter the nation's third century.

We believe the American people . . . understand that positive new approaches must be developed on a fiscally sound basis and that these objectives need not be mutually exclusive.

A State of the Union Message responding to this call is certain to have the enthusiastic and strong support of the country.

The vice president's presentation was a strongly made, last-ditch effort to assert the need for a positive approach to solving the nation's problems and addressing its needs. The clear, but unstated, conclusion was that failure to adopt such an approach would burden the Ford presidency with a negative image and suggest a failure of leadership, an image that would be highly problematic in an election year.

Having fulfilled his assignment to develop proposals for the 1976 State of the Union Message with the submission of his recommendations and his report on the Domestic Council Forums,[90] the vice president officially withdrew on December 16 from active involvement with the work of the Domestic Council. His withdrawal indicates the extent to which he recognized the futility facing his proposals for the State of the Union, coming as it did before Ford's final decisions on the 1976 package. Certainly his judgment cannot be called into question on this: when Ford announced his State of the Union proposals on January 19, 1976, virtually all of Nelson Rockefeller's recommendations were conspicuous—by their absence.[91]

· 4 · VICE PRESIDENTIAL POLICY MAKING: THE CASE OF ENERGY INDEPENDENCE

Within the domestic-policy role he acquired as vice chairman of the Domestic Council, Nelson Rockefeller saw his principal function to be the development of administration proposals to meet the policy needs of the nation. This chapter considers Rockefeller in his role as a problem solver, examining specifically his proposal to create a federal energy development corporation to accelerate and promote domestic energy production. This proposal was expansive and highly controversial, and it brought Rockefeller into conflict with prominent members of the Ford administration.

ACHIEVING ENERGY INDEPENDENCE: A VICE PRESIDENTIAL PROPOSAL

In a nationally televised address on January 13, 1975, previewing his first State of the Union Message, President Ford discussed the major problems facing the nation:

Since becoming your president five months ago, economic problems have been my foremost concern. Two elements of our problems are long range—inflation and energy. Both are affected not only by our actions but also by international forces beyond our direct control. The new and disturbing element in the economic picture is our worsening recession and the unemployment that goes with it.

Americans are no longer in full control of their national destiny, when that destiny depends on uncertain foreign fuel at high prices fixed by others. Higher energy costs compound both inflation and recession, and dependence on others for future energy supplies is intolerable to our national security.[1]

The energy problem outlined by Ford was of fairly recent origin. As late as the 1960s, the nation had enjoyed a surplus capacity in domestic energy supply. But the situation changed dramatically in the early 1970s as domestic energy production (particularly of crude oil) failed to keep pace with rapidly rising demand levels. The immediate consequence of this was that the United States found itself increasingly dependent on imported oil to meet domestic energy needs.[2] Moreover, this dependency quickly proved to be a serious problem in the face of massive crude oil price increases announced by OPEC in 1973 and 1974[3] and an oil embargo imposed on the United States by Arab members of OPEC in the period from October 1973 through March 1974.[4]

To deal with the problems of insufficient domestic energy production, President Ford outlined the following national energy goals in his first State of the Union Message to Congress on January 15, 1975:

First, we must reduce oil imports by one million barrels per day by the end of this year and by two million barrels per day by the end of 1977.

Second, we must end vulnerability to economic disruption by foreign suppliers by 1985.

Third, we must develop our energy technology and resources so that the United States has the ability to supply a significant share of the energy needs of the free world by the end of this century.

The president's program to achieve these goals comprised a mixture of proposals to increase production of existing energy supplies, to encourage energy conservation, and to facilitate research and development of new energy resources. Over a ten-year period, Ford envisioned 200 major nuclear power plants, 250 major new coal mines, 150 major coal-fired power plants, 30 major new oil refineries, 20 major new synthetic fuel plants, the drilling of many thousands of new oil wells, the insulation of 18 million new homes, and the manufacturing and sale of millions of new automobiles, trucks, and buses that used much less fuel. Expressing his belief that the goal of energy independence could be attained by 1985, Ford recalled a previous challenge confronted by the nation: "In another crisis—the one in 1942—President Franklin D. Roosevelt said this country would build 60,000 [50,000] military aircraft. By 1943, production in that program had reached 125,000 aircraft annually. They did it then. We can do it now."[5]

In many respects, Ford's program was similar in shape and objectives to the program announced by President Nixon in November, 1973. Then, Nixon had called for an effort to achieve energy self-sufficiency by 1980, a goal he labeled "Project Independence." Nixon's proposals for the attainment of energy independence had called for the creation of a Department of Energy and Natural Resources and an Energy Research and Development Administration (ERDA).[6] Although Congress failed to act upon the proposal to create a cabinet-level energy department, the ERDA proposal was adopted, and the ERDA was established by passage of the Energy Reorganization Act of 1974.

The ERDA was primarily a research vehicle that had a developmental role limited to the "demonstration of commercial feasibility and practical applications of the extraction, conversion, storage, transmission, and utilization" of new energy resources. However, absent from Nixon's program was a vehicle for promoting massive investment in production of energy from new energy resources and technologies that had been demonstrated to be commercially feasible but that lacked the large capital outlays required for production development. As Ford outlined his energy program in January, 1975, the same defect surfaced: while the goal of energy independence by 1985 was clearly stated, the means of achieving the goal appeared to be missing.

The practical aspect of attaining energy self-sufficiency in the 1980s was a consideration that had intrigued Nelson Rockefeller in 1974. His Commission on Critical Choices for Americans had established, as one of six study panels, a panel concerned with "Energy and Its Relationship to Ecology, Economics, and World Stability." Under the direction of Dr. Edward Teller, Rockefeller's long-time science adviser, the energy panel assessed various methods and approaches of dealing with the energy crisis from both domestic and global perspectives.[7] On the problem of domestic energy production, the panel considered the accelerated development of energy resources through the commercial use of new technologies to be vital for achieving American energy self-sufficiency.[8]

In the course of the panel's discussion in the fall of 1974, it was suggested by commission member George D. Woods that the federal government could directly make a major contribution to the development of adequate domestic energy supplies in the form of financial assistance for the commercial application of new energy technologies. As a former president of the World Bank, Woods was concerned about the capital investment funding available for energy projects that projected high or uncertain risk factors to a capital market already lacking confidence and investment funds. Pondering Woods's suggestion in December, 1974, at a time when Ford's State of the Union proposals for energy independence were being finalized, Rockefeller decided to employ it for the purpose of developing a vehicle for the attainment of the president's goal of energy independence by 1985.[9]

Shortly after his confirmation and swearing in as vice president, Rockefeller had his staff begin an examination of the practical needs of a program to achieve energy self-sufficiency. In late December, a preliminary outline was prepared that discussed four major areas for programmatic action:

• Capital flow

• Conservation

• Research and development

• Facilitating production

Since Rockefeller had expressed an interest in capital-flow problems, the staff considered possible governmental responses to deal with the needs of the capital markets, particularly as these affected energy production. Two specific approaches were developed for the vice president's consideration: first, the creation of an "energy trust fund to hold energy-related federal receipts out of general funds of the United States," and, second, the creation of an "RFC-like government-sponsored agency to seek long-term capital funds from OPEC or other sources." The effect of both sets of proposals would be to increase capital funding for investment in energy production and development, while at the same time avoiding excessive competition for scarce capital resources with other sectors of the economy.[10]

These considerations continued to exercise the vice president's mind throughout the month of January, 1975. On January 22, he was advised by Alan Greenspan, chairman of the Council of Economic Advisers, that

The issue which has got to be gotten across is that national economic policy no longer has the luxury of focusing on the very simple question of whether the unemployment rate is 4½ percent or 6½ percent or regrettably even 8 percent.

Now the real world is beginning to press in on the average American and could very well devastate family life and standards of living if we do not confront our longer-term problems and protect the United States from the ever-increasing potential dangers to which it is becoming exposed.

The immediate problem is oil, although I would list our national defense posture and fiscal erosion as equally critical.[11]

In early February, Rockefeller broadened his consideration of the energy problem to embrace the issue of unemployment. He moved to examine the employment effects of various levels of energy production.[12] However, according to information supplied by his staff, the indications were that in the heavily capital-intensive energy sector, "even with a major energy development effort, labor requirements . . . will remain under 1½ percent of the U.S. labor force." But, on the positive side, it was pointed out that the immediate employment effects of a dynamic energy program would be felt in the construction trades, where "employment levels . . . could more than double from 1975-1980." Furthermore, without any significant energy program, it was stressed that American employment levels would remain vulnerable to a future oil embargo. Regarding such an eventuality, the vice president was reminded that "the Arab embargo of 1973-74 put 200,000 people out of work between October and January."[13]

Looking at the president's energy goals of building 200 major nuclear power plants, 150 major new coal-fired power plants, 30 major new oil refineries, and 20 major new synthetic fuel plants by 1985, Rockefeller considered these in the context of current problems of capital market shortages and record levels of unemployment. It was his conclusion that the condition of the investment capital markets was such that the massive investment in constructing energy facilities required by Ford's program could not be supplied by the private sector alone. Here, George Woods's suggestion of governmental financial assistance for development of an energy program prompted serious consideration of a federal government entity patterned after the Reconstruction Finance Corporation (RFC) of Roosevelt's New Deal.[14] To develop this proposition more fully, Rockefeller had a staff associate, Richard Parsons, prepare a discussion paper setting out a range of recommendations regarding a new RFC type of agency.

On February 27, Parsons presented to the vice president a review of the problems arising from the outpouring of U.S. dollars for imported energy, the tight credit situation in the domestic money markets, inflation, and unemployment. To deal with these problems, he proposed the establishment of a Resources Policy and Finance Corporation (RPFC). As Parsons outlined them, the functions of the RPFC would be to promote and assure:

Economic stability, by helping to insure liquidity of private sector financial institutions.

Full employment, by directing investment into areas where the unavailability of capital has restricted growth of important industries and areas where additional capital will substantially increase employment opportunities.

The attainment of energy self-sufficiency, by directing investment into private sector initiatives for the development of new energy sources and by encouraging (or in some cases undertaking) plant conversions or use of excess plant capacity to manufacture products essential to the achievement of energy independence.

Maximum utilization of natural resources and raw materials, by directing investment in technological initiatives to discover new resources or to promote more efficient consumption of existing resources.

If possible, the raising of funds for the forgoing purposes through the sale of government-guaranteed obligations in capital surplus areas abroad.[15]

The scale of the RPFC venture as considered by the vice president was ambitious and breathtaking, even by Rockefeller standards. Initially, it was proposed that RPFC be capitalized "through the sale of $5 billion common stock to the U.S. Treasury," but with "power to issue up to $200 billion in government-guaranteed obligations."[16] As for specific RPFC functions, it was recommended that the RPFC "have broad powers to lend and invest in financial institutions, utilities, industrial corporations, and public authorities; and be authorized to establish subsidiary corporations to undertake special projects, such as the construction of power-generating facilities or industrial facilities for the manufacture of products essential to the achievement of energy independence."

As Parsons outlined the RPFC proposal, there were several benefits to be derived from such a federal entity. First, it would work toward the restoration of confidence in the business and financial communities as a concrete demonstration of governmental resolve to prevent "major catastrophe" in the private sector. Thus the RPFC would provide an ongoing institutionalized mechanism for economic regeneration in contrast to piecemeal, ad hoc measures exemplified by the federal loans made by the Nixon administration to the Lockheed Corporation in 1971. Second, if the RPFC were designed to take account of the needs of foreign investors it would be possible to finance the proposed corporation with only minimal impact on the domestic money markets. Furthermore, receipt of foreign investment funding would provide a useful means of recycling "petro-dollars," "without allowing direct investment in businesses by foreign nations." Last, but by no means least, the RPFC would provide a vehicle for financing the energy plant and production facilities essential for attaining the president's energy program objectives.[17]

Parson's RPFC proposal was developed further by the vice president's counsel, Peter Wallison, who supplemented its organizational framework with a provision that

Management of the RPFC would be vested in a board of directors consisting of five (5) persons appointed by the president, with the advice and consent of the Senate. Of the five, not more than three could be members of any one political party and not more than one could be from any one Federal Reserve district.

Wallison added a further provision, recommending that the RPFC's authority to make or guarantee loans, or to invest in capital stock, be terminated within five years of the establishment of the corporation.[18]

On March 6, Rockefeller met with the president to discuss the broad framework of his thinking about the problems and needs of the financial and energy sectors of the economy. In particular, he reviewed with the president his proposal to deal with the problems of unemployment and private sector confidence by means of an RFC type of federal entity aimed at revitalizing private industry and accelerating energy production. Ford indicated an interest in having the proposal developed further and requested Rockefeller to refine it in consultation with members of the Domestic Council.[19]

Heartened by the president's interest in getting further development of the RPFC concept, Rockefeller proceeded to review the range of problems that the proposed corporation might be usefully employed to resolve. In the field of energy production, he was made aware of the difficulties encountered in getting energy-related construction projects completed expeditiously because of delays created by the regulatory process. On the problems facing energy projects, Richard Dunham advised him that:

In addition to the delays caused by capital insufficiency, some critical energy-related projects are being delayed by a variety of agencies, both federal and state, with overlapping jurisdictions in regulation of energy projects and companies. Specifically, an energy project, such as a large nuclear power plant or a deepwater tanker port, cannot be constructed until approvals are obtained from several agencies.[20]

In Dunham's view, there was real merit in consolidating all regulatory functions into a single agency in order to get more coherent and expeditious consideration of energy-related projects. Considering this suggestion, the vice president saw possibilities in employing the RPFC as a vehicle to speed up the regulatory process for such projects.

Meanwhile, although Rockefeller had hoped to secure quick approval of his RPFC proposal,[21] he continued the work of refining it and building support for the RPFC both within and outside the administration. In late April, he looked at the potential for support within the labor constituency, which had a vested interest in any proposal designed to affect positively the unemployment situation. Accordingly, both Labor Secretary John Dunlop and AFL-CIO President George Meany were viewed as important actors in moving the RPFC project forward. Outside of labor, Federal Reserve Chairman Arthur Burns showed sufficient interest in the proposal to be considered by Rockefeller a potential ally in winning presidential endorsement of the proposed corporation. Finally, the vice president moved to sound out the business and financial communities whose support was vital to the ultimate success of the venture; therefore, he arranged to meet with David Packard, chairman of the Business Council, at a May 2 breakfast with Arthur Burns.

THE VICE PRESIDENT'S ERFCO PROPOSAL

In the main, the delay throughout the month of April in getting movement toward a recommendation for submission to the president was a product of Ford's directive to the vice president concerning consultation with members of the Domestic Council. The results of that consultation had been decidedly mixed. Although no one had directly opposed Rockefeller's RPFC proposal, some council members had been decidedly lukewarm about it. In particular, Treasury Secretary William Simon, chairman of the Council of Economic Advisers Alan Greenspan, and Director of the Office of Management and Budget James Lynn had all indicated serious reservations about the size and scope of the RPFC, while at the same time expressing interest in the concept of a federal corporation to provide assistance to the private sector. Despite this mixed reaction, but having carried out the consultation desired by the president, Rockefeller decided on May 2 to proceed with submission of a presidential recommendation.

The proposed federal corporation outlined for President Ford by Vice President Rockefeller on May 2 was, in its essentials, similar to the RPFC recommended by Parsons on May 27 and subsequently refined by Wallison. However, the scope of the corporation had been sharpened to focus more explicitly on energy. As Rockefeller explained the functions of his proposed corporation to the president, these were to provide a self-liquidating financing mechanism sponsored and chartered by the federal government that could: "(1) achieve the president's goal of energy and self-sufficiency by 1985; (2) assure adequate supplies of essential raw materials or their substitutes; (3) assure the provision of essential transportation services; and (4) have the capacity to finance the conversion of vacant or underutilized plants to produce materials essential to achieve the above."

Although Rockefeller discussed the various elements of his proposal concerning the corporation's operations, powers, financing, organization, and termination period, he deliberately refrained from submitting it to Ford as a straightforward recommendation for decisive presidential approval or disapproval. Rather, his May 2 recommendation was drawn very narrowly, reflecting his acute awareness of the division within the administration about the size and scope proposed for the corporation's operations. What he recommended for President Ford's approval was the creation of a Domestic Council review group on "Energy and Resource Policy and Finance." The basic purpose of this review would be to develop further the proposed federal corporation, with the specific goal of developing concrete illustrations of how the corporation would function in practice. More broadly, creation of the review group would assist in building support for the corporation within the administration.

Concerning the establishment of the review group, Rockefeller stressed to the president that it would have to be done "on a very confidential basis to avoid leaks." Proposed as members of the group were Economic Policy Board Executive Director William Seidman, Federal Energy Administration Administrator Frank Zarb, Council of Economic Advisers Chairman Alan Greenspan, and representatives of the Office of Management and Budget, the Federal Reserve Board, and the Departments of Commerce, Labor, and Treasury. In addition to the internal work of the review group, Rockefeller disclosed that he was engaging in external consultations about the proposal. Specifically, he informed Ford that David Packard had agreed "to get together a top group from business, industry, and finance to meet with me confidentially at the Business Council Conference a week from today in Hot Springs, West Virginia, to get their thoughts on the subject." Meanwhile, he recommended a target date of May 16 for presidential submission of the review group's report.[22] President Ford gave his approval, and the Domestic Council's Energy and Resource Policy and Finance Review Group was established.

Essentially, Rockefeller's decision to employ the device of a review group operating under the auspices of the Domestic Council for developing his corporation proposal was made for the same reasons as the decision to employ a review group for his social programs review. Within the Domestic Council's general framework, the review group would have access to the council's staff and financial resources. In addition, the arrangement would provide the development of the proposal with a considerable measure of legitimacy within the administration. Beyond these considerations, the review group provided an institutional framework to allow the inclusion of lukewarm and even hostile participants for "due process" purposes, on a basis controlled and directed by Rockefeller.

Anxious to get the work of the review group off to a fast start, the vice president assigned a staff associate, Richard Allison, to meet with James Cannon and Richard Dunham of the Domestic Council on May 3 to establish an agenda for the first meeting of the review group, which was scheduled for May 5. Their agenda proposed that the vice president begin the review group meeting with a discussion of the purpose of the review. He would be followed by Dunham, who would review a prepared list of specific illustrations of objectives that the proposed corporation could undertake.[23] Finally, the agenda proposed the following timetable for adoption by the review group:

May 14	—	Submit study to the vice president
May 16	—	Submit study to the president
Week of May 23	—	Presidential Address and submit legislation to Congress
June 1-August 1	—	Enactment of enabling legislation
June 1-August 1	—	Discussions with investors
August	—	Establishment of the corporation.[24]

When the review group met on May 5, the vice president impressed on the various participants the need for urgency in carrying out the review requested by the president. To emphasize this point, he asked each institutional participant to provide within two days: first, "brief but authoritative assessments of five of the most important energy projects which are currently delayed—with serious implications for the future strength and vitality of our economy," and, second, "for each of these five projects, the type of financing that could be developed by the financing vehicle which we are contemplating; and, in response to the president's request, how that financing would actually work."[25]

While the work of the review group was getting underway, Rockefeller was preoccupied with a further problem: maintaining exclusive direction and control of the development of his proposal. This problem was occasioned by a request from the Energy Resources Council (ERC) to have the review group operate as a joint ERC-Domestic Council review exercise. The basis for the ERC's request lay in authority granted to the ERC under its enabling executive order of October 11, 1974, which clearly contemplated that the ERC would have the lead role in the development of national energy policy. Accordingly, the ERC's request for joint sponsorship of the review group had on its face considerable merit.

As Rockefeller saw the situation, the problem was compounded by the fact that his review group had under consideration not only energy policy considerations but also large economic concerns regarding the investment capital markets. As a consequence, yielding to the ERC's request would immediately entail granting joint sponsorship to the Economic Policy Board since the EPB's role in the economic sphere was approximately contiguous with the ERC's in the energy area. However, such a grant to the EPB would be disastrous for Rockefeller's position since the EPB came under the direction of Treasury Secretary Simon, who was emerging as a leading opponent of the vice president's proposal.

Reviewing these problems for Rockefeller, Peter Wallison argued that the president had already designated the Domestic Council as the lead agency of the corporation proposal. Therefore, it followed that the appropriate role for the ERC was as an institutional participant with the others in the work of the review group. Referring to the Domestic Council revisions of February 13, 1975, Wallison argued that the memberships of the ERC and the EPB within the Domestic Council suggested a subordinate role for these two groups under the Domestic Council's "broader gauged authority for policy development." The ERC request for joint sponsorship of the energy and finance review group constituted, in his view, the first test of such a proposition. Therefore, he advised the vice president:

The Domestic Council's authority to create a review group on [Energy and Resource Policy and Finance] was assigned to it by the president; to the extent that any other agency or group had a similar general assignment from the president, it has been superseded. In the future, the question of whether a review group should be jointly sponsored should be presented to and resolved by the president.[26]

Acting upon Wallison's advice, Rockefeller added the ERC and the EPB to the formal institutional membership of the Domestic Council's review group. In addition, three other institutional actors with related areas of concern were brought in as review group members: the Departments of Interior and Transportation, and the Energy Research and Development Administration.[27]

On May 9, the vice president held his confidential meeting with the group of leaders of business, finance, and industry assembled by David Packard at the Business Council Conference at Hot Springs. This proved to be a disappointment for Rockefeller, who had hoped to collect a positive endorsement from the private sector for the proposed federal energy corporation. Although there was an expression of some favorable sentiment, which viewed the corporation as a useful financing vehicle "of last resort" for commercial development of energy projects whose size and scope made them unattractive risks for private investment capital, the overwhelming response from the private sector leaders was negative. Essentially, two sets of arguments were leveled at the vice president's proposal. First, it was regarded as unnecessary since it was believed no actual energy crisis existed, and, in any case, the functions of the proposed corporation could be accomplished by established federal agencies (e.g., the ERDA). Moreover, the proposal did not address what for business was the real problem: restrictions on incentive caused by excessively low, regulated energy prices. Second, the proposed corporation was viewed as harmful to the best interests of the private sector because it would be a major competitor for scarce investment capital and because it would inevitably become another interfering and intervening governmental agency working to restrict the freedom of business and industry.[28]

Within the review group, matters were no more encouraging. It quicky became evident that Simon, Greenspan, and Lynn were totally opposed to the vice president's proposal on essentially similar grounds to the opposition encountered by Rockefeller from his critics at Hot Springs. Indeed, commenting on the massive scale of Rockefeller's proposals (with a total financing in excess of $200 billion) Treasury Secretary Simon joked to the vice president that he would rather become chairman of the proposed corporation than be President of the United States: in his view the corporation's chairman would possess a greater measure of direct power to act upon the U.S. economy.[29] Nevertheless, despite the opposition from such critics, Rockefeller proceeded with the work of the review group and in mid-May had drafted a developed proposal for submission for presidential decision.

The recommendation that Vice President Rockefeller delivered to the president on May 21 focused on the creation of a federally sponsored Energy Resources Finance Corporation (ERFCO). Basically, ERFCO would act as "a financing vehicle designed to catalyze the private sector into undertaking the massive scale of investment needed to achieve the administration's energy independence goals of the next decade." The financing of ERFCO would be at a total authorized capitalization of $220 billion, of which $20 billion would comprise capital stock (equity subscribed by the U.S. Treasury) and the remaining $200 billion comprised of borrowing authority (including loan guarantees).

As recommended to the president, the financing operations proposed for ERFCO were aimed at three broad areas of energy production:

Large projects, with long lead times, where present delay stems partly because of technical uncertainty and partly because capacity might not be needed unless first stage projects are completed first. Uranium fuel enrichment plants are typical of this situation.

Projects that require financing that will accept deferred payment of interest charges and abnormal balloon "back end" maturities. The construction and lease of a conventional nuclear power plant to a utility would be typical of this category of investment. The corporation could, through a subsidiary, cause this plant to be built and would "carry it" until completion, when it could be either sold or leased to the user utility.

Projects that are either demonstrational in nature or are uncertain as to commercial feasibility. Such projects could bear a much higher degree of investment risk and would be limited to an amount equivalent to the equity capital of the corporation. They would be undertaken as "second stage" efforts, after development financing by the ERDA and/or R & D sponsored by private industry. Such projects might presently be in areas such as coal gasification and liquefaction and eventually in thermal- and solar-type projects.

The general powers and term proposed by Rockefeller for the corporation were essentially those outlined in the earlier draft of the RPFC proposal: ERFCO would cease to make new loans or investments after a five-year term and would be required to liquidate and sell all assets within ten years. Management of ERFCO would be vested in a board of five directors appointed by the president, with the advice and consent of Congress. These directors would be responsible for devising "an investment strategy designed to implement the national energy policy and program set forth by the president and his delegated agent[s]." Accordingly, because the ERC, the FEA, and the ERDA all possessed "statutory roles in the development of overall energy strategy," ERFCO would "attempt to make investment commitments that expedite the national energy goals put forth by these agencies." ERFCO would also have power to certify energy-related projects as "of critical importance" to the goal of national energy independence, for the purpose of expediting the regulatory process. Certified projects would have to be processed by regulatory agencies within a period of six months.[30]

Realizing that the dimensions of his proposal were vast and venturesome, Rockefeller addressed himself to the justification for such an administrative initiative in his covering memorandum to President Ford:

Evidence to date suggests that we are alarmingly stalled on efforts to implement your energy self-sufficiency goals. Investment spending which must precede the development of new and expansion of old sources of energy are seriously lagging. The bureaucracy abounds in thoughts, plans, and schemes to attack this problem, but unfortunately there is an abundance of equally strongly held views and rationalization as to why such plans will not work. *The net result is inaction.*

To date, you have been forced to back economic measures that, while stimulative to the economy, have had no impact on increasing our productivity or improving our competitive position in the world. Your efforts to hold back the inflationary impact of these programs by keeping a tight rein on the size of the federal deficit have been courageous, but have the unfortunate side effect of casting the administration in a negative tone. We are against a runaway deficit because we recognize the inevitable inflationary implications, but our program lacks the positive counterbalance of a new effort that will channel expenditures in an inflation-fighting, job-producing manner.

Having presented the president with a political rationale for adopting ERFCO as an administration program, Rockefeller addressed the basic features of the corporation and its role in the private sector in an effort to portray the ERFCO concept as one that was wholly consistent with Ford's own deep-seated belief in the free enterprise system. Accordingly, he argued that ERFCO should be seen essentially as a dynamic free market catalyst possessing the following features:

It will work through, not around or as a replacement for, private enterprise.

It will have a limited life, with no new investment commitments after five years. Consistent with its catalytic, bridge financing role, it will, by law, go out of business when its mission is completed.

In addition to its financing role, it will have legal powers designed to at least shorten, and in some cases eliminate, the myriad of regulatory impediments which currently impede and stall energy-related investment.

It is being formed to attack a current problem, is designed to have a finite lifespan and therefore should be able to attract the type of entrepreneurial managerial talent from the private sector that led to the success of World War II synthetic rubber plant and Manhattan-type projects of the past.

Mindful of the opposition that was mobilizing within the administration against the ERFCO proposal, Rockefeller discussed this in the context of the need for a prompt presidential initiative:

Several of the concerns and objections to such a project . . . have some merit. I am convinced, however, that the refutation judgments carry the day. We could go on for months or years refining the pros and cons—but delay beyond the early part of the summer will put the project that much closer to 1976, and the political attack and/or legislative blockage which predictably will emerge as a matter of presidential politics.

Your early public announcement of the decision to submit enabling legislation will mobilize the considerable talents within the administration to a concerted program to enlarge, flesh out, and improve the precise scope and structure of the corporation. . . . With the galvanizing effect of such a decision now, I believe we can have a final program ready within a month.[31]

ERFCO: AN EMBATTLED VICE PRESIDENTIAL INITIATIVE

As the vice president himself had indicated in his ERFCO proposal to the president on May 21, serious opposition to the initiative had developed within the administration. The hard-line critics of ERFCO were, as already noted, the president's leading economic and budget advisers (William Simon, Alan Greenspan, and James Lynn), who opposed the size and scope of the proposed venture as well as its propensity to "crowd out" the capital investment markets. The effect of this opposition was to delay a presidential decision on acceptance or rejection of the proposed initiative. Ford was caught in an ambivalent position on ERFCO's merits. On the one hand, he accepted Rockefeller's arguments for creating a federal corporation to assist in providing the necessary financing of an expensive energy development program essential for achieving the administration's goal of energy independence by 1985. Yet, on the other hand, he shared the concerns of Arthur Burns, who endorsed the general aims of the ERFCO concept but had serious doubts about the corporation's magnitude and broad scope. Accordingly, Ford informed Rockefeller that if acceptable changes to the proposal could be worked out with Burns it would be given presidential clearance.[32]

Thus, while the ERFCO initiative had not been accepted by the president, it had not been rejected either. Rockefeller had been given a grace period in which to generate support for the proposal and to negotiate acceptable modifications to it for ultimate presidential clearance. Assisting him in his efforts to engage in a dialogue on ERFCO's merits within the administration was a public endorsement of the initiative published in the *Washington Star* on May 20, in the form of an article by Charles Bartlett entitled "Rockefeller on Energy." As Bartlett informed his readers:

Viewed from the outside, Nelson Rockefeller is making no special contribution as vice president. Viewed from the inside, he is taking a venturous political risk to force critical choices on the energy issues.

Rockefeller is pushing a . . . proposal that will bring the government into the front lines of the struggle to build tomorrow's energy supply. The government will plunge in wherever private companies are not doing their job, whether the task is building nuclear power plants or reviving railroads to carry coal. The concept is that the government must do what is being neglected by free enterprise.

This is a bold proposal in the old Rockefeller tradition, and it will reflect well on the vice president when it surfaces.

On May 23, Rockefeller met with key members of the administration to discuss ERFCO and the objections to the form of his proposal. Present at this meeting were Arthur Burns, Richard Dunham, Alan Greenspan, James Lynn, Rogers Morton, William Seidman, and Frank Zarb. As the discussion progressed it quickly became apparent that Greenspan and Lynn were unalterably opposed to ERFCO, whereas Burns, Morton, and Zarb saw some merit in the corporation despite considerable reservations about key aspects of its functions.[33]

Briefly summarized, the arguments against ERFCO were as follows:

- Money is not really the problem; instead it is the inhibiting impact of regulations.
- The project will become:
    a Christmas tree;
    a crowd-out (absorbing too much of the available capital);
    a super-central bank, allocating capital;
    a bailout;
    a permanent institution that we won't be able to get rid of;
    another ad hoc solution devised to win an election, but not solving the energy problem.
- Even if the political arguments in favor of the project are conceded, is *this* project the most appropriate vehicle to achieve those political goals?
- Ultimately, the project will lead to more, not less, control and signal that the free enterprise system is finished.

Despite these criticisms, the meeting provided Rockefeller's proposal with some positive support. Rogers Morton voiced a strong concern about the negative image of the administration and expressed interest in the political benefits to be gained for the president from an ERFCO initiative that dealt with the problems of unemployment, energy, and the capital markets. As Morton bluntly expressed himself on Ford's political situation: "He's got to kick this thing in the ass a whole lot harder or he's not going to get elected!"[34] Arthur Burns had some practical questions that he thought should be addressed to allow full consideration of the proposal's merits. In particular, Burns expressed concern about the following areas:

Size: Assuming that the project is viable (the figures aren't clear), do we really need this much?

Role: How does this project fit into the president's overall energy program—is it a supplement or a replacement?

Function: How would the entity actually function financially? Wouldn't it be operating at a loss—at least for the first few years?

Feasibility: Examples of what projects would be financed ought to be worked out in great detail by engineering and financial experts.

Finally, Frank Zarb shared a concern voiced by Burns that the corporation would become primarily a central lending bank. However, Zarb conceded that President Ford had set out basic energy goals that had to be met and that the existing vehicle (the ERDA) for achieving these goals was inadequate. Given the necessity of meeting energy goals that required expensive energy development projects, he indicated that he could support the ERFCO initiative if it could be modified with a more limited and less flexible charter.[35]

Following up on this May 23 meeting, Rockefeller met with Arthur Burns separately on May 28 in an effort to win him over to endorsing the ERFCO proposal. In this effort, he was largely successful. Although Burns had concerns about ERFCO's propensity to become essentially a banking entity, he conceded merits in the proposal. As he explained to the vice president, the prime consideration for the United States was "to achieve independence in the energy area so we can shape our own destiny." Therefore, he agreed that action had to be taken during the next twenty years to achieving energy self-sufficiency. The start on such an effort could be done on a relatively modest but convincing scale: the important thing, Burns stressed, was not the size of the endeavor but its soundness.

Because of the overriding importance of the national security reasons for gaining immunity to future oil embargoes, Burns agreed to give the ERFCO project his endorsement as a necessary vehicle in assisting the private sector in developing the nation's energy resources. In Burns's view, the corporation should comprise three components: "some banking functions—to provide assistance, but not subsidies, to accelerate private sector activities; some subsidy functions—to get the private sector involved in activities not otherwise undertaken; and some complete cost-underwriting functions—to provide facilities (such as oil storage) that were essential to the national interest. However, Burns made it clear to the vice president that his endorsement was conditional on clearing the details of ERFCO's structure and functions with Frank Zarb, who had the prime responsibility for the president's current energy program.[36]

With Burns's conditional endorsement in hand, Rockefeller arranged to meet with Zarb to resolve Zarb's outstanding reservations about the proposal. The meeting with Zarb on May 29 proved to be highly fruitful. Although he had expressed real concern about ERFCO's proposed size and scope, Zarb was anxious to employ the corporation as a means of meeting the very real capital needs of the energy industry. In particular, he was concerned about the immediate financing needs of two energy projects that could benefit from ERFCO investment assistance: the construction of new nuclear power plant facilities (including uranium enrichment and disposal of nuclear waste), and construction of plants for coal conversion, gasification, and liquefaction.

To meet the concerns both Zarb and Burns had expressed about the magnitude of the proposed corporation, the vice president indicated at the outset a willingness to cut the recommended ERFCO borrowing authority in half, from $200 billion to $100 billion, with the capitalization level correspondingly reduced from $20 billion to $10 billion. However, Zarb, in addition to his doubts about funding levels, had other concerns about the eligibility standards for ERFCO assistance as well as standards for governing ERFCO's operations. But, in general, he declared himself in broad agreement with the vice president's proposal, stressing the need to be thorough in preparing it in final version. It was his view that ERFCO supporters had to avoid making the initiative "vulnerable to sharpshooting." Above all, he declared to Rockefeller, "We have to make it the sine qua non for the accomplishment of the president's energy goals, but . . . the project has to be laid out in precise terms."

Accepting Zarb's points, the vice president nonetheless insisted on " . . . a need to stake out the concept, and then work out the details later." Unless the proposal emerged from the administration fairly quickly, he argued, the president would find that others (including Senators Jackson and Bentsen) would "beat him to the punch" with energy proposals of their own. Consequently, Rockefeller proposed that "the president should give a speech setting forth the governing idea and then saying that he has asked Frank Zarb to work out a detailed scheme."

After further discussion, Zarb and Rockefeller concluded their meeting with agreement that Zarb should undertake the preparation of a revised ERFCO proposal for submission to the president by June 5. This new plan would outline the following:

- Clarification of the relationship of ERFCO's activities to existing FEA programs.

- Examples of how ERFCO's financing would work in practice.

- A revised limitation of ERFCO's borrowing authority to a level of about $60 billion.[37]

On June 4, Rogers Morton and Zarb submitted a joint memorandum to the vice president, enclosing a draft presidential press statement. The essence of the proposed statement was an announcement that the president had directed the ERC to consider ways in which the federal government could assist in promoting "necessary investment over the short term" to assist the private sector. Specifically, the press statement would announce that:

The concept to be examined by the Energy Resources Council includes the creation of what may possibly be called the Energy Resources Finance Corporation. The primary mission of such an agency, if adopted, would be to invest or loan funds or guarantee loans in order to inactivize [sic] prompt development of needed energy facilities. Such a program will, of course, provide thousands of jobs in mines, oil fields, utility facilities, construction projects, and so on.

Complete details and options are to be developed by the council and submitted to the president no later than July 20. It is important to note that the president has not decided to go ahead on such a program or on any of its details. The purpose of his direction to the Energy Resources Council is to insure that adequate staff work is completed to analyze its viability and potential methods of operation.[38]

While the Morton-Zarb approach of June 4 clearly undercut aspects of the vice president's endeavors on behalf of ERFCO (their draft presidential announcement implicitly stated that the ERFCO proposal had been inadequately considered and was underdeveloped), their action was welcomed by the vice president's staff. Long-time Rockefeller aide William Ronan declared that "Morton-Zarb can be read as an attempt to keep the project alive in the face of strong opposition elsewhere." Moreover, Ronan argued, a new opportunity had now been created for the vice president to take up the proposal with Ford. However, he cautioned that "the approach to the president on ERFCO must be basically political—the opportunity to seize leadership, to revitalize the energy program, and put a call again to the Congress to act."[39]

Acting on Ronan's advice, Rockefeller took up the ERFCO proposal at his weekly meetings with the president successively on June 6 and June 12.[40] However, Ford indicated that he was not ready to commit himself decisively either positively or negatively on the proposal. Part of the president's problem was that the contours of what he was being asked to endorse were in a constant state of flux. He had received a developed ERFCO proposal from the vice president on May 21, but this had been attacked on all sides, and the vice president had been subsequently charged with the task of securing acceptable revisions to it. Meanwhile, Morton and Zarb had requested that the ERC develop a revised options paper for presidential submission by July 20.

Following his meeting with the vice president on June 12, President Ford decided that the logjam on the ERFCO proposal should be broken. On June 16, Rumsfeld's deputy, Richard Cheney, was instructed to request James Connor, the secretary to the cabinet, to obtain the ERFCO proposal of May 21 and arrange to have it "staffed out" for response to the president within a week.[41]

However, when Connor approached the vice president's counsel, Peter Wallison, on June 16 for a copy of the May 21 proposal, he was informed that "modifications were being made to it" and a copy would be sent to him "as soon as possible." Two days later, on June 18, Connor obtained a copy of the proposal (but "in the form of a memorandum from Dick Dunham to Jim Cannon"). This he then distributed to the following members of the administration: Philip Buchen, William Seidman, John Marsh, James Lynn, and Frank Zarb, with Seidman and Zarb respectively requested to secure the views of members of the EPB and the ERC.[42]

The reluctance of Wallison to provide Connor with a copy of the May 21 ERFCO proposal was based on the straightforward grounds that the vice president had agreed to make major modifications to that particular version of ERFCO and that, consequently, the May 21 draft was no longer a valid decision memorandum. This position was generally adopted by ERFCO supporters who refused to treat the May 21 draft as an appropriate paper for a presidential decision. Therefore, Connor was considerably frustrated in his efforts to obtain responses, as his own chronology makes clear:

June 26: Jim Cannon and Frank Zarb were queried on the status of their responses; both indicated that they had questions as to whether this paper was the appropriate one to use for decision making and that they would discuss the matter with the vice president.

June 30: Frank Zarb and Secretary Morton sent me a memorandum indicating that they had met with the vice president the previous week and had agreed with him that a different course of action should be followed. They suggested that instead of responding to this specific proposal, a broader options paper incorporating this suggestion and others be prepared for the president's decision. I asked for a schedule of such activities.

July 7: I met with Frank Zarb and Jim Cannon, and they reiterated that both they and the vice president agreed that a broader options paper would be appropriate. They indicated that a schedule would be available on July 9.

July 9: Frank Zarb and Secretary Morton responded with . . . [a] schedule in the form of a memorandum to the vice president.[43]

For Rockefeller, Cheney's request to have the May 21 ERFCO proposal circulated to the senior staff to comment and make recommendations for a presidential decision hoisted a storm warning about the perils facing the whole ERFCO initiative. In response to Ford's direct request, the vice president had begun a process of consultation about and modification of his May 21 recommendation. Therefore, it appeared that this process was being undermined by White House insistence on getting a decisive outcome on ERFCO based on a weakened and outdated proposal. Accordingly, Rockefeller took steps to consolidate his position with the other prime ERFCO supporters within the administration: Morton and Zarb.

On June 25, Rockefeller met with Morton and Zarb to discuss the development of a mutually acceptable revision of his ERFCO proposal of May 21. In the course of the meeting, the vice president conceded that it was the general feeling that "this subject was so very much in the area of responsibility of ERC." Accordingly, he suggested to Morton and Zarb that they assume responsibility for the preparation of a revised presidential options paper. Morton and Zarb both indicated that they would undertake such a paper.[44]

The following week, they informed Rockefeller about an upcoming report on a synthetic fuel commercialization program that would contain incentives to spur production of coal gasification and liquefaction, oil shale, and other fuels. In their view, it would be highly desirable to integrate this ERC program with the ERFCO proposal. Therefore, to achieve this they proposed the following schedule:

July 15   — Presentation of synthetic fuels commercialization program findings to the ERC.

July 30   — Draft presidential decision memorandum integrating synthetic fuels program and the ERFC presented to the ERC.

August 15   — Final decision memorandum delivered to the president.

September 1 — Presidential statement on new initiative (prior to Congress' return from the August recess).

As for the revised options paper which Rockefeller had requested, they indicated that: "The decision memorandum will lay out the rationale for choosing whether ERFCO should cover all energy investments, just synthetic fuels, or some middle ground. It will also discuss the appropriate financing instructions, levels of government involvement, and the organizational structure of the corporation."[45]

ERFCO II: REVISION OF A VICE PRESIDENTIAL PROPOSAL

Throughout the month of July, the FEA worked under the direction of Morton and Zarb to produce a new ERFCO options paper. Meanwhile, the vice president reported to the president that the paper would be ready on his return from Europe,[46] and that following a presidential decision the necessary materials and legislation on the selected options could be prepared for submission to the Congress after Labor Day (September 1). Ford responded that Labor Day "might afford . . . the opportunity to make a speech on the importance of unemployment in the private sector, and the stimulation which an Energy Resource Finance Corporation could give the economy."[47]

At the end of July, the FEA completed its eagerly awaited ERFCO options paper. As expected, the FEA's ERFCO proposal differed considerably from the vice president's proposal of May 21 in terms of the size and scope of the corporation's activities. The FEA proposal incorporated the change in borrowing authority first suggested by Rockefeller, putting forward a borrowing ceiling of $100 billion in place of the original $200 billion, and an equity capital level of $10 billion rather than $20 billion as originally proposed. Moreover, while Rockefeller's proposal had proposed ERFCO assistance for transportation and other nonenergy economic sectors, the FEA proposed to narrow ERFCO's activities to energy projects. The basic elements of the FEA's ERFCO proposal were as follows:

ERFCO Organization: ERFCO would be established as an independent federal corporation with authority to provide financial support of up to $110 billion for energy or energy-related projects. The board of directors, consisting of five members, would be appointed by the president and be confirmed by the Senate, would serve at the president's pleasure, and would include no more than three members of one political party. The chairman and the president of ERFCO would be two of the board members.

The chairman of ERFCO would be a member of the president's Energy Resources Council (ERC) and the Economic Policy Board (EPB), and would consult with the ERC and the EPB on broad direction and specific projects. The chairman of ERFCO would be the corporation's chief executive officer; he would report directly to the President of the United States.

ERFCO would be self-liquidating and have a specific, limited life of ten years, with new commitments only in the first seven years of its existence. After the seventh year, ERFCO would develop a liquidation plan for all of its investments. Any remaining obligations after the ten-year life would be transferred to the Department of the Treasury for liquidation.

A Statutory Advisory Committee would be established to assist the board and would consist of outstanding representatives from consumer, environmental, government, labor, and business organizations.

ERFCO Financial Structure: ERFCO's sources of finance capital would be off-budget; it would have authorized equity capital of $10 billion and the ability to borrow up to $100 billion.

Scope of ERFCO Investments: ERFCO would concentrate on the financing of large-scale energy projects deemed critical to our national energy objectives. It would have broad discretionary authority to support the projects approved by the board without case-by-case outside review.

Generally, ERFCO would evaluate proposals against the following criteria:

(1) *Credit Elsewhere Test*—Is the proposed project unable to be financed elsewhere under terms and conditions which would allow other entities, private or public, to undertake it economically?

(2) *Energy Impact Test*—Is the proposed project consistent with, and does it advance, national energy goals and policies; and does its energy impact justify financial assistance from ERFCO?

The options components of the FEA's ERFCO proposal came in a section discussing projects that could be sponsored by the corporation. As indicated above, these were basically limited to the energy sector of the economy but encompassed the "full spectrum of energy development and conservation programs." As FEA listed them, the projects options were as follows:

Option 1—Synthetic Fuel Technology Commercialization: The emphasis here would be upon the application of technology, which has been proven at the R & D phase, to plentiful energy resources such as coal and oil shale, and to the conversion of solid waste materials into liquid fuels. The projects to be supported would be high-risk ventures, which could not be undertaken without government support, and are vital to the achievement of the president's synthetic fuels goal. Major processes would include: synthetic gas from coal; synthetic crude oil from coal; crude oil from western shale; and synthetic gas and liquids from solid waste.

Option 2—Other Emerging Technologies: Suitable projects in this area would include other high technology processes, also proven at the R & D phase, which are ready for full-scale commercial development. Major projects would consist of: geothermal energy; production of energy from Devonian shale and tight gas formations; solar energy applications; and conservation equipment such as heat recovery processes and energy storage units.

Option 3—Conventional Technologies: Within this category the focus would be on the application of new technology to improve the efficiency of conventional energy development, and use of financing as a lever to accelerate significantly the development of conventional energy supply and conservation technologies. Specific projects could consist of: conservation technology to improve efficiency of energy processes; floating nuclear power plants; uranium enrichment and spent-fuel reprocessing; mass production of conservation equipment such as insulation or time-of-day electric meters; and energy parks.

Option 4—Related Projects to Reduce Energy Development Constraints: This would include support of major categories of infrastructure and equipment that might otherwise constrain energy development. For example, the production potential of Alaskan oil and gas is of no benefit unless costly pipelines and logistical systems are put in place rapidly. Exploration and development of resources in the Outer Continental Shelf may be delayed by a shortage of mobile drilling rigs. Consequently, ERFCO could support projects aimed at relieving major bottlenecks such as these.

Finally, in its proposals concerning ERFCO's authority, the FEA retained the vice president's proposed employment of the corporation as a vehicle for expediting the regulatory process as it impacted on energy-related projects. Emphasizing that ERFCO would have no power to override regulatory decisions made at the federal or other levels of government, the FEA recommended that:

ERFCO would be empowered to certify projects as essential to national energy goals; this certification would have the effect of requiring final regulatory determinations by federal agencies within twelve months of submission of applications or within an appropriate shorter time, with an extension of up to six months for good cause granted by ERFCO at the regulatory agency's request. ERFCO could enforce these time limits for expedited processing by seeking a court order.[48]

Reviewing these options for the president on August 6, the vice president stressed that the first three dealt primarily with research, development, and pilot commercial demonstration plants. His estimate of the total potential increase production inherent in Option 1 activities was one million barrels per day by 1985, and for Option 2 activities at around two million barrels increased production by 1985. While Option 3 would encompass the areas of Options 1 and 2, the additional activities prescribed related solely to demonstration plants and facilities that would not make any significant contribution to increasing energy production beyond the level of increase of Option 2. Accordingly, Rockefeller argued that these three options, either singly or in combination, failed to deal with the commercial production of energy on a scale necessary for the attainment of the goal of energy independence by 1985. However, the fourth option did, in his view, address the needs of production as well as the essential promotion of research and development, and pilot and demonstration plants. Option 4 encompassed all of the areas of the first three options with the addition of "conventional technology production plants in the energy area as well as elements like pipelines, coal rail lines, equipment of various kinds and materials which otherwise would be so scarce or unobtainable and constrict the possibility of achieving the program." The total potential increased production of energy from Option 4 was estimated at twenty million barrels per day by 1985.

Accordingly, the vice president made two recommendations for the president's consideration: first, that the research, development, and pilot activities described in the first three FEA options be assigned to the ERDA; second, that the production financing activities outlined in the FEA's fourth option become the responsibility and mission of ERFCO. As for the level of ERFCO financing, Rockefeller proposed for presidential decision a range that encompassed his own May 21 level and the FEA revised level: on authorized capitalization he recommended a range of $10-$20 billion, and on borrowing capacity he proposed a range of $100-$200 billion.[49]

Turning to the political considerations inherent in adoption of the ERFCO proposal, Rockefeller recommended that Ford should emphasize it as an administrative initiative that tackled the major problems of energy and unemployment. In Rockefeller's view, a major public announcement of ERFCO by the president scheduled for Labor Day could:

a. provide the political initiative needed for energy and unemployment;
b. break the stalemate with Congress over energy;
c. blunt the ability of the Democratic congressional majority to grab the post-veto initiative;
d. attract labor support;
e. encourage sectors of business to move ahead with plans for construction and inventory replenishment;

f. put enormous pressure on the returning Congress to respond; and

g. give the OPEC countries and the rest of the world tangible evidence of U.S. determination to diminish its reliance on imports.

On the public impact of the ERFCO initiative, Rockefeller made the point that the president's original energy program had lost most of its initial impetus in the eight months of haggling between Congress and the White House, and, consequently its features had become blurred to the public eye. In sharp contrast, the ERFCO proposal would be clearly and easily understood by the public. Moreover, he advised the president, "Even if the ERFCO proposal should not be adopted (although this is not likely), you would have the credit for a major leadership issue."[50]

Meanwhile, the basic hurdle that the revised ERFCO proposal had to overcome concerned the financing levels and budgeting features built into the corporation's structure. The FEA, for example, was dissatisfied with the level of equity capitalization: at a proposed $10 billion, this would be insufficient for the needs of the FEA's synthetic fuels program, which required some $25 billion of investment financing. Rockefeller, as noted above, had advised Ford to eliminate the synthetic fuels program from ERFCO's activities, an approach that risked the loss of FEA support for ERFCO. As for the vice president's recommendation that the borrowing authority be in the range of $100 to $200 billion, this was not calculated to appease ERFCO's critics at the treasury, the CEA, and the OMB.

Some of the concerns of the critics of ERFCO had begun to surface in the press. On August 15, the *Wall Street Journal* published an article by Dennis Farney entitled "After a Quiet Year Rockefeller Is Ready to Step into the Limelight," which reported widespread disagreement within the administration over the vice president's ERFCO proposal. Farney noted an ominous connection made by ERFCO critics concerning Rockefeller's proposals: "Skeptics see a scary resemblance, in ERFCO's reliance upon leverage, to another Rockefeller creation, New York State's Urban Development Corporation, which came perilously close to financial collapse." A more neutral piece on ERFCO was published by the *New York Times* on August 21. The *Times* article gave a broad outline of the initiative and noted that President Ford had asked that the proposal "be honed into something more specific." However, the *Times* was seriously in error in stating that "Treasury Secretary William Simon was also reported to be enthusiastic [about ERFCO]." Finally, the *Washington Star* published an editorial comment on August 25 which gave ERFCO moderate encouragement. The *Star* declared:

A plan presented to President Ford the other day to create a quasi-public energy corporation to pump up to $100 billion into development of U.S. energy independence is an interesting proposal. Vice President Rockefeller seems to have had the major hand in developing the plan. . . .

It is too early to say with certainty that the creation of a largely independent agency with enormous financial backing is the way to go. Not enough is known about it yet, and President Ford wisely has asked that the proposal "be honed into something more specific." Rockefeller and the others should get busy on the honing so that it can be brought to public debate as soon as possible.

The revised ERFCO proposal submitted to the president on August 7, and discussed above, was sent out to the senior staff members of the administration in late August for response to the president. One of the first responses came from the vice president, who addressed himself to what he termed "open issues" in a memorandum to the president on August 26. To meet the FEA's objection that ERFCO's equity base of $10 billion was inadequate to fund the synthetic fuels program, Rockefeller suggested a revised equity total of $20 billion. However, he made clear his reluctance to include such a program within ERFCO with a caveat to the president that: "Too much emphasis on synthetic fuels and high-risk endeavors would seriously jeopardize [the] self-liquidating nature of ERFCO."

On some other controversial aspects of ERFCO Rockefeller was unyielding. He defended the absence of OMB review procedures generally required for federal agency operations, noting that in ERFCO's case, "it would be impossible to run this type of investment operation with prior review constraint." Similarly, he endorsed strongly the absence of control or review by the treasury secretary of the loan guarantees to be issued by ERFCO, emphasizing the impossibility of making investment commitments "if they were subject to prior review of outside authority." Finally, he was supportive of the "off-budget" financing nature of ERFCO's borrowing authority and advised the president: "This is as it should be. The corporation is designed to be self-liquidating."

Although Rockefeller defended the major features of the revised ERFCO proposal, there were three areas of concern that he expressed to the president. First, concerning the lack of prohibition on "ERFCO guarantees on tax-exempt municipal bonds," he saw a potential problem of linkage to the New York City financial crisis and advised that such an ERFCO provision "would raise a serious political issue in Congress." Second, he objected to the provision that ERFCO have a split leadership with a chairman and chief executive officer as well as a president and chief operating officer. His own recommendation was that:

The president should appoint a five-member board of directors, and designate one member as chairman and chief executive officer. The chairman should have full control in selecting his operating staff, including his deputy or number-two man, who should not be a member of the board. The four outside directors should be part time, to assure maximum flexibility in selection of topflight people and to avoid any confusion or second-guessing by a full time director not involved in management.

Third, regarding the provision for an ERFCO advisory committee of "representative citizens," Rockefeller advised Ford: "Drop. Just asking for trouble."[51]

As at previous steps in the development of the ERFCO initiative, the principal critics of the proposal were the president's chief economic advisers—Simon, Greenspan, and Lynn. It was Simon's judgment that:

The ERFCO proposal would result in a massive incursion of the federal government into the private sector. . . . With annual outlays of, say, $17 billion, ERFCO would account for between 20 and 45 percent of annual capital requirements for the energy sector over the 1976-82 period as estimated by the FEA. The clear result would be to socialize a large part of the capital going into the energy sector. Such a move would mark a major and undesirable shift away from a private market economy in the United States. Further steps in that direction would likely follow (transportation, basic industries). This is precisely the type of reasoning and action that has led to the present state of the British economy.[52]

Greenspan shared Simon's views, declaring that:

ERFCO will not lead to additional capital formation. To the extent ERFCO succeeds in directing more capital to energy, the energy "shortage" will be replaced by shortages in other sectors, which will lead to further attempts to redress the distortions that ERFCO created in the first place.

ERFCO will have large if not yet quantifiable budgetary impacts. . . . However camouflaged at first, [ERFCO] subsidies must be supported ultimately by transfers from taxpayers to energy consumers. We cannot have the program both ways: If ERFCO has any effect on energy output, it will be largely because of on-budget subsidies; if ERFCO does not have any on-budget costs, it will have little impact on energy output.

Greenspan's conclusion was that ERFCO offered no advantage that could not be had without it, and, moreover, its "small and questionable" benefits would outweigh its "large and almost certain costs."[53]

Lynn conceded some preliminary points in ERFCO's favor regarding the stalemated condition of the president's energy program, but he immediately pronounced that "no convincing case has been made for a need for ERFCO." Like Simon and Greenspan, he expressed concern about the governmental channeling of capital in the private sector and reiterated Greenspan's objection to the "off-budget" aspect of ERFCO's financing. A major objection Lynn leveled at the proposal was its propensity to function as a "Christmas tree" vehicle for a Democratic Congress to load up with additional features unwanted by the administration. His assessment was that ERFCO would emerge from Congress with "a perpetual life: significant congressional control; significant limitations of Civil Service, Davis-Bacon, etc.; mandated proportional uses of its fund, e.g., solar, geothermal, and other congressional favorites; little, if any, effect on the regulatory process; and emphasis on public ownership of energy facilities—such as uranium enrichment and oil and gas exportation."[54]

As expected, the ERFCO proposal received endorsements from Rogers Morton and Frank Zarb, but both expressed qualifications in their recommendations to the president. Morton's concern was unrelated to the substance of the proposal but was directed rather at the question of its timing. He counseled Ford against an immediate public announcement, declaring: "I would withhold action until we know where we stand [with Congress] vis-à-vis allocations, controls, windfall profits, and rebates but be prepared with a completely fleshed-out version prior to the Congress adjourning this fall."[55]

Zarb indicated general support for the proposal but recommended to the president the following modifications to ERFCO's design:

Its total size be reduced from $120 billion to $75 billion with $50 billion of debt and the equity raised to $25 billion.

That clear legislative language be provided to limit its activities to preclude financing conventional energy production facilities, but allow:

- commercializing new technologies or concepts, e.g., synthetic fuels, advanced nuclear projects or demonstrating new institutional concepts such as energy parks;

- financing large-scale, risky projects which would not be put together otherwise, e.g., uranium enrichment or a trans-Canada oil pipeline.

While the Energy Finance Corporation [EFC] should be a separate organization, its autonomy should be restricted by:

- designating as its board of directors the administrators of the FEA and the ERDA, the secretary of the treasury, chairman of the ERC, and the president of the EFC;

- not exempting it from the normal agency review processes of the ERC or the OMB with respect to policy, priorities, or programs.

Conditional upon Ford's adoption of the ERFCO proposal as an administration program, Zarb recommended the following sequence for proceeding with ERFCO: "(a) indicate your final decision to your senior advisers; (b) prepare the detailed legislative and organizational proposals;[56] and (c) develop a public statement for use in an appropriate forum later in September."[57]

ERFCO BECOMES EIA: ADOPTION OF A
VICE PRESIDENTIAL PROPOSAL

From the vice president's standpoint, the threat to the ERFCO proposal came not from its outright opponents, but rather from a major source of ERFCO support: Frank Zarb. Rockefeller had previously found the president to be sympathetic to the general conception of ERFCO based upon the national security considerations underlying the goal of energy and self-sufficiency and, consequently, felt that Ford would not be swayed by the free market arguments of Simon, Greenspan, and Lynn. However, Zarb presented a different consideration because Ford had indicated the need for the vice president to clear ERFCO proposal details with Arthur Burns, who had in turn conditioned his endorsement on Zarb's agreement. In consequence, Zarb was a pivotal actor for gaining presidential adoption of the proposal.

The problem posed by Zarb was that all of his recommended modifications were unacceptable to the vice president, who thought that ERFCO needed autonomy of action, free from treasury or OMB review, to carry out its functions as well as a mission that included development of large-scale commercial production of conventional energy resources. Therefore, Rockefeller's response to the president on Zarb's ERFCO amendments was of great importance.

Dealing with the proposed modification to the corporation's structure and autonomy in a memorandum to the president on September 3, Rockefeller advised: "I don't have any comment on the question of an in-house board of directors and budgetary and review controls except to say that I am totally opposed to this way of structuring the corporation and its procedures."

On Zarb's proposal to limit the total financing of ERFCO to a level of $75 billion ($25 billion of equity and $50 billion of loan authority), he suggested a compromise total of $100 billion as reasonable. To go below that level, he cautioned Ford, "would destroy the impact of the program."[58]

On Zarb's amendment to restrict ERFCO to commercializing only *new* technologies, developing demonstration projects, and the financing of large-scale, high-risk energy projects, the vice president declared himself to be "totally opposed." To exclude the financing of *conventional* energy facilities, he counseled the president, would severely undercut the major objectives of the ERFCO proposal. Such an exclusion would result in reduced development of energy production and as a consequence delay achievement of energy independence (and thus the national security objective inherent in energy independence). Moreover, he informed Ford, limiting the corporation to "experimental production . . . would destroy the possibility of making the corporation self-liquidating."[59]

Rockefeller was not only concerned about the form of an ERFCO proposal for presidential adoption, he was also anxious about getting it adopted promptly. Accordingly, he urged Ford to employ a scheduled news conference in Seattle, Washington, on September 4 as a vehicle for public announcement of the initiative. Informing Ford that Rogers Morton concurred in the need for an immediate announcement, the vice president outlined several reasons for expediting the matter: "(1) mounting pressure from labor for action to create jobs; (2) various presidential aspirants, particularly Jackson, are readying announcements of similar plans any day now with the possibility of stealing the leadership from you;[60] and (3) to announce a positive program before the New York City situation breaks."[61] Meanwhile, Rockefeller proposed to the president that the name of the proposed federal corporation be changed from Energy Resources Finance Corporation (ERFCO) to Energy Independence Authority (the EIA).[62]

However, President Ford was being pushed and pulled on all sides and was not ready to act decisively on the proposal. The ongoing nature of the division within the administration was publicly highlighted in a *New York Times* article on September 4 entitled "Rockefeller Plan Splits Ford Aides." To effect some resolution of the conflicting arguments before him Ford arranged to have Richard Cheney compile a list of the major criticisms of the ERFCO proposal and get these answered by the vice president's staff. However, the list of critical questions compiled and submitted to the vice president's office by Cheney on September 4 was simply a rehash of questions dealt with by Rockefeller at much earlier points of the ongoing debate with his critics.[63] Consequently, Cheney's list was quickly dealt with and returned.

The president's basic uncertainty about the proposal at this stage centered on the disagreements between Zarb and the vice president. In a commendable effort to resolve matters himself, Ford arranged a joint meeting with them, acting personally as a broker. For Zarb, this proved to be an almost overwhelming experience. As he explained: "Here I was, a poor boy from Brooklyn, debating *Nelson Rockefeller*, vice president of the United States, with the president intervening to break the deadlock between us."[64] The outcome of this session with president was the removal of all outstanding disagreements between Zarb and the vice president.

The terms of the Zarb-Rockefeller agreement on disputed issues concerning ERFCO (which Zarb now agreed should be renamed the Energy Independence Authority [the EIA]) were set out in a followup memorandum to the president, as follows:

A. FUNCTIONS

EIA will concentrate primarily on the following types of projects in support of your 1985 energy independence goals:

• New technologies either to support or directly produce, transport, or conserve energy.

- Technologies essential to the production of nuclear power.

- Conventional technologies if they are directly related to production, transportation, or conservation of energy and are of such size or scope that they would not otherwise be financed by the private sector, or represent institutional or regulatory arrangements which are not in widespread use.

EIA will not undertake projects which (a) can be financed without government assistance, (b) are not commercially viable, or (c) will produce energy which would be produced by the private sector in any event.

B. AUTONOMY

EIA would be a new, autonomous federal authority which reports directly to the president.

A five-man board of directors would be designated by the president, subject to the advice and consent of the Senate.

The chairman of the board would be the chief executive officer of the corporation, and the president at his discretion would choose full- or part-time members from either private or public service.

Although autonomous, the corporation's programs would be subject to an annual OMB management and financial review, and treasury concurrence in the timing and terms of the issuance of debt; however, the corporation's actual financing and expenditures would be off-budget.

FEA, ERDA, and ERC would be given advance notice of pending project approvals to allow for executive branch coordination and specific presidential disapproval if warranted.

On the size of the EIA, Zarb accepted Rockefeller's earlier compromise level of $100 billion, broken into $25 billion of equity and $75 billion of borrowing authority.

With all outstanding issues agreed upon, Rockefeller and Zarb proposed to the president the following schedule for getting the EIA initiative launched:

- Convene an early meeting of your economic and energy advisers to inform them of your basic decision.

- Develop a strategy for notifying and involving the Congress.

- Announce the objectives and the basic elements of your proposal at an appropriate forum, including a decision on the corporation's name.

- After the speech, circulate the draft legislation for several days of interagency review. This will allow further refinement and clearance to occur without premature leaks.[65]

- Submit the legislation to the Congress as soon as possible after your announcement.[66]

On September 16, at his regular weekly meeting with the president, Rockefeller stressed the importance of the EIA as a stimulant to the economy and job creation and strongly urged Ford to decide affirmatively on the initiative.[67] Pondering the merits of the EIA over several days, President Ford finally decided to adopt the proposal as an administration program and arranged to announce this publicly at the AFL-CIO Building and Construction Trades Department's Convention at San Francisco on September 22.

Unveiling the EIA proposal on that date, Ford told his labor union audience:

Let's spend here at home for American jobs some of the billions we have been spending abroad for foreign oil and foreign payrolls. We can create construction jobs for workers, capital for industrial expansion, and new energy for all Americans. That is what independence is all about.

In response to those nations which would control our energy supplies and prices and hence our future, I say to industry, to construction workers, and to all Americans: Let's go into business for ourselves. Let's produce American energy in America with American workers and do it as soon as possible.

Describing the essential features of the EIA as a ten-year, self-liquidating federal government authority financed at $100 billion, Ford went on to declare:

My vision is of dramatic action to produce oil and gas from coal, safe and clean nuclear and coal-generated electrical power, harness the energy of the sun and the natural heat within the earth, and build numerous other energy facilities throughout our great country. The Energy Independence Authority would act to finance those projects vitally needed for America's energy independence that will not be financed even by America's great private capital resources.[68]

Despite the fact that the EIA was now a formally adopted and publicly announced presidential program, there was still residual controversy within the administration about various details of the EIA's structure and functions. A signal of the lingering disagreements was seen in the absence of a fact sheet (a normal accompaniment to announcement of a presidential program initiative) following Ford's EIA announcement.[69]

The issues that were reopened at the eleventh hour were handled swiftly by Frank Zarb, who prepared a presidential options memorandum on September 24 as a means of decisively disposing of them. The options outlined by Zarb for the president were accompanied by the recommendations of the senior staff, as follows:

Issue 1: Board of Directors   *Recommended by:*

Option 1   —   Full-time directors   Lynn, Morton,
                                                  Greenspan

Option 2 — Presidential authority to have either   Vice president, Zarb,
full¹ or part-time directors   Simon, Seidman

Issue 2: Inclusion of EIA
Employees in Civil Service and
Executive Appointments System

Option 1 — All employees as in executive departments   Zarb

Option 2 — EIA excluded from all executive   Lynn, Simon,
limitations   Seidman

Option 3 — Hybrid compensation for EIA   Vice president,
Morton, Greenspan

Issue 3: Scope of EIA Investments

EIA to finance: — transportation of energy
— nuclear power technology
— energy pipelines
— electric power not derived from oil or gas
(e.g., coal, nuclear, geothermal)

Option 1 — Do not preclude other types of projects   Vice president

Option 2 — Limit to projects listed above   Lynn, Simon, Zarb,
Morton, Greenspan,
Seidman

Issue 4: Treatment of EIA for
Budget Purposes

Option 1 — Initially request entire $75 billion in   Vice president,
borrowing authority without   Zarb, Seidman
congressional appropriations

Option 2 — Request borrowing authority be
appropriated by Congress and request $75
billion initially

Option 3 — Request borrowing authority be   Lynn, Greenspan,
appropriated, but request portions of $75   Simon, Morton
billion over time as needed.[70]

The vice president was able to make full use of his weekly meeting with the president to lobby for the above options he personally recommended, and he pressed hard for these when he met with Ford on September 25.[71] The measure of his success can be gauged from the fact that the president ultimately decided in favor of all the vice president's recommended options.

By the end of the first week in October, all of the outstanding reopened EIA issues had been settled. On October 10, President Ford transmitted to the Congress a draft of the administration's proposed Energy Independence Act of 1975.[72] In a covering letter of transmission to the President of the Senate and the Speaker of the House of Representatives, Ford declared:

America cannot permit the excessive delays associated with the commercialization of unconventional energy technologies. New production is essential. Our national security and economic well-being depend on our ability to act decisively on energy.

The Energy Independence Authority Act of 1975 will give the United States the tools necessary to achieve energy independence. I urge its prompt enactment by the Congress.

ENDGAME: EIA STALEMATE ON CAPITOL HILL

Vice President Rockefeller's success in winning presidential adoption of his energy corporation proposal as an administration program was little short of spectacular, coming as it did against the combined efforts of Treasury Secretary William Simon, CEA Chairman Alan Greenspan, and OMB Director James Lynn. However, this achievement was tempered by the realization that the EIA legislation faced stiff opposition in a Congress that had shown itself throughout 1975 unwilling to enact Ford administration energy proposals. The plain fact was that legislative hearings were not likely to be held until the early part of 1976, an election year in which the Democratic majorities in the House and Senate would be highly resistant to proposals coming from a Republican administration.[73]

Reviewing the EIA's legislative prospects during a major address at a Washington, D.C., energy conference with business executives on October 6, Rockefeller put a brave face on the situation. Underscoring his stated belief that the proposal had good prospects of going through Congress, he declared:

This is something that labor wants very badly. It is jobs through industry and not jobs through dole.

Therefore, I am pretty sure labor is going to give it very strong support. If industry at the same time feels it is desirable and worthwhile and gives it support, then I think its passage has got very great potential.

If industry is opposed to it, that will nullify labor support and probably nothing would happen.[74]

Because he was anxious about the level of information about, and support for, the EIA proposal, Rockefeller approached the president at their regular weekly meeting on October 8 to obtain clearance for a series of vice presidential appearances in support of the EIA.[75] Ford readily assented and authorized Rockefeller to proceed in seeking support for the proposal in the labor and business communities and in Congress.

The vice president's endeavors on behalf of the EIA in the winter of 1975 and the spring of 1976 invoked the usual Rockefeller panoply of intimate dinners at his Foxhall residence in Washington, D.C., working breakfasts, and vice presidential luncheons. In the process, congressmen, business and finance leaders, and labor leaders were assiduously courted in a sustained effort by Rockefeller to build support for the EIA and get hearings on it begun on Capitol Hill.

With business and financial leaders, the vice president met with scant success. The influential *Wall Street Journal* had set the tone for the private sector regarding its attitude to the EIA proposal in an editorial published on September 25. In the *Journal's* view, the EIA represented "government preemption of the private sector, credit allocation, fiscal gimmickry, bigger bureaucracies, and multibillion-dollar subsidies." Although Rockefeller was able to secure a limited endorsement of the EIA from some financial leaders,[76] the private sector as a whole rejected the proposal as an unwarranted expansion of governmental interference with the free enterprise system.[77] Of particular significance was the fact that the major energy-producing corporations declared themselves to be totally opposed to the EIA concept.

As expected, Rockefeller's lobbying efforts with labor union leaders were considerably more successful. From the outset, he had framed his arguments in designing the proposal to highlight the jobs benefits to be gained from large-scale energy construction projects financed by a federal energy corporation. The major endorsement sought was that of the AFL-CIO, and this was forthcoming in November, 1975, with a public declaration of support from AFL-CIO President George Meany. Announcing the AFL-CIO's endorsement of the EIA on November 14, Meany declared:

Private industry, left to itself, cannot and will not resolve the energy crisis. . . . Government must provide the initiative and incentive for development of energy projects that will place this nation on the road to energy independence.

While the AFL-CIO does endorse the creation of an Energy Independence Authority and the basic program set forth in the bill, we expect to have a number of proposals for improvements in the specific terms of this measure.[78]

All of the vice president's efforts on behalf of the EIA through speeches around the nation and his meetings with leaders from business and labor groups were tilted toward Capitol Hill. The ultimate aim was to secure passage of the EIA legislation, but the first essential step was to generate some momentum for congressional hearings.

As the lead agency on the EIA within the administration, the FEA had responsibility for guiding the EIA bill through the legislative hearings stage of the congressional process. Accordingly, the FEA drew up plans for getting congressional action on the EIA proposal, which included the following elements:

Developing a team of administration spokesmen who would testify together before the appropriate congressional committees; the team would include Zarb, Lynn, and Simon, or someone else from the treasury;

Making sure that the White House's regular briefings for interest groups and others include a briefing on the EIA by Zarb or Sausner;

Attempt to secure joint referral of the legislation to committees in the Senate and the House other than the banking committees; the banking committees will receive the initial referral in each House, but are not expected to be favorable to the legislation.[79]

However, although the EIA was an announced administration proposal of major dimensions, little was being done by senior members of the administration to push for legislative hearings. Republican Senator Charles Percy complained about this state of affairs in a meeting with Peter Wallison in the latter half of November. According to Wallison: "Senator Percy seemed to be most concerned about whether the president and the administration were going to back this legislation. He indicated that he had seen no signs of substantial administration support, and seldom hears of the president or any of his energy spokesmen referring to this legislation."[80]

But, while Wallison did his best to reassure Senator Percy that the EIA proposal was indeed a concern of the administration, the fact is that John Veneman could report essentially the same criticism two months later. On January 27, Veneman informed Rockefeller: "There is no evidence that an overall strategy for promoting the EIA either on the Hill or among the public has been developed." Veneman proposed that the vice president involve himself, in consultation with Zarb and Elliot Richardson (who had become Rogers Morton's successor as commerce secretary), in establishing a strategy and timetable for getting the EIA hearings started.[81] Rockefeller adopted Veneman's suggestion and, in effect, undertook the lead role in the legislative lobbying effort for the proposal.

On the House side, the vice president's efforts met with total frustration. Throughout the months of February through May, Rockefeller and his staff were hopeful that a commitment to hold hearings could be obtained from three key congressmen, all of whom chaired committees or subcommittees with jurisdictional responsibilities encompassing the EIA's subject matter area: Congressman Henry Reuss (chairman of the House Committee on Banking, Currency, and Housing); Congressman Lud Ashley (chairman of the Economic Stabilization Subcommittee of the House Banking Committee); and Congressman John Dingell (chairman of the Energy and Power Subcommittee of the House Committee on Interstate and Foreign Commerce). However, while the vice president pressed hard, no hearings were forthcoming in the House committees.

On the Senate side, the endeavor to get hearings started met with some success. Senator William Proxmire, chairman of the Committee on Banking, Housing, and Urban Affairs, agreed to hold hearings before the full committee and arranged for these to be held on April 12, 13, and 14. However, this piece of good news was tinged considerably by the fact that the Banking Committee was not expected to be disposed favorably toward the EIA proposal. In fact, as noted above, the FEA at the outset had hoped that the EIA bill would be referred to some other committee.

As a joint lead-off witness with FEA Administrator Frank Zarb, Vice President Rockefeller made a rare vice presidential appearance as a hearing witness. Only three vice presidents had previously given congressional testimony in the history of the office, and Rockefeller's personal appearance, therefore, served to underline his role in advancing the EIA proposal.[82] Also testifying in favor of the proposal on behalf of the administration were Assistant Secretary of the Treasury for International Affairs Gerald Parsky and two FEA officials. Testifying in general support were Walt W. Rostow; John Simpson, chairman of the Atomic Industrial Forum; Russell Cameron, a synthetic fuels expert; Andrew Biemiller, director of the Department of Legislation, AFL-CIO; Monte Canfield, Jr., General Accounting Office; Peter Peterson, president of Lehman Brothers; John Harper, former chairman, Alcoa; and Robert Nathan, a Washington, D.C., economic consultant. Testifying in opposition to the EIA were Barry Commoner, environmentalist; Ralph Nader, public citizens' activist; Joe Browder, Environmental Policy Center; and Murray Weidenbaum, economist.[83]

Conspicuously absent from the hearings were Treasury Secretary William Simon and OMB Director James Lynn. Given the massive nature of the administration's proposal, the absence of such influential witnesses (who would normally have been expected to appear in support of the administration) served to underscore the disputed nature of the EIA within administration circles.

However, although the debate over energy problems and solutions generated by the hearings got into substantive discussion of the capital scarcity problems of energy production and the need to develop new energy resources, the fact was that they were, in reality, perfunctory hearings. They did not lead to any kind of committee report, much less to movement of the bill to the Senate floor.

Given the set of circumstances surrounding the development and presentation of the EIA proposal in 1975 and 1976, it would have been unrealistic to have expected a different outcome. First, the proposal had generated much heat and division within the Ford administration, which lingered after the EIA's adoption by the president. Consequently, the woeful absence of major administration figures (with the exception of the vice president) advocating the EIA around the nation and on Capitol Hill gave the proposal a "lukewarm" appearance. Second, apart from labor, there was no large constituency nationally to apply pressure to get action on the proposal in the Congress. The plain truth was that the EIA generated more opposition than support, and the opposition comprised powerful lobby groups: energy producers, banking and financial interests, industry, and environmentalists. Third, given the manner in which the Democratic majority in Congress had stalled the energy proposals submitted by President Ford in January, 1975, there was never any real prospect that a proposal of the size and scope of the EIA would receive more than cursory treatment on Capitol Hill in the year of a presidential election.[84]

· 5 · ROCKEFELLER IN A VARIETY OF VICE PRESIDENTIAL ROLES

Although Nelson Rockefeller's major policy contributions as vice president within the Ford administration centered principally on the domestic-policy review under the direction of John Veneman, and on his proposed federal energy corporation (which became the Energy Independence Authority proposal), he made other contributions that, while of a lesser degree of magnitude, throw further illumination on the nature of his vice presidency. The first of these concerns the establishment of a White House Office of Science and Technology Policy, an endeavor in which Rockefeller's role was central and which provides a further case study in successful vice presidential policy development. Second are the contributions made by Rockefeller to the debate within and outside the administration on the role of the federal government in assisting New York City resolve its fiscal crisis in 1975. This issue brought Rockefeller into an open, though minor, conflict with the president's position, and shows the extent to which the vice president felt he had freedom to advocate policy positions publicly. Finally, some consideration is given to what may be called the more conventional side of Rockefeller's vice presidency, outlining the various commissions on which he served.

THE ESTABLISHMENT OF A WHITE HOUSE
SCIENCE ADVISORY UNIT

Among the various vice presidential assignments Rockefeller received from President Ford on December 21, 1974, was the "study of whether the system of a White House science adviser, or board of advisers, should be revived, and if so, in what form."[1] Ford requested that this be done quickly, asking the vice president "to have his recommendations in on the question of a new science adviser, or advisory board, in a month or so."[2]

Rockefeller acted promptly to bring together an advisory group from the scientific community to devise a set of options from which a vice presidential recommendation could be developed. At the outset, this group comprised individuals who had been associated with the Commission on Critical Choices for Americans.[3] Directing the work of the group were two long-time Rockefeller associates: Henry L. Diamond, chairman of the Critical Choices Commission, and Oscar Reubhausen, a commission member.

Within two weeks, Diamond had prepared a set of three preliminary options for the vice president's consideration, as follows:

- Strengthen the role of the director of the National Science Foundation as science adviser to the president. By formal appointment, make him a member of the National Security Council and the Domestic Council, and give him a White House office and direct access.
- Appoint a full-time science adviser to the president with a small White House staff and with reliance on the other science agencies for staffing.
- Reconstruct the science advisory function in the White House with a full staff headed either by a single science adviser or a council of three.[4]

These options were given further attention and development throughout January, with particular consideration given to the extent to which a White House science adviser should participate in broad policy concerns rather than exclusively within the more narrow confines of purely science matters.

On January 31, Rockefeller indicated in a memorandum to the president that he hoped to submit his recommendations within a week. Meanwhile, reviewing the work already undertaken, he advised Ford:

There is general agreement that unless a science adviser, with or without a council, has continuing access and can participate on a day-to-day basis in policy formulation at the White House level, it would be better not to make such an appointment.

The revitalization of the Domestic Council along its original lines would provide one of the logical places for scientific and technological advice in relation to domestic matters.[5]

On February 5, the vice president submitted the results of his study of the merits of a White House science advisory unit, with the recommendation that:

While the federal departments and agencies have, and should have, scientific and technological competence of high quality, the president should have available to him an *independent source* of scientific and technological judgment of the very highest quality. The organization set up to provide such a source for the president must not be, or be perceived as, the representative of the scientific and technical community in the president's office.

An Office of Technology and Science should be established by congressional action and should be headed by a director who should also have the title of science and technology adviser to the president. The office should be made a part of the executive office of the president.

To assist the director of the proposed Office of Technology and Science (OTS), the vice president's recommendation proposed a deputy, up to five assistant directors, and a professional staff not to exceed a dozen, with additional support staff. It was further recommended that the OTS be given authority to organize ad hoc panels of outside consultants. Finally, to fund the operations of the OTS the vice president suggested an annual budget in the range of $1 to $3 million.

As for proposed functions for the OTS, Rockefeller outlined for the president some ten areas of possible OTS activities but advised that not all of these were in any way essential at the outset. Rather, he counseled, "the functions of the office should be allowed to grow, as the president may require, as relationships with the departments and agencies of government develop, and as emerging national programs, policies, and issues may make desirable and useful."[6]

However, the vice president's recommendations of February 5 did not meet the format requirements demanded of presidential decision memoranda established by Donald Rumsfeld in his capacity as White House coordinator.[7] In this case, Rumsfeld objected strongly to the advocacy nature of Rockefeller's memorandum and arranged to have it redone as an options paper. This assignment was given to James Cavanaugh of the Domestic Council, who submitted a memorandum to the president on February 12 outlining the following options:

- Create an Office of Technology and Science.
- Strengthen the existing arrangements.
- Appoint a science adviser with limited staff.
- Explore further the development of a broad policy analysis capability.

However, Cavanaugh's options memorandum was itself no less an advocacy paper than that submitted by the vice president on February 5. Although it presented four options, only the third option, to appoint a science adviser with limited staff (which was identified as having the support of Brent Scowcroft, National Security Council deputy director; James Lynn, director of the Office of Management and Budget; Paul O'Neill, OMB deputy director; Philip Buchen, White House legal counsel; and Buchen's deputy, Philip Areeda) was presented favorably and carried Cavanaugh's personal recommendation. The vice president's recommendation to create an Office of Technology and Science was presented as the first option and discussed as virtually identical to a bill (S.32) promoted by

Senator Edward Kennedy and passed by voice vote in the Senate in October, 1974. The remaining two options were given minimal discussion and were clearly makeweight in nature.[8]

When he discovered that his vice presidential recommendation to the president had been redone by Cavanaugh on Rumsfeld's instructions, Rockefeller blew up. Discussing his response to this turn of events, Rockefeller stated:

So by now I was head of the Domestic Council, so I went to Rumsfeld and said, "Look, Rummy, what the hell is this?" And he said, "Well, your paper was an advocacy paper and this is an option paper, and this is the way we do things here." "Well," I said, "look, to begin with, the president didn't ask me for an option paper. He asked me for my judgment as to what he should do, and I gave it to him. And this paper is for the birds." I said, "It just happens that I am head of the Domestic Council, so I will rewrite this and if he wants some options we will give him honest ones."[9]

Adopting Rumsfeld's decision paper format, Rockefeller arranged to develop a set of options for submission to the president. The alternatives considered by his staff were as follows:

- Option 1: An individual science adviser to the president, supported by a professional staff.
- Option 2: A council of scientists and engineers, supported by a professional staff.
- Option 3: An office, headed by a director (who would also have the title of science adviser), supported by a professional staff.

Basic to each of these three options was a provision for ad hoc panels of external consultants to engage in studies of major policy or program issues involving science and technology.[10]

On March 3, the vice president submitted a memorandum to the president presenting in more developed form the three options outlined above. Dealing first with an option to create a Council of Technology and Science Advisers (Option 2), Rockefeller identified this as essentially the approach embodied in the Kennedy Bill (S.32). Next, he discussed his own proposal to create an Office of Technology and Science (Option 3). Finally, he presented the option of having a presidential adviser with a small staff of one to three professionals.[11]

Meanwhile, Rumsfeld approached James Cannon, the newly appointed executive director of the Domestic Council, and gave him a directive to "redo," as an option paper, the vice president's "advocacy" memorandum of February 5. As a close Rockefeller associate, this assignment put Cannon in a difficult position he described as follows: "Here I was, lately

[Rockefeller's] . . . employee, rewriting something which he had sent to the president."[12]

Walking a difficult line between his responsibilities on the one hand as an assistant to the president (on which Rumsfeld's "redo" directive was based), and on the other as executive director of the Domestic Council over which Rockefeller exercised supervision as vice chairman, Cannon's tack was to move slowly on developing the assigned options paper. Discussing his progress with the president in mid-March, Cannon assured Ford, "I'm working on this and I'll get it to you just as fast as I can." As Cannon recalled the conversation, Ford then made it clear that he wanted an options paper and not an advocacy piece. Cannon then inquired, "Is there any particular thing that you would like stressed in this, Mr. President?" Ford responded: "I'll tell you what I would like to do, very simply. I would like to know what previous science advisers actually accomplished for the president they served."[13]

Consequently, Cannon set in motion an inquiry to determine from past science advisers the nature of their accomplishments.[14] However, his main task was still the preparation of an options paper for the president. This was completed and submitted to the president on April 24. His memorandum to Ford emphasized the strong likelihood that Congress would give passage to a bill to establish a "strong, effective, and visible scientific advisory group" within the executive office of the president. Accordingly, selection of a presidential option should be made with that prospect in mind. The options reviewed by Cannon were essentially the three options presented in the vice president's own options memorandum of March 3, with the addition of a proposal for the appointment of a scientific and technology liaison adviser to the president. These options had been presented to the White House senior staff for comment, and Cannon reported the following responses:

- Option 1: A council of technology and science advisers with up to twenty assistants.
  Recommended by: [no one].

- Option 2: A single director of technology and science with up to seventeen assistants.
  Recommended by: James Cannon, Russell Train, Russell Peterson.

- Option 3: A science and technology adviser with up to three assistants.
  Recommended by: John Marsh, Robert Goldwin, Frank Zarb, Paul O'Neill, Alan Greenspan, Max Friedersdorf.

- Option 4: A scientific and technology liaison adviser with no staff.
  Recommended by: William Seidman, Philip Buchen.[15]

Ford's decision was to accept Option 2 and proceed with developing an administration initiative to create an Office of Technology and Science. Although he had selected the OTS option recommended by the vice president, the president in fact wanted to establish the OTS on a smaller scale than Rockefeller had envisaged. As he explained to Cannon:

Nelson may not like my going this way, but I'll tell you what I'm gong to do. I want to go with a group this size (up to five assistants), and I want to be able to call in consultants. But I don't want to have [the OTS] as big as Nelson wants to have. But I want to do it by legislation, because if Congress—which wants to do it this way—goes through the process of legislating it for the future, we won't have what happened under Nixon, when the guy gets mad and throws [the adviser] out of the White House. If it's institutionalized, the people in the science community . . . will always have their representation.[16]

On May 13, the president met with the vice president, Donald Rumsfeld, James Lynn, and James Cannon to discuss the details of his decision to support creation of the OTS. He indicated his preference to have an OTS staff at a lower level than the seventeen professionals called for in the option as Cannon had presented it on April 24. It was Ford's view that the OTS might begin with a staff of five assistants. After discussion, it was decided further that the president should arrange to meet with the various sponsors of science advisory unit proposals in the House and Senate to outline the administration's initiative and "express the hope that they will follow [this] proposal for legislation."[17]

On June 9, having held his planned discussions with the key legislative actors on the initiative, Ford submitted his legislative proposal to the Congress. In all of its essentials, the administration bill was virtually identical to the vice president's proposal (including a proposed staff level of up to fifteen professionals),[18] but the name of the advisory unit was changed. The president proposed creation of an Office of Science and Technology Policy (OSTP) headed by a director who would also serve as science and technology adviser to the president.

Underscoring the strength of his personal commitment to the proposal to create the OSTP, the vice president appeared the following day, June 10, before the House Committee on Science and Technology to introduce and outline the administration's bill. Describing the main features of the proposal, Rockefeller declared:

Probably the thing that the science community was most anxious about . . . is that [the adviser] must have access to the White House staff and organization which is preparing and doing the staff work for the president, so that he is geared in, whether it is the National Security Council or the Domestic Council, where the thinking and planning at the staff level is being done, so that those ideas will fit in and their problems are fed back to him and can go back to the scientific communities. This way, you get the most intimate meshing of the problems and the policy decisions with . . . the scientific knowledge that exists in this nation.[19]

Having personally launched the administration's OSTP initiative on Capitol Hill, Rockefeller turned his attentions to the practical problems of planning for areas of activity to be covered by the OSTP. Therefore, at his weekly meeting with the president on June 12, the vice president discussed the idea of forming task forces of scientists to advise on study areas for the OSTP. To develop this effort, he proposed to the president that he approach Dr. Hans Mark of NASA-Ames Laboratory (who had been a member of the first vice presidential advisory group to study the merits of a science advisory unit) and Dr. Simon Ramo, vice chairman of the board of TRW, Inc.

With the president's general approval, Rockefeller proceeded to work with Mark and Ramo to bring together a leadership group from the scientific community to assist in shaping a role for the OSTP. The first meeting of this group was convened on July 17 in the Cabinet Room at the White House. Determined to convince the scientific community of the responsiveness of the administration to its needs, the vice president persuaded the president to address the group and underline the administration's commitment to creating the OSTP.

However, the meeting of July 17 was of a decidedly general and preliminary nature. To develop more substantive results concerning OSTP functions, Rockefeller directed Mark and Ramo to arrange for a further group of scientists and technologists to meet and discuss specific OSTP study areas. This second group met on September 4 and provided some concrete suggestions for action. In particular, the group advised that, in the light of "the confluence of interests between the administration, the Congress, and the scientific and technological community," the administration should proceed with the establishment of one or two specific consulting groups in anticipation of favorable action by the Congress.[20]

Following up on this proposal, Rockefeller approached Ford on September 16 with a recommendation that he be directed "to bring together groups of scientists and other experts as part of the planning for the establishment of the contemplated Office of Science and Technology Policy." These groups would advise and consult on issues regarding the OSTP under two main headings: "Anticipated Advances in Science and Technology" and "Technology Policy and Economic Growth." To assist in the work of these groups, Rockefeller advised the president that the National Science Foundation, under its director, Dr. H. Guyford Stever, had agreed to provide staff and logistical support. President Ford approved the vice president's recommendation and directed that the panels be developed.[21]

Meanwhile, progress on the legislation to create a White House science advisory unit was delayed on Capitol Hill by a disagreement between Congress and the administration about the precise organizational nature of such a unit. Members of the House Science and Technology Committee preferred to establish an advisory panel, whereas the proposal submitted by the president called for the creation of the OSTP with a single director. However, by the latter part of October, a compromise was worked out to provide for an OSTP director who would have up to four assistant directors. With this agreement, the committee reported out a clean bill (H.R.10230) on October 29. With minor modifications, this basically conformed to the administration's proposal creating the Office of Science and Technology Policy within the executive office of the president. On November 6, without debate, the House overwhelmingly passed H.R.10230 by a 362-28 vote.

Meanwhile, the vice president proceeded with the task of organizing the advisory groups approved by the president. By mid-October, he had developed a list of proposed task force members and submitted this for presidential clearance. With some minor delay this was approved, and on November 12, the White House announced the establishment of two OSTP advisory groups. The first group, under the direction of Dr. Simon Ramo, was to consider issues and opportunities under the heading "Contribution of Technology to Economic Strength," while the second group, to be directed by Dr. William A. Baker, president, Bell Laboratories, would consider "Anticipated Advances in Science and Technology."[22]

Although the House had passed OSTP legislation in November, the Senate did not take action on similar legislation until February, 1976. This delay reflected a desire of Senate sponsors of the Kennedy Bill (S.32) to strengthen some aspects of the House-passed measure (H.R.10230).[23] On February 3, the three senate committees sharing jurisdiction (i.e., Labor and Public Welfare, Commerce, and Aeronautical and Space Sciences) reported out an amended version of H.R.10230 containing some provisions of S.32. These provisions specified more sharply the responsibilities of the White House science adviser and also included programs to retrain scientists and to give support to state science advisory programs. On February 4, by voice vote, the Senate passed H.R.10230 as amended in committee.

At the subsequent House-Senate Conference, the House conferees prevailed in getting these additional Senate provisions dropped or amended, and the conference reported out the bill on April 26. The conference version was rapidly approved by both Houses: the Senate passage came on April 27, while the House gave its approval on April 29.

On May 11, the bill was signed into law by President Ford as the National Science and Technology Policy, Organization, and Priorities Act of 1976. The act created the OSTP within the executive office of the president. The OSTP was to be headed by a director, who would also serve as adviser to the president on science and technology. The director was further named as a member of the Domestic Council and as an adviser to the National Security Council.[24]

As provided by the act, the primary function of the OSTP director was to provide advice on the scientific, engineering, and technological aspects of issues that required attention "at the highest levels of government." The specific functions of the OSTP, as outlined in a White House fact sheet on the legislation issued on May 11, included the following:

Preparing an annually updated five-year outlook that highlights current and emerging problems, which have been identified through the results of scientific research, and opportunities for the use of science and technology to contribute to the achievement of federal objectives and national goals.

Assisting the Office of Management and Budget in reviewing funding proposed by federal agencies for research and development.

Assisting the president in preparing an annual science and technology report.

Although the initial vice presidential assignment Rockefeller had received from the president on December 21, 1974, was confined to making a study of, and submitting recommendations on, the restoration of a White House science advisory component, the vice president's own tenacity and interest in pursuing the assignment greatly expanded its early scope. The assignment brought him into conflict with some of the president's senior aides (notably Rumsfeld—although Buchen and Seidman were opposed to the scope of the vice president's proposal on its merits), but Rockefeller had held firm. With the diplomatic assistance of Cannon, the vice president's proposal received the president's approval with its integrity intact. His sponsorship of the administration's proposal on Capitol Hill provided a signal to the Congress that the administration was indeed serious about providing the scientific community with a restored voice in the White House.

NEW YORK CITY'S FISCAL CRISIS

A political issue of importance that captured the attention of the Ford administration throughout much of 1975, and that brought the president and the vice president into a measure of public disagreement, was the fiscal crisis that threatened New York City with imminent bankruptcy. At the outset of the crisis, both men had been in complete accord on the denial of federal assistance to meet the city's immediate financial needs. However, as the crisis continued, Ford remained resolutely opposed to reconsideration of that denial while Rockefeller moved (at first, privately, within the administration, and later publicly) toward advocacy of some limited form of assistance.[25]

The public division between Rockefeller and Ford is an interesting one because, however minor it may have been, it provided an illustration of the extent to which Rockefeller felt he had freedom as vice president to speak his mind on positions not endorsed by the president. For Rockefeller this aspect of his vice presidency was of sufficient importance to be raised with the president at the outset. As he has explained the situation:

I described my position in the very beginning at the time I took the office, after talking to the president, that the only function is presiding over the Senate. Anything else is a staff job. That I would support him in his administration's positions—I would give him any thoughts I had and would support him in his positions. If I disagreed mildly, I might not say anything. But if I had a very serious disagreement, I would feel I [would have] to speak up. He said, "That's fine."[26]

The fiscal crisis, which produced an open disagreement between the president and vice president, developed rapidly in late April, 1975, as New York City found itself unable to borrow in the municipal bond market to meet various long-term obligations that were falling due and to finance the more normal provision of municipal services. Without further financing, the city contemplated not only the interruption of vital services, but the real possibility of declaring bankruptcy in the face of default on obligations that were now due.[27]

Early in May, there were suggestions that the federal government should come to the assistance of the city. This was a concern put to the vice president at a press conference at the Business Council Meeting at Hot Springs, West Virginia, on May 9. His response indicated a firm belief that the city's problems stemmed from mismanagement and that more could be done by city authorities to remedy the situation. Outlining his views, Rockefeller declared:

Well, I suppose I've dealt with New York City and its financial problems as governor for a great many years—that they've used up about all the rinky-dinks and rollovers and gimmicks that there are. Now they're going down to a very tough situation of income and outgo which are out of balance. And this is one of those tough situations, really, where the bonds—I would have to think from what the banks said—were not saleable, or at least the measures that have been taken have not created the confidence in the bond market that they are competitive.

The steps [the mayor] has taken have not as yet convinced those who handled their finances that they're adequate.[28]

On May 13, New York City Mayor Abraham Beame and New York Governor Hugh Carey met with President Ford to request administration support for federal legislation to provide the city with a short-term loan of $1 billion for a period of ninety days. Such a bridging loan, they argued, would grant the city a grace period in which to obtain increased taxing authority from the New York State Legislature, an authority that would enable the city to adopt a balanced budget for the fiscal year beginning July 1, 1975.

Also present at the meeting was the vice president. As governor of New

York State over a fifteen-year period, he had considerable knowledge of the city's problems and, therefore, could provide Ford with informed advice on the request before him. Rockefeller's counsel to the president was that the arguments presented by Beame and Carey in support of federal aid failed to provide the total picture. Recalling his role in the discussion, Rockefeller reported:

I commented, I intervened when I thought that information being presented to the president was incorrect. The governor implied that federal help was their last resort, their last court of appeal. He didn't use those words, but that was the meaning. I said, "Mr. President, you ought to know that the State of New York has the capacity to do exactly what the governor is asking you to do."[29]

It was, he explained to Ford, his position that the state had the necessary authority to provide the bridging loan sought by the city and could do so on the issuance of short-term loan notes. However, this approach was rejected by Governor Carey, who alluded to New York State's own weakened fiscal situation by asking rhetorically: "Do you think we are going to destroy the credit of the State of New York to help bail out the city?"[30] Nonetheless, Rockefeller insisted to the president that the provision of immediate financial aid for the city was the responsibility of the state and not the federal government. In any case, he observed of a point made by Mayor Beame, if New York City's credit was really as good as Beame claimed, then immediate loan assistance could be obtained from the city's accumulated pension funds.[31]

Rockefeller's intervention in the meeting with the president and the mayor and governor had the effect of stiffening Ford's resolve not to support the request for federal assistance for the city. And when the president wrote to Mayor Beame the following day to respond to the mayor's request, he employed the vice president's arguments as the basis for denying federal support. As he informed the mayor:

. . . in regard to your request to me for support of congressional legislation to provide federal backing and guarantee of city debt, I believe that the proper place for any request for backing and guarantee is the State of New York. For such "bridge loan legislation," it seems to be both logical and desirable for the State of New York to arrange under its laws a "bridge loan" to the city in the amount that you estimate will be needed during the city's fiscal year.

In view of the foregoing considerations, I must deny your request for support of your federal legislative proposal.

I have asked Secretary Simon to follow closely the credit situation of the City of New York over the next few weeks and to keep me informed.

The Federal Reserve Board, under its statutory responsibilities, will, I am sure, likewise monitor the situation very closely.[32]

Publicly, the vice president strongly supported the position he had advocated in the private meeting with Ford, Beame, and Carey. At a council luncheon of the National Republican Heritage Group in Washington, D.C., on May 16, he responded to an argument that since Albany Republicans were opposing consideration of increased taxing authority for the city, the consideration of federal aid had become imperative, declaring:

That's not what I'm talking about. They said they would not give new taxes to the city because they are afraid taxes in the city are already so high that they have driven out jobs and lost 500,000 jobs. This is the serious problem they face. Therefore, I was not talking about increased taxing power. I'm talking about a first instance advance to the city, which the state has the power to do to help them through this period while they put their budget in order.

But the state doesn't want it. The governor doesn't want to recommend it. He'd like to pass the buck to Washington. But they have the power. There's also one other source. If the credit of the city is as good as they say—as the mayor took it to the president—then Arthur Levitt and the Teachers' Pension Fund have the power to buy the notes or the bonds, and the funds to do it.[33]

Although he had adopted a firm stance against federal assistance for the city, and publicly defended the position throughout much of May, Rockefeller privately began to shift ground and move toward some consideration of federal guarantees of municipal bonds. He still retained his commitment to the proposition that it was the responsibility of the state to assist the city in meeting its financial needs, but now sought to provide a means of insuring that the execution of such a responsibility was not harmful to the state. On June 3, he outlined to the president a proposal to assist the city with a federal guarantee program, which would require action by the state before going into effect. With a reaffirmation of his position on the primary responsibility of the state, Rockefeller made the following recommendation:

Although I believe it is a responsibility of the states, and not of the federal government, to meet the pressing needs of cities, if the federal government stands by without a program while the City of New York defaults on its obligations the political consequences could be severe.

It seems to me that the best policy for the federal government would be one which puts pressure on the states to act, but still demonstrates a federal concern for the welfare of city residents.

I believe both these objectives may be accomplished by legislation which provides for federal guarantees of a municipality's obligations only in cases where these obligations have first been guaranteed by the state in which the municipality is located.

Senators Javits and Buckley have introduced legislation which would provide federal guarantees without a prior state guarantee, but I believe this legislation would transfer to the federal level a responsibility which is properly that of the states.[34]

However, President Ford took no action on the vice president's guarantee proposal and remained privately and publicly opposed to any consideration of federal aid for New York City.

Meanwhile, New York State did take direct action to assist the city. First, in late May some $800 million in state aid scheduled for the city in the fiscal year beginning July 1 was advanced to meet immediate city needs. Second, the state created the Municipal Assistance Corporation (MAC) to change the city's short-term debts into long-term obligations. With an initial borrowing authority of $3 billion, it was anticipated that the MAC would provide sufficient short-term assistance to allow the city to meet its obligations until October when, it was hoped, the city could sell a new bond issue on its own behalf. However, despite the backing of New York State and a high tax-exempt interest rate, the MAC bonds were sold with great difficulty, and a further MAC bond issue in August failed to attract buyers for half of the total amount offered.

New York State's experience with the MAC bonds provided some support for Rockefeller's position that some federal guarantee was needed for municipal bonds. However, within the administration his was a lone voice.[35] The view of the administration was publicly articulated by Secretary Simon, who declared in late June, "Under our system of government, it is not, and should not be, the job of the federal government to manage the affairs of state and local government." While this position was not any different from the vice president's basic premise, Simon's view of the outcome was very different. Defending the decision of the administration to deny aid to New York City, the secretary insisted that the economy could sustain the effects of a city bankruptcy occasioned by default on municipal obligations.[36] And it was this outcome that Rockefeller was anxious to avoid.

The first public hint of any difference of position between the vice president and the administration came in remarks made by Rockefeller at a meeting with White House summer interns on August 5. In response to a questioner, Rockefeller declared:

What can the federal government do? One thing I think it may come to would be, if the state takes such responsibility to supervise [the city]—and the cities and the towns and the villages are creatures of the state—if you want to put in sound management of cities and then want a guarantee, I think the federal government could reguarantee bonds to get a lower interest. But I think the state has to take the primary responsibility.[37]

On September 2, Governor Carey met with President Ford to discuss a financial aid package he was about to propose to the New York State Legislature. The elements of this package included a new borrowing authority for the MAC to provide New York City with $2.3 billion in further assistance through December and the creation of an Emergency Financial Control Board to operate the city's finances and to balance the city's budget by fiscal year 1978. Carey felt that, in addition, he needed some federal guarantees to back up the state's position and renewed his request for federal assistance. But the president held firm against such consideration.

Advising the vice president of the Carey-Ford meeting of September 2, Richard Dunham, deputy director of the Domestic Council, counseled that the Carey package "only has a slim chance and only [then] if some moral and/or tangible support by the federal government is evident." Considering the perilous situation facing both New York State and New York City, Dunham made the following observations:

The Carey financial package is extremely shaky for a whole variety of reasons, and it increases substantially the risk of a New York State default either now or in December.

The impact of a New York City default will in our opinion grossly increase the risk of a default in September of the State H.F.A., other authorities later in the fall and possibly the state itself.

Governor Carey in the event of default is likely to blame the default largely on federal insensitivity and lack of cooperation.[38]

Following up on this assessment by Dunham at his weekly meeting with the president on September 3, Rockefeller proposed the establishment of a joint Domestic Council-Economic Policy Board task force operating under Dunham's direction. The mission of this task force was outlined as follows:

- To review all ways the federal government can cooperate with New York State if the present plan proposed by Governor Carey goes forward.

- To review all federal, state, and city actions that are possible or may be required if New York City goes into default and/or bankruptcy.

- This review will not include the regular relationships and responsibilities of treasury with financial institutions.[39]

However, Ford gave this proposal the same negative response that he had given to Governor Carey the day before and remained absolutely unyielding in his opposition to granting federal assistance for the city's woes.

On September 5, the vice president publicly discussed the consequences of a New York City default. Speaking at a press conference at Rochester, New York, he clearly enunciated his disagreement with the assessment of Secretary Simon, who had suggested that a default was manageable. In Rockefeller's view,

a default by New York City would have very serious implications in terms of the ability of the municipalities to sell bonds. The repercussions would be hard to estimate because this has never happened in modern history and certainly not in the largest city in our country. Therefore, it is very serious and very tragic.

However, Rockefeller went further than disagreement with the administration view on the consequences of a default. Despite the fact that the president had made clear his continued opposition to federal assistance for the city, the vice president left reporters with the distinct impression that such aid could not be ruled out, observing that: "The federal government and the president are deeply concerned about the question. As you know, under the present laws of the federal government, there is nothing the president can do directly without the action of the Congress. That is a question which is before Congress."[40]

On September 9, the New York State Legislature approved Governor Carey's rescue package to provide a new MAC bond issue and establish a state-controlled board to manage the city's fiscal affairs. When reporters inquired at the White House whether this measure would alter the president's stance on federal aid, Press Secretary Ron Nessen curtly informed them: "There is no plan to provide federal financial assistance in New York City."[41]

However, the Carey package proved to be the unreliable rescue vehicle foreseen by Dunham on September 2. Private investors and city and state pension funds investors balked at purchasing the new MAC bonds, while the state (which was directly committed to a $750 million loan to the city) found its own borrowing abilities increasingly circumscribed.[42]

As New York City's crisis worsened, pressures grew in Congress for some federal assistance. At a hearing of the Joint Economic Committee on September 24, the president of the U.S. Conference of Mayors, New Orleans Mayor Moon Landrieu, called for federal guarantees of municipal bonds or the provision of emergency federal loans to cities about to default on their obligations. Denver Mayor William McNichols described the New York City crisis as a variant of the domino theory: "Every city in the nation is like a tenant in the same building. If somebody says the third floor is going to collapse, you can't say that's not going to bother me because I'm on the second floor."[43] The Mayors' Conference also met with President Ford later that same day to press their demands for some federal measures to resolve the crisis, but reported no change in Ford's position.

Concerned about the deteriorating situation as the Carey package floundered in late September, the vice president broached a new proposal at his weekly meeting with the president on October 2. What Rockefeller outlined was a presidential initiative to provide a bridging loan for the city, which would be conditional on the approval by the Emergency Financial Control Board of a plan to balance the city's budget by June 30, 1978. Building on his earlier argument that the president could do nothing until

Congress had acted, Rockefeller had tailored his proposed initiative to reflect the need for prior congressional action. Accordingly, he recommended a presidential initiative urging:

the prompt establishment of a Joint Select Committee of the U.S. Congress, or that standing committees of the Congress be designated, for the purpose of becoming thoroughly familiar with decisions of the Emergency Financial Control Board, and the corrective actions that are adopted by the mayor and the City Council to restore sound management and the fiscal integrity of the city.

The committee and the Congress should consider what, if any, federal legislation may be necessary to help bridge this temporary situation between the time actions have been taken by the city to restore fiscal integrity and investor confidence has been regained.[44]

As before, the vice president failed to convince the president to yield on the issue of federal assistance. Ford simply refused to countenance any proposal that had as its basic purpose the provision of aid from the federal government.[45]

Having failed to win his case within the administration, the vice president went public with his bridging proposal. At a luncheon for local editors and publishers in Portland, Oregon, on October 3, he discussed the budgeting and bond refinancing measures to be adopted by the state-controlled financial management board. He then went on to declare:

. . . nobody can do anything to help solve this situation but themselves to put this house in order. But after they have done that, they have still got this $3.2 billion in the short-term float and they won't be able to sell those notes. They have got to turn those into long-term bonds to give them time after what they have done what is necessary to get a reestablishment of their credit. . . . And there is this period that somehow there has got to be help somewhere to bridge that. But the president has no power and only the Congress of the United States is going to be in the position to take action.

A questioner at the luncheon detected some differences between this assessment and the position of the administration and pointedly asked about these. Rockefeller responded (in part) as follows: "I have said nothing on this issue up to now, and I am simply analyzing the issue, not trying to get ahead of my boss or the administration. But I am simply saying he [the president] has no power to do anything."[46]

To some extent, support for the vice president's position came begrudgingly from Federal Reserve Board Chairman Arthur Burns in testimony before the Joint Economic Committee on October 8. Although he made plain his own general unreceptivity to the question of federal aid for New

York City, he told the Joint Committee that Congress should act more expeditiously if it intended to assist the city. It was his assessment that "protracted congressional debate will keep the markets uncertain and in turmoil,
and congressional indecision might keep New York from doing what it
should."[47]

At a presidential news conference on October 9, President Ford showed
some signs of moving from his previously inflexible position. Responding to
a question on a presidential veto of congressional legislation to provide a
"federal bailout of New York City," the president said:

I don't think any legislation that I have heard people comment about or any legislation that I have read about would justify approval by myself. The legislation that I
have heard about is a long way from getting through the Congress.

So, I think it is very premature to make any comment other than nothing I have seen
so far seems to fit the bill.

Although the above answer continued his past refusal to endorse legislation designed to aid the city, at the same time Ford did not actually rule out
the possibility that some future proposal might secure his approval. This
slight shift was underscored in an answer to a subsequent question about the
conditions necessary for presidential support of short-term aid proposals.
Commenting on the undesirability of "bailing out" a city, the president
observed:

Unless they come in with a balanced budget, unless they get some state aid from the
State of New York by some means or other, I am just very reluctant to say anything
other than "no" until I see the fine print, until I see what New York City has done.
And, it is interesting to note that the "Big Mac" committee has turned down Mayor
Beame's program as being not sufficient. So, it hasn't gotten by the state yet, much
less come back down to Washington.[48]

Ford's hint of possible flexibility on the question of federal assistance
was quickly followed, two days later, by an outright call from the vice president for immediate congressional action on legislating aid for the city, once
the state control board and the city government had taken the necessary
measures to restructure the city's debt obligations and to balance the city
budget. To a highly receptive Columbus Day Dinner audience in New York
City, Rockefeller declared:

It is, therefore, essential that under these circumstances, the Congress as a whole
focus on the problem now and enact appropriate legislation. . . .

Time is of the essence and the resolution of this immediate New York City situation
is crucial. After the State Emergency Financial Control Board and New York City

have acted to restore fiscal integrity it will be the true test of the responsiveness of our congressional system as to whether the Congress can act in time to avoid catastrophe.[49]

The now-evident conflict between the views of the vice president and the president became the main focus of questioning at a vice presidential press conference held at Columbus, Ohio, on October 15, four days after the Columbus Day Dinner speech. Describing the disagreement between himself and the president as one consisting only of "minor differences," Rockefeller set out for the reporters what these differences amounted to:

The minor differences relate to his concern that there should be no bailout of New York City, a concern which I share. My concern is that New York City must put its house in order. He feels the same way. So we are totally in agreement.

We then get to the point where after New York City has taken the action to restore fiscal integrity, even then—now here is where the differences lie in the estimates—some people say when that is done, their credit will be restored. Other people say when that is done, they are still going to have trouble selling their bonds until that three-year period has been passed through.

I happen to be of the second school. Therefore, I wanted to call the attention of the Congress to the fact that if I am right, and the others happen to be wrong that things will all then be hunky-dory, that they better have some legislation on the books so that we don't have a catastrophe. Because that catastrophe could not only affect New York but could spread to other parts.[50]

However, any hopes that the pressures within Congress for legislation to assist the city, combined with the public support for such eventual legislative action given by the vice president, might effect an early change in the official stance of the Ford administration were short-lived. On October 29, in a nationally broadcast address to the National Press Club in Washington, D.C., President Ford announced in the bluntest terms:

I can tell you, and tell you now, that I am prepared to veto any bill that has as its purpose a federal bailout of New York City to prevent a default.

I am fundamentally opposed to this so-called solution, and I will tell you why. Basically, it is a mirage. By giving a federal guarantee, we would be reducing rather than increasing the prospect that the city's budget will ever be balanced.

What President Ford offered as his alternative to federal assistance was a proposal that the federal bankruptcy laws be amended to provide the federal courts "with sufficient authority to preside over an orderly reorganization of New York City's financial affairs—should that become necessary." The proposal would allow the city, with the state's approval, to petition for bankruptcy. This petition (which would not require the consent of city creditors) would include a budgeting plan to adjust debts and bring the budget into balance. To meet the short-term needs of the city, the federal court would have power to issue "debt certificates" to raise new loans for the city, which would be paid out of revenues ahead of other creditors.

As the president presented this proposal, he indicated the benefits that it held for New York City: "First, it will prevent, in the event of default, all New York City's funds from being tied up in lawsuits; second, it will provide the conditions for an orderly plan to be developed for payments to New York City's creditors over a long term; and third, it will provide a way for new borrowing to be secured by pledging future revenues."[51]

At the time that Ford gave his National Press Club speech, the vice president was in Tampa, Florida, conducting the second in the series of Domestic Council Public Forums. Questioned within minutes of the conclusion of Ford's announcement of his bankruptcy law revision proposal, Rockefeller was at pains to point out his own opposition to a bailout, indicating that he favored bridging loan guarantees after decisive budgeting action had been taken by the city. However, he was pressed hard about his differences with the president's position. In particular, he was asked what he thought the president's action said about the nature of his influence on administration policy, to which he responded:

Obviously there is some honest difference of opinion. But it just happens he is the President of the United States and I am Vice President of the United States. Therefore, I will always, as I [have] said on all occasions, give him the best advice or reactions I have. But when he makes the decision, that is it. He is the one who is President of the United States.[52]

Three days after his November 3 letter to President Ford, indicating his "unavailability" for the 1976 Republican vice presidential nomination, the vice president discussed his situation at a press conference in the old executive office building adjoining the White House. As in Florida, he found himself questioned closely about his differences with Ford about the appropriate method of dealing with the city's fiscal problems. Indicating that he felt "very strongly" about his own approach, Rockefeller provided an impromptu analysis of the alternatives presented, as follows:

If the city takes the steps that are essential to bring their budget in balance in three years, which is the best they can do, then there is going to have to be a period during that three years to help . . . somebody has to help them bridge over their financing. I said I thought the Congress ought to focus on it and act so that that could be done.

He feels they won't take the steps and that, therefore, the only course will be to go into bankruptcy and that, therefore, they are going to need legislation.

They need legislation in either case, and more or less the same actions will be taken. I think the trustee on bankruptcy, the federal judge, when he issues certificates which the president said he will do, those certificates will have to be guaranteed by the federal government. So it is going to come out more or less the same. It is just a different course of action.

On the political aspects of Ford's decision to eschew a financial-aid approach, opting instead for an orderly bankruptcy procedure, Rockefeller indicated that this did not proclaim that the president had "written off" New York in the 1976 presidential election. However, he did concede that it would cost Ford heavily in lost support throughout the state.[53]

Despite the renewed opposition of the Ford administration to any proposal remotely suggesting a federal bailout of New York City and the announced intention of the president to veto any such legislation, Congress proceeded with consideration of proposals to guarantee payment of the city's bonds.[54] On November 3, the House Committee on Banking, Currency, and Housing reported out a measure (H.R.10481) to provide federal guarantees for bonds issued to meet the city's expenses, and floor debate in the full House was scheduled for November 17 or 18. On the Senate side, the Committee on Banking, Housing and Urban Affairs passed its own bill (S.2615) to provide for slightly different bond guarantee assistance. Further action on this bill was expected on the Senate floor after the House considered H.R.10481.

In mid-November, Governor Carey called the New York State Legislature into special session to consider a new package of measures to deal with the city's problems. Carey's new package comprised several elements designed to provide a further $6.8 billion to meet city needs for fiscal years 1976-1978, including financial pledges from municipal union pension funds and city banks; extension of short-term notes due on June 30, 1976; new city taxing authority; changes in contribution levels in municipal pension funds; and adoption of additional budget cuts by the city government. At the same time, Carey wrote to Treasury Secretary Simon outlining this new package and requesting federal loan guarantees to supplement the state's actions.[55]

In the light of these considerations and the prospect of imminent congressional action to provide bond guarantees, the president issued the following statement on November 19:

I am gratified that the leaders of New York appear to have accepted primary responsibility for solving the financial problems of the city and are proceeding in the direction of a long-term solution. . . . I am impressed with the seriousness of their intentions as described by Governor Carey in his letter to Secretary Simon and await further concrete actions by the state and the other parties concerned.

The bailout bill now before the House of Representatives is irrelevant because it does not address the current situation and I would veto it.

I am convinced that if New York continues to move toward fiscal responsibility, all parties concerned can look forward to a satisfactory resolution despite the current obstacles.

If they continue to make progress, I will review the situation early next week to see if any legislation is appropriate at the federal level.

In the meantime, should New York leaders fail to implement their intentions, New York City could still be forced into legal default. Therefore, I am asking the Congress once again to enact special amendments to the federal bankruptcy laws which would ensure that such a default, if it occurs, would be orderly.[56]

Although Ford did not promise concrete federal assistance measures backed by the administration, his announced intention to "review the situation . . . to see if any legislation is appropriate" was a clear incentive to force the pace in the legislature in Albany, New York. The immediate effect the statement had in Congress was postponement of House action on H.R.10481 (the bill threatened by presidential veto) until after the Thanksgiving recess.

Prodded by Ford's announcement, the New York State Legislature approved the Carey package in its entirety on November 25. Governor Carey notified the president of this action the following day and requested that immediate consideration be given to appropriate federal support to bolster the state's own measures to assist the city.

The president's response to Carey's request was announced in a nationally broadcast news conference on the evening of November 26. Ford declared that he was now prepared to propose a federal program of seasonal loan assistance to provide funding for New York City during the July-March period when revenues fail to match city expenses. Anticipating charges that he was endorsing the very bailout approach that he had so roundly condemned previously, he claimed to the contrary that he had succeeded in getting the city and state governments to accept their responsibilities in the matter. As he put it:

Only in the last month after I made it clear that New York would have to solve its fundamental financial problems without the help of the federal taxpayer has there been a concerted effort to put the finances of the city and state on a sound basis. They have today informed me of the specifics of New York's self-help program.

Underlining his determination to avoid any appearance of a bailout, Ford cautioned: "if local parties fail to carry out their plan, I am prepared to stop . . . the seasonal federal assistance."

Essentially, Ford proposed the short-term bridging assistance that Rockefeller had called for several months earlier. Providing a maximum amount of $2.3 billion in assistance for each of the next two years, Ford's initiative called for direct treasury loans rather than the loan guarantee proposed in the bills currently awaiting action in the House and the Senate. Questioned about the use of loan assistance rather than guarantee, the president explained:

The reason we made it a loan rather than a loan guarantee is very simple. It is a much cleaner transaction between the federal government and the state and/or the city. If you have a loan guarantee, you involve other parties. And we think we have much better control over it, if we make it a direct loan from the federal government.[57]

Ford's seasonal loan proposal was promptly moved through the Congress. On December 2, the House passed the loan bill (H.R.10481—amended to substitute direct loan assistance for the bond guarantees it previously provided) by a narrow 213-203 vote, while the Senate approved the measure on December 6 on a 57-30 vote after invoking cloture on a filibuster. On December 9, the president signed the legislation, and New York City was given the federal assistance necessary to meet its seasonal cash-flow needs.[58]

With the establishment of the administration's loan assistance program, the president turned to the vice president for regular advice on New York City's financial situation. At their regular weekly meeting on January 8, Ford requested Rockefeller to "keep him fully informed on a confidential basis as to developments in the New York City/State fiscal situation."[59] The vice president accepted this assignment and arranged for the production of a weekly report detailing for the president the ongoing status of the city's fiscal situation and providing highlights and analysis of associated political and fiscal developments. These reports were hand delivered by Rockefeller at his weekly meetings with Ford throughout 1976.

CONVENTIONAL VICE PRESIDENTIAL DUTIES

The role that Rockefeller undertook to play as vice president in the Ford administration was rather novel from the outset. The arrangement of having the vice president function with policy-planning responsibilities gave an unconventional cast to Rockefeller's incumbency. As a "staff assistant" to the president, Rockefeller involved himself as a major contributor within the policy processes of the Ford White House and thus brought the vice presidency into the mainstream of presidential politics. However, at the same time there were other assignments undertaken by Rockefeller that of their very nature were traditional vice presidential chores, and which gave an otherwise novel incumbency a conventional veneer.

The range of conventional vice presidential tasks is fairly broad and includes such activities as foreign trips to promote goodwill and understanding abroad; representing the president at the funerals of foreign leaders;

speech making on behalf of the administration throughout the nation; and service on national councils or commissions. Beyond these, there is, of course, the one duty prescribed for the vice president by the Constitution—the duty of presiding over the Senate. For an underemployed incumbent, some of these activities hold within them relief from the vacancy of an office devoid of inherent substance. However, for a vice president committed to employing the office as a vehicle for substantive policy involvement within the administration, such activities surely come, at best, as an unwanted distraction.

In his short tenure as vice president, Rockefeller was called upon to undertake his share of these conventional activities. He spoke on behalf of the administration throughout the country, made some foreign goodwill trips, and attended three state funerals abroad.[60] He presided over the Senate on an occasional basis, as do most vice presidents. But the most time-consuming of his conventional responsibilities was his service on national commissions.

Although the practice of assigning the vice president to national councils or commissions is of relatively recent origin,[61] it has become a useful device for achieving various presidential aims: to add symbolic luster to particular national study groups; to maintain an administration presence for monitoring or control purposes; or simply to occupy the time and talents of an otherwise underemployed official. In the case of Vice President Rockefeller, his commission assignments were made to achieve the first two presidential objectives: to add the luster of the Rockefeller experience and prestige and to maintain a reliable administration presence on studies of vital importance to the administration.

However, for Rockefeller the commission assignments he received from President Ford were essentially peripheral to what he perceived to be his central role in the administration. For him, commission responsibilities constituted a distraction from the program policy activities he preferred to pursue. Of his experience with them he observed:

Now, these were major time-consuming operations. And if it hadn't been that I had a lifetime of organizing and studying commissions, I could have been kissed good-bye and lost in the morass . . . of any one of them. But I went right after them and I got the best people . . . in every case I got topflight people.[62]

Rockefeller served on five national commissions during his vice presidency, but since this service was not central to his policy-making role within the administration, each commission is merely sketched-in briefly below to indicate the vice president's mission as a presidential appointee.

Commission on the Organization of Government for the Conduct of Foreign Policy. Established in 1972 as a result of congressional concerns about the increasing dominance of the executive branch in the area of foreign relations, the commission was created to consider and make recommendations on the relationship between the executive and legislative branches in foreign policy making. Jointly sponsored by the Congress and the president, the commission was comprised of twelve members: four each appointed by the president, the Speaker of the House, and the president of the Senate. Chairing the commission was Robert D. Murphy, a former undersecretary of state.

Rockefeller was appointed to the commission on December 21, 1974, as a presidential appointee in place of Anne Armstrong, who had resigned her membership. The vice president's appointment came at a time when the commission's charter had only six more months to run (it expired on June 30, 1975), and his mission on behalf of the administration was to protect the position of the president in the vitally important task of writing up the commission's report and recommendations. As Rockefeller has described his position: "This commission was what is known as getting out of hand, and I was asked to go in and try to rescue the operation."[63] To assist him in this endeavor, Rockefeller recruited General Andrew F. Goodpaster, who was at that time retiring from service with the North Atlantic Treaty Organization.

On June 27, 1975, the commission issued its report. Its principal recommendation was the creation of a Joint Committee on National Security, which would be a congressional counterpart to the National Security Council and would provide a mechanism for dealing with the executive under the War Powers Act. The basic recommendations concerning the executive branch were as follows:

- The separation (in the future) of the positions of assistant to the president for National Security Affairs and secretary of state.
- Greater emphasis to be given to international economic policy in the state department, the White House, and the National Security Council.
- Changes within the state department to improve its capabilities in the areas of economics, science, and defense.
- Upgrading the Arms Control and Disarmament Agency.
- Reorganization of the programs of the USIA, the Voice of America, and the cultural affairs unit of the state department.
- Restricting claims of executive privilege to those of the president himself.
- Reconstituting the Central Intelligence Agency as the Foreign Intelligence Agency (to emphasize its central function), with a director appointed from the outside.
- Establishing the post of director of Central Intelligence, with the responsibility of serving as the president's intelligence adviser.
- Restricting covert activities and requiring that they be reported to the proposed Joint Committee.[64]

Commission on CIA Activities within the United States. Created by President Ford on January 4, 1975, in the wake of news reports of illegal domestic activities carried out by the CIA,[65] the commission was established to determine whether the CIA had acted illegally and beyond the scope of its charter, and to make appropriate recommendations to the president. Including the vice president, who was named chairman, the commission had a membership of eight, as follows:

Nelson A. Rockefeller, vice president (commission chairman);

John T. Connor, chairman of the board, Allied Chemical Corporation, and former secretary of commerce;

C. Douglas Dillon, managing director, Dillon, Read & Co., and former secretary of the treasury and former ambassador to France and undersecretary of state;

Erwin N. Griswold, lawyer, former solicitor general;

Lane Kirkland, secretary-treasurer, AFL-CIO;

Lyman L. Lemnitzer, general, U.S. Army (Rtd.), and former chairman of the Joint Chiefs of Staff;

Ronald Reagan, political commentator, former governor of California;

Edgar F. Shannon, Jr., commonwealth professor of English and former president of the University of Virginia.

Although Ford had named the vice president as commission chairman, Rockefeller was not consulted about the president's selection of commission members.[66] Nor was he consulted on the choice of David W. Belin as the commission's executive director.[67] Thus, despite the fact that the commission was popularly referred to as the Rockefeller Commission, Rockefeller had no impact on the shape of the commission nor the ready means of directing its staff work.

Besides the absence of prior consultation at the outset, Rockefeller was unhappy with the assignment largely because he assessed (correctly, as it turned out) that it would make great demands on his time. His intention, after the extremely lengthy confirmation process had been concluded, was to get the work of the Domestic Council moving quickly (under his direction) to develop new program policy options for adoption by the administration. Much of this effort could be hampered in its formative stages by the demands of a major investigative commission on the vice president's time and energies.

However, the vice president was unhappy about the commission assignment for a further reason. The fact that the commission would make large demands on his time was not entirely benign in his view: he detected in the assignment a means of blunting his policy role in the administration. His comment that "I could have been kissed good-bye and lost in the morass" of commission work is indicative of such a perception. More telling on this point is Rockefeller's description of a presidential request that the commission broaden the scope of its inquiry to include investigation of past presidential involvement in CIA assassination plots against foreign leaders. Since this would get into the question of John F. Kennedy's alleged involvement with a plot to assassinate Fidel Castro of Cuba, Rockefeller was convinced that the request was "another way of chopping my head off and of getting me out there where I was the one who was putting the finger on the Kennedys, as chairman of the commission."[68]

The commission issued its report on June 6, 1975, concluding that:

A detailed analysis of the facts has convinced the commission that the great majority of the CIA's domestic activities comply with its statutory authority.

Nevertheless, over the twenty-eight years of its history, the CIA has engaged in some activities that should be criticized and not permitted to happen again—both in light of the limits imposed on the agency by law and as a matter of public policy.

Some of these activities were initiated or ordered by presidents either directly or indirectly.

Some of them fall within the doubtful area between responsibilities delegated to the CIA by Congress and the National Security Council on the one hand and activities specifically prohibited to the agency on the other.

Some of them were plainly unlawful and constitute improper invasions upon the rights of Americans.

The agency's own recent actions, undertaken for the most part in 1973 and 1974, have gone far to terminate the activities upon which this investigation has focused. The recommendations of the commission are designed to clarify areas of doubt concerning the agency's authority, to strengthen the agency's structure, and to guard against recurrences of these improprieties.[69]

National Commission on Productivity and Work Quality. Established in reconstituted form by President Ford on December 30, 1974, the commission comprised twenty-four members appointed by the president and representing in equal numbers members from business, labor, the public, and government. The objectives of the commission were "to help increase the productivity of the American economy and to help improve the morale and quality of work of the American worker."

Ford's appointment of the vice president as commission chairman on March 17, 1975, came as a consequence of the acceptance by John T. Dunlop, the outgoing chairman, of the cabinet post of secretary of labor. Dunlop in fact remained on the commission as a government representative, giving up the chairmanship because the labor department post required this for reasons of "seemliness." Rockefeller's appointment can be viewed as an effort to add luster and prestige to a little-known national body.

The commission involved Rockefeller only peripherally. It actually expired with legislation establishing a National Center for Productivity and Quality of Working Life, which was signed into law by President Ford on November 28, 1975. This legislation transferred all of the functions of the commission to the center. On December 10, the president announced: "Because of the importance I personally attach to this center, I am delighted that the vice president will continue his leadership as chairman of the board."[70]

The President's Panel on Federal Compensation. President Ford established the panel on June 12, 1975, "to ascertain any needed changes in federal compensation policies and practices, keeping in mind our goal of a system that is fair and equitable both to the employees and to the public." Since this panel was essentially an in-house executive branch unit to consider federal compensation, all six panel members appointed by the president came from departments and agencies of the federal government and included the vice president, who was named panel chairman. Again, Rockefeller's appointment lent prestige (and public service experience that related directly to the work of the panel) to an otherwise undistinguished body.

The work of the panel was completed in less than nine months, and its report was submitted to the president on December 2, 1975. Among the various recommendations of the panel were proposals to provide:

- The creation of separate grade and pay schedules for professionals and clerical/technical federal employees.
- The abolition of basing in-grade pay increases on longevity rather than merit.
- Salary increases for senior government executives.[71]

National Commission on Water Quality. Rockefeller's service as chairman of the commission was not the result of an assignment he received as vice president: he was in fact chairman when he accepted the president's offer of the vice presidential nomination in August, 1974. His intention on acceptance of Ford's offer of that nomination was to announce his resignation of the commission chairmanship on completion of the vice presidential confirmation process. However, the other members of the commission prevailed on him to remain, arguing that his status as vice president would enhance the status of the commission.

Therefore, Rockefeller continued as chairman until the work of the commission was completed in March, 1976. On March 18, 1976, the commission submitted its report to the Congress, setting various recommendations regarding revisions to the 1977 and 1983 federal water quality standards and goals.[72]

As the chapter shows, Rockefeller attempted to play an active role of total involvement in the activities of the administration, while at the same time carrying out the conventional duties associated with the office of vice president. To a considerable degree, he was successful in these endeavors and is to be commended for his efforts to expand the dimensions of the vice presidential office. Yet there is here some sense of a contradiction built into his vice presidency. On the one hand, he was clearly insistent on maintaining a "portfolio," with his oversight responsibility for the Domestic Council; on the other hand, he seemed bent on fulfilling the role of "minister without portfolio," accepting and performing a multiplicity of competing assignments. This is a matter that will be taken up in the succeeding chapters.

· 6 · ROCKEFELLER AND THE POLITICS OF ADVERSITY

In many ways, the vice presidency of Nelson Rockefeller presents itself as a study in adversity. First, as a nominee under the terms of the Twenty-fifth Amendment, he underwent a confirmation process that proved to be highly controversial, was drawn out, and almost outlasted his own ability to endure.[1] Second, his delayed entrance as vice president into the Ford administration was met with considerable dispute and acrimony over the precise terms of his Domestic Council role. Third, the organizational structure of the Ford White House was one that promoted competition and conflict; therefore, his efforts to develop coherent, comprehensive policy proposals became the subject of considerable controversy and opposition. Fourth, the duality of his positions as staff assistant to the president and as vice president not only enlarged his overall role within the administration, but also placed exhausting demands upon him and subjected him to the punishing turbulence of mainstream administration politics. Finally, although his relationship with President Ford was, on the surface, close and warm, Ford's indecisiveness and reluctance to intervene in disputes had the effect of undercutting Rockefeller's position to the ultimate point of withdrawal as a potential Ford running mate in the 1976 election.

THE CONFIRMATION DELAY

Perhaps the single most important factor in determining the development of Rockefeller's vice presidency was the delay in effecting his confirmation in the Congress. The months of September through December, 1974, were vital months for the fledgling Ford presidency. Excluded from the administration by his confirmation hearings, he was thus prevented from playing any part in the reorganization of the White House structure and in the policy planning for the State of the Union Message given in January 1975. Moreover, he also was kept at arm's length from Gerald Ford as he embarked on the vital task of establishing himself as President of the United States.

As Richard Neustadt has noted in the preface to the original edition of his classic study, *Presidential Power*: "When we inaugurate a President of the United States we give a man the powers of our largest public office. From the moment he is sworn the man confronts a personal problem: how to make those powers work for *him*."[2]

In Ford's case, the problems of making the powers of the presidency work for him were if anything more acute than those normally encountered by an incoming president. Coming as it did at the climax of a long period of pressure for the resignation of President Nixon, the transition to the Ford presidency was unique in American history and brought in its wake unique problems. Although Vice President Ford, as constitutional heir, was not thrust suddenly into the presidential office on the uncontemplated death of an incumbent president as had eight of his predecessors, neither had he been able to ready himself for the transition when it did come. For excellent reasons of politics and propriety, he had not allowed his vice presidential staff to prepare for the practical aspects of a future Ford administration. Moreover, when he did assume the office of the presidency, Ford was dependent at the very outset on the cabinet and White House staff chosen by a discredited predecessor, from whom he was immediately obliged to dissociate himself in order to establish his own sense of legitimacy. In short, Ford's accession to the presidency posed with dramatic acuteness Neustadt's problem: "how to make [presidential] powers work for him."

At the very outset of his presidency, Ford displayed considerable ambivalence concerning the structure of the Ford White House. According to Rockefeller, in their telephone conversation of August 17, Ford described his vice presidential role as follows: "I want you on the domestic, and Henry [Kissinger] on the foreign and then we can move on these things."[3] Rockefeller took this to be a clear statement of presidential intent that as vice president he would have preeminence in domestic-policy concerns in the same way that Kissinger enjoyed dominance over national-security and foreign-policy concerns. The concept of White House organization thus implied was clearly hierarchical, with Rockefeller and Kissinger serving as first among equals in their respective areas of concern.

However, at the same time Ford had set in motion a reorganization study of White House staff structures to be undertaken by his transition team.[4] This team developed an organizational framework for restructuring the White House that included the following elements: first, the differentiation of presidential staff by subject matter specialization, with lateral equality between resultant White House units, and, second, the installation of a White House coordinator to insure coordination of the paperwork in place of an all-powerful chief of staff.[5]

The problem here was that the White House structure contemplated by the president's transition team, with its principle of lateral equality between units, was in conflict with the hierarchical structure implied by Ford's discussion with Rockefeller on August 17. While this clearly suggested a certain ambivalence on Ford's part, publicly he endorsed the transition team's structure. At his first presidential news conference on August 28, he declared:

There will be no tightly controlled operations of the White House staff. I have a policy of seeking advice from a number of top members of my staff. There will be no one person, nor any limited number of individuals, who make decisions. I will make the decisions. I will make the decisions and take the blame for them or whatever benefit might be the case.[6]

In practice, Ford adhered to a diffused White House structure, with the creation of the Economic Policy Board and the Energy Resources Council as additional units in the executive office of the president. The effect of setting up these additional units was to decrease the jurisdictional area of the Domestic Council, which ceded coordination responsibility for energy and economic policy concerns respectively to the ERC and the EPB. Thus Ford's White House structure began to take shape as a highly differentiated whole composed of relatively coequal parts.

Developed over the course of several months, the completed structure of the Ford White House was not announced publicly until mid-December. In a press office statement issued on December 18, it was announced that the reorganization of the White House was based upon "the working style of this president. . . . It implements his concept of leadership and management of the executive branch and conforms to the way President Ford operates."

The major features of the reorganization were, first, that there would be four cabinet-rank advisers who would be available to the president on the full range of policy issues. Each adviser would also have staff responsibilities. Second, nine key staff directors would report directly to the president, as follows:

- An assistant to the president for Management and Budget and director of OMB;

- An assistant to the president for Economic Affairs and executive director of the Economic Policy Board, L. William Seidman;

- An assistant to the president for Domestic Affairs and executive director of the Domestic Council;

- An assistant to the president dealing with national security affairs, Henry A. Kissinger;

- An assistant to the president heading the White House Operations Office and with responsibility for coordination of White House staff operations, Donald Rumsfeld;

- A counselor to the president principally responsible for congressional relations and public liaison, John O. Marsh, Jr.;

- The press secretary to the president, Ronald H. Nessen;

- A counselor to the president principally responsible for the editorial office and political affairs, Robert T. Hartmann; and

- The legal counsel to the president, Philip W. Buchen.[7]

The striking feature of the structure of the Ford White House is that, despite the designation of Rumsfeld, Hartmann, Marsh, and Buchen as cabinet-rank advisers, there is an in-built egalitarian cast to it. Moreover, there is nothing in the White House organizational chart (see figure 3) to suggest the primacy of the Domestic Council implied by Ford's August 17 discussion with Rockefeller.

Unless there was in Ford an ongoing ambivalence about his conception of White House structure, it can be inferred from the structure announced on December 18 that he had abandoned his earlier intention to have the foreign- and domestic-policy areas dominated respectively by Kissinger and Rockefeller. While the national security apparatus under Kissinger was left intact by the White House reorganization, that was not true of the domestic-policy area that saw a diminished Domestic Council sharing domestic jurisdiction with other units.

From Rockefeller's standpoint, the unfortunate aspect of the apparent shift in Ford's conception of White House organization was that it occurred during the period when he was cut off from the administration by a cordon sanitaire created by his confirmation hearings on Capitol Hill. Thus he was afforded no opportunity to make any contribution to the president's deliberations on White House reorganization.

Beyond an inability to counsel Ford on the reshaping of the White House, Rockefeller's delayed confirmation had a further adverse effect on his eventual entry into the administration as vice president. By the time of his swearing in on December 19, many of the senior staff and staff structures of the Ford White House had been in place for several months and had become fairly well established. Discussing Rockefeller's arrival as vice president, Philip Buchen makes the important point that:

By that time everybody was geared to working for Ford. . . . Rumsfeld was already in place, we were all organized . . . the show was running. [We were not] waiting for someone else to come in to fill the vacuum.

[Normally] if you were elected, there is a lag between election and inauguration. If you had the vice president in on the planning, he is a part of it. [Rockefeller's] situation was the worst situation for a vice president to break in. It was a less auspicious circumstance for a vice president than normal. Everybody was in place, the machinery was all working without a vice president.[8]

FIGURE 3. FORD'S WHITE HOUSE STAFF ORGANIZATION
(AS AT DECEMBER 18, 1974)

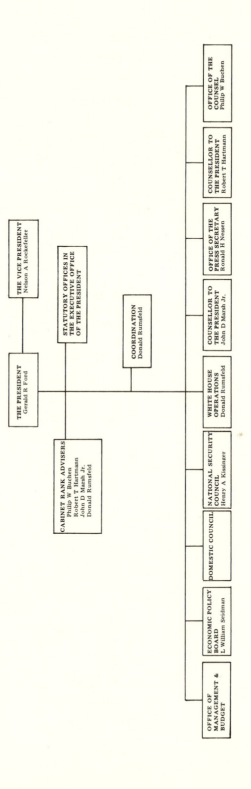

Thus Rockefeller was faced with the unenviable task of establishing himself in a White House structure within which all of the other participants had already established themselves.

The confirmation delay also prevented Rockefeller from making any contribution to the policy deliberations that fashioned Ford's first State of the Union Message delivered in January, 1975. For the policy areas within which Rockefeller subsequently developed administration proposals this had adverse consequences, particularly for energy policy and the president's declared goal of achieving energy independence by 1985. Peter Wallison has argued that had the Energy Independence Authority proposal been developed for inclusion in the 1975 State of the Union Message, it would have been less vulnerable and isolated and would have been pushed into the legislative process much sooner than subsequently was the case.[9] As for social programs, it is difficult to consider the extent to which Rockefeller might have made any significant contribution had his confirmation been completed sooner. Ford's administration certainly had little time in which to prepare much of a legislative agenda for 1975, given the few months with which it had to work following Nixon's resignation in August. However, it is possible that Rockefeller could have provided some opposition to the budget concerns that produced the president's declaration, in the 1975 State of the Union Message, that "no new spending programs can be initiated this year, except for energy."

Beyond the absence of vice presidential contributions concerning the restructuring of the White House and the policy deliberations on the 1975 State of the Union Message, the delayed confirmation further prevented Rockefeller from developing a close working relationship with Ford during the formative period of his presidency. The months of September through December were vital months of learning and adjustment, as Ford sought to establish himself in the White House as the nation's chief executive. With a background comprised exclusively of experience in the legislative politics of the House of Representatives, Ford's major adjustment concerned the decision-making demands of executive politics. Commenting on his early experiences at the beginning of 1975, Ford observed:

The experience, the training I had in the Congress has been invaluable. We have been going through the same process in the development of a plan for our energy program, or the economy program, the same way you almost do it in Congress. You listen to Bill Simon, to Arthur Burns, to Alan Greenspan. They have ideas, and you sort of—well, you have to make a judgment—you mesh here or you modify there. The only difference is, when you're in this office, among people on your staff or in your administration, if you make the decision it's supposed to stick. In the Congress, you don't have quite that authority. But the process isn't too much different.

The experiences, again, I had in Congress I think were helpful in giving me the way of working with people in the executive branch, the same as you have to work with people in the legislative branch.[10]

Ford's growing grasp of the decision-making aspect of executive politics was the most tangible evidence of his development as president. James Cannon has commented on this development, noting that: "By the time Ford had been in the White House six months or so . . . he had moved all the way over from being a sudden president to the point where he was feeling, 'It is my responsibility to make the decisions, I will do it.' "[11]

In Cannon's view, this movement was of major significance for Rockefeller and his relationship with Ford. As Cannon explained the situation:

Rockefeller really thought he was going to make decisions and indeed hoped he was. But the fact is, between the time that Rockefeller was nominated and the time he was confirmed, Ford became a very different person as the president. I recognized that, because I had seen this through the eyes of Jack Marsh and various other people I was working with at the White House. I had seen this change, but I don't think Rockefeller did.[12]

ROCKEFELLER AND THE DOMESTIC COUNCIL

The major difficulty encountered by Rockefeller as he entered the administration to take up the Domestic Council assignment announced by the president on December 21 was that the dimensions of that assignment were unclear. The dispute that developed over the size and scope of his council role was decidedly acrimonious and was the product of several factors: first, the failure on the part of the president to define clearly for himself, the vice president, and senior White House staff members the dimensions of the vice president's council assignment; second, the resistance offered, for a variety of reasons, by some senior presidential staff members to Rockefeller's proposal to assume active personal leadership of the council's staff and policy functions; third, the refusal on the part of Rockefeller to accept that the changes effected in structure and staffing in the four months of his confirmation hearings implicitly required some redefinition of the role outlined to him by the president in August, 1974.

Central to the difficulties encountered in establishing Rockefeller's Domestic Council responsibility was Ford's management style. According to his long-time associate Robert Hartmann (who had served with Ford in Congress and in the vice presidential office before becoming a counselor to the president), Ford "never liked precisely to define responsibility. He never precisely defined anybody's. He gave you assignments, missions to carry out, but just because you did it this time didn't mean you'd do it next time."[13] This did not necessarily denote the absence of administrative principles. In fact, Ford considered his approach to be administratively sound. As Hartmann explained:

The principle is a common one, and certainly a common one on Capitol Hill. He [Ford] is the only one . . . who knows everything that's going on. Nobody else knows everything . . . they know parts of it, they know what they need to know the job. But he's the only one who has the total picture.[14]

Despite Ford's own dislike of precisely defined responsibilities, the White House structure shaped by the transition team and announced by Rumsfeld on December 18, 1974, provided concrete definition of the individual responsibilities of the president's senior staff. But in the structure Rumsfeld outlined, there were two omissions: first, there was no indication of the vice president's responsibilities;[15] and, second, the position of executive director of the Domestic Council was vacant. At his December 18 briefing on White House reorganization, Rumsfeld indicated that both areas would be taken up directly by the president with the vice president after Rockefeller's confirmation.

Meanwhile, President Ford had given his staff no indication of the scope of the role he had discussed with Rockefeller in August concerning domestic policy and the Domestic Council. The absence of such discussion with the staff was underscored by Philip Buchen, who noted that, in December, "I don't think anyone thought that his role would be any different from any previous vice president."[16] This view is supported by Hartmann, who declared that Ford "did not ever make Rockefeller's role clear."[17] While John Marsh did anticipate Rockefeller playing a role of some importance, he has provided support for Hartmann's discussion of Ford's dislike of precisely defined responsibilities. As Marsh recalled the situation: "I have never understood how we got so wrapped around the axle on the Domestic Council. I am not sure it was ever clearly defined . . . Ford and Rockefeller knew what they wanted the vice presidential role to be, but they never fully translated it precisely to the staff."[18]

The failure on the part of the president to communicate with his staff about his intentions regarding Rockefeller's role in domestic policy was disastrous. It was directly responsible for the adverse reaction of the senior White House staff to the vice president's several proposals to implement his Domestic Council role. While Rockefeller's initial proposal to assume personal direction of the council was unambiguously based on the broad grant of authority outlined by Ford in their telephone conversation of August 17, no such understanding on the part of the senior White House staff was possible. Rather, the vice president's proposals appeared as a violation of, and even a threat to, the White House staff structure already in place and ordered on the basis of lateral equality. Since the president had approved that structure, any proposal such as that of the vice president's could be legitimately and vigorously opposed.

A further concern on the part of some senior presidential staff members was that the vice president could well emerge as a "first among equals." In a status-conscious White House, in which individual staff members drew reassurance from the structure of lateral equality, such a specter was one that had to be resisted. In Philip Buchen's view:

The only way staffers around the president can work is if they are equals. Maybe a different kind of a vice president might have come down and been one of the boys, but certainly not Nelson Rockefeller. After all, he hadn't been a staffer to anyone for *years*!

The very position the vice president holds puts him at an advantage. [And add to this] the kind of a man Rockefeller is: he is a leader who likes to have his own way and gets impatient with long assignments and quibbling, [or] anything else that goes on when you're dealing with equals.[19]

The Ford staff already had some experience with a staff member who did not regard himself simply as equal. It had been clear from the outset that Henry Kissinger, as the president's national security adviser and secretary of state, was not prepared to subject himself to the rules and strictures applied to the president's staff by Rumsfeld as White House coordinator. Kissinger was par excellence a "first among equals," as the following description by Robert Hartmann makes clear:

The demonstration that we witnessed every day, of Kissinger disappearing into the oval office, [with] everybody else waiting patiently while their appointment times came and went—stacking everybody else in the government four or five deep—till he finished his long monologue instructing his new pupil in the Byzantine intracacies of the world, was not a happy example in terms of another one like this.[20]

The Ford staff member who had the greatest institutional concern about the vice president's Domestic Council leadership role was Donald Rumsfeld. Although his position within the White House was formally to function as the coordinator, Rumsfeld was in all but name a chief of staff who insisted that everything destined for the president be routed through him. Consequently, Rockefeller's intention to coordinate domestic-policy matters personally, as head of the Domestic Council, posed a serious threat to Rumsfeld's position. If, as the vice president proposed, domestic-policy matters for the president were routed through the Domestic Council, bypassing the central coordination system, Rumsfeld would be deprived of much of his function (and thus his power base in the Ford White House). Accordingly, the ensuing dispute between Rumsfeld and Rockefeller directly concerned the considerations of "first among equals"; but in their case it involved distinctions respectively between covert and overt primacy.

An interesting question poses itself here: why did President Ford not take steps to resolve the dispute within White House circles concerning

Rockefeller's Domestic Council role? Clearly two avenues of approach were open to him to deal decisively with the situation. On the one hand, the president could have simply announced to his senior staff that he had an agreement with Rockefeller and that the vice president's Domestic Council proposal represented the means of implementing that agreement. On the other hand, he could have indicated to Rockefeller that, because he had adopted a White House staff structure contrary to that implied by their August agreement, some reconsideration of the vice president's domestic-policy role was now necessary. Either approach would have prevented the debacle that developed between Rockefeller and the senior White House staff (particularly Rumsfeld and Buchen).

It is extremely difficult to assess why Ford refrained from intervening decisively one way or the other to resolve the dispute. Rockefeller was sufficiently upset by the protracted wrangling to give the president an ultimatum to support him on an amended proposal or else face his withdrawal from any Domestic Council role. And it was only at this point that Ford directly involved himself. One explanation, suggested by Philip Buchen, has the merit of accounting for Ford's apparent lack of concern about the organizational contradictions inherent in the dispute. As Buchen recalled the situation: "I certainly explained my views on it to the president. But Ford was not that much interested in *how* things operated: he'd never had any administrative experience to speak of. And I don't think he realized how important this tuning of a staff is."[21]

As for Rockefeller, at no time did he concede that the role outlined for him by the president in August, 1974, might require some redefinition given the organizational structure adopted for the Ford White House. His determination to oppose efforts by the president's senior staff to curtail his proposed personal assumption of Domestic Council leadership was based on the conviction that his proposal reflected the commitment made by Ford on August 17. In this, Rockefeller was a victim, as were the senior White House staff, of Ford's inability or unwillingness to make clear his intentions about the vice president's role.

The Domestic Council compromise finally agreed upon by Rockefeller and imposed upon the White House staff by the president proved to be conceptually flawed. The compromise plan called for the appointment of two Rockefeller associates, James Cannon and Richard Dunham respectively, as executive director and deputy director of the Domestic Council, with the vice president assuming oversight responsibilities as the council's vice chairman. However, as executive director, Cannon also functioned as assistant to the president for Domestic Affairs and was required to report directly to Ford as a senior White House adviser. Therefore, from the outset Cannon had a dual responsibility—to the president as adviser on domestic-policy matters and to Rockefeller (in his vice chairman's capacity) as the council's executive director. However, because of the presidential service functions performed by the Domestic Council's staff, Cannon became increasingly drawn into the White House circle.[22] As Rockefeller withdrew from direct involvement in the staff work of the council,[23] Cannon's White House gravitation became complete.

Rockefeller's abortive efforts to secure the domestic-policy role outlined by Ford in their August 17 telephone conversation were based on considerations that included but also transcended personal ambition. The fact was that Rockefeller had long held the view that the White House structure required a centralized unit for efficient and coherent handling of domestic affairs. In 1965, he had proposed the establishment of an Office of Executive Management for the purpose of integrating the various presidential concerns of budgeting, legislation, policy planning, personnel matters, and organizational activities.[24] The extent to which Rockefeller remained committed to such a conception of a centralized White House domestic policy apparatus was revealed in a memorandum to the president on December 16, 1975, at the time he announced formally his withdrawal from his oversight role as the Domestic Council's vice chairman. This memorandum, which was marked "personal and private," set out for Ford the vice president's analysis of the White House organizational structure as a mistaken structure for meeting domestic-policy needs.

Commencing his analysis with a discussion of the responsibilities and functions of the Domestic Council, Rockefeller proceeded to advise the president as follows:

As the president's office is currently organized, there is a striking contrast between the administrative arrangements for the two principal presidential roles—national security and domestic policy.

On the national security side, the National Security Council staff serves as a funnel through which information flows in an orderly way to your desk, and through which your decisions return for followup treatment. There is a consistency of approach here, a recognizable policy, and a sense of progress even in the face of complexity.

This is not so on the domestic policy side. In addition to the Domestic Council, you are advised by the Economic Policy Board, the Energy Resources Council, the Council of Economic Advisers, and the Office of Management and Budget. Each of these bodies has profound impact on aspects of domestic policy.

As a result, there is no overall conceptual planning and staff responsibility on the domestic front to assist you. The interrelation of the various elements is not given proper weight and major areas can be overlooked.

The present system actually divides consideration of these elements among a number of units, and thus works against the creation of a coherent approach.

The problem is compounded by the organization of the administrative staff, which is headed by a coordinator. Almost by definition, a coordinator responds but does not initiate. As matters percolate up through the proliferated staff system, a coordinator sees to it that they are superficially reviewed by all interested parties, but there is no strong staff leadership direction. It is not the role of a coordinator to see that initiatives are commenced or that matters which are to be handled at subordinate levels are actually being dealt with in a timely and effective manner.

As a result, the coordinator system cannot compensate for the organizational deficiencies of the domestic policy apparatus. It cannot create an orderly and consistent process of policy formulation, it cannot give direction in the development and staffing of initiatives.

I have great respect for the abilities and dedication of your staff, but they operate in an organizational environment which makes them effective only in response to outside stimuli and random initiatives. They are unable in this context to perform the broader duties which are essential to the proper discharge of your responsibilities— long-range, creative, conceptual planning, and strategic actions on an integrated basis relating to the various economic, social, and fiscal areas.

I, therefore, recommend that you centralize staff responsibilities for all economic, social, and fiscal policies under the Domestic Council as originally conceived, and that the relationships and responsibilities among the Domestic Council, Office of Management and Budget, counsel's office, and the Office of Legislative Affairs be clarified.

I would be glad to share with you further thoughts on this subject, should you so desire.[25]

However, President Ford declined either to discuss further Rockefeller's analysis or to give consideration to his recommendations.

THE STRUCTURE OF POLICY MAKING IN THE FORD ADMINISTRATION

While Rockefeller's critical analysis of the Ford White House organizational structure owed much to his commitment to a centralized approach, at the same time it was also clearly the product of his own experiences as a policy developer within the Ford administration. In the light of these experiences, it is certainly tempting to concede Rockefeller's arguments and adopt his conclusion that the Ford administration would have been much better served by a more coherent, centralized, domestic policy structure directed by an experienced policy planner (i.e., Rockefeller), who would coordinate all domestic-policy concerns on behalf of the president. Although he did not employ these in his memorandum of December 16, two policy proposals developed by Rockefeller provide useful illustrations of his analysis: first, the abortive domestic programs policy review of 1975, and, second, the Energy Independence Authority (EIA) proposal.

Considering first the domestic programs policy review of 1975, this presents itself in Rockefeller's terms as a clear-cut example of a systematic policy endeavor that was negated by a wholly unsystematic decision. The facts of the case are relatively straightforward. Rockefeller, with the express approval of the president, directed the activities of a domestic policy review group under John Veneman to produce a set of program policy options for the 1976 State of the Union Message. This endeavor proceeded onward from May, 1975, and was reaching the point of compiling a completed proposals package when the president announced a commitment to limit the federal budget for fiscal year 1977 to a ceiling of $395 billion. Because this ceiling demanded program spending cuts of $28 billion (which would be offset by corresponding cuts in federal taxes), the effect of the announcement was to damage fatally the domestic policy options package, which contained proposals for revised and new federal programs.

For this discussion, the significant point about the president's decision to propose a budget ceiling of $395 billion lies in the way that Ford reached his decision. Although it had profound consequences for all domestic programs and for Rockefeller's options development for the 1976 State of the Union Message, the president made his decision on the exclusive advice of Alan Greenspan, chairman of the Council of Economic Advisers; James Lynn, director of the Office of Management and Budget; Donald Rumsfeld, White House coordinator; and Rumsfeld's deputy, Richard Cheney.[26] No other advisers were consulted or given the opportunity of counseling Ford on the advisability of the budget ceiling.[27] In short, it was a presidential decision that had considerable implications for a wider range of domestic policy and political and electoral considerations, but that was arrived at on narrow budgetary grounds. From the standpoint of Rockefeller's analysis it exemplifies well his point that, under the Ford White House organizational structure, "the interrelationship of the various elements [on the domestic front] is not given proper weight and major areas can be overlooked."[28]

The second case for consideration here concerns the proposal to create a federal energy development finance corporation and provides a good illustration of Rockefeller's analysis that the Ford White House structure "divides consideration of . . . [policy] elements among a number of units, and thus works against the creation of a coherent approach."[29]

The original conception Rockefeller had of a vehicle to meet the administration's goal of achieving energy independence by 1985 was one that went far beyond narrow energy considerations. His first RFC-type of structure, the Resources Policy and Finance Corporation (RPFC) would, in addition to energy development, promote economic stability, full employment, and maximum utilization of natural resources and raw materials. Thus his RPFC proposal, at the outset, straddled the jurisdictions of the following executive office units: the Energy Resources Council, the Economic Policy Board, the Council of Economic Advisers, and the Office of Management and Budget, in addition to the Domestic Council of which he was vice chairman.

The fact that the Domestic Council (under whose organizational auspices Rockefeller developed his RPFC proposal) did not have complete jurisdiction of the policy areas covered by the RPFC proposal insured conflict. Rockefeller's efforts to develop the proposal as a personal initiative within the administration had the effect of arousing instincts of "territorial imperative" within units that perceived these efforts as trespass on their own areas of jurisdiction.[30] Consequently, as the proposal proceeded through its various stages of development (with RPFC becoming the Energy Resources Finance Corporation [ERFCO], which in turn became the Energy Independence Authority [EIA]), the opposition from the various institutional actors became increasingly intense and proved to be difficult and time-consuming to overcome.[31]

Although Rockefeller recognized that the Domestic Council had at best a shared jurisdiction over domestic-policy concerns with other executive office units, his actions did not reflect such a recognition. Many of the problems encountered in developing his energy corporation proposal sprang from his determination to maintain exclusive jurisdiction (formally under Domestic Council auspices) over it. It was only when he was faced with complete impasse in proceeding with ERFCO that he relinquished exclusive control and coopted Rogers Morton and Frank Zarb to proceed with its further development.

The outcome of the internal conflict and disputation was a delayed presidential iniative that conspicuously lacked a broad base of support within the administration, aspects that contributed to the negative reception given to the proposal in Congress. In consequence, the incomplete jurisdiction possessed by the Domestic Council had the effect not only of legitimating, but also of promoting, institutional conflict over the proposal's development.

Concerning White House decision making, Theodore Sorenson has made the point that: "Procedures do . . . affect decisions. They especially affect which issues reach the top and which options are presented, and this may, in the last analysis, matter more than the final act of decision itself."[32] This is certainly a viewpoint strongly endorsed by Rockefeller, whose experiences in the Ford administration in the two cases discussed here underscore its validity. It is clear from these examples that the structure of the Ford White House promoted piecemeal, ad hoc decision making and fragmented and disputed policy outcomes. Thus the domestic policy options package for the 1976 State of the Union Message became a casualty of a decision that was taken on exclusively budgetary grounds, while the EIA proposal emerged as an administration initiative fatally delayed and compromised by internal conflict.

Rockefeller's concern with the organizational structure of the White House surfaced again in a private meeting with the president in the spring of

1976—a meeting held in the lame-duck period of his vice presidency following his withdrawal as a possible running mate in November, 1975. Rockefeller was worried about a situation in which he perceived "the cabinet . . . becoming increasingly demoralized, [while] the White House was totally demoralized." Although much of the administration's demoralization was closely connected with the string of Reagan primary victories that commenced with the defeat of the president in North Carolina, the vice president prescribed an organizational remedy which had a highly novel appearance. What Rockefeller proposed was that he should personally assume the role of White House chief of staff, indicating to Ford: "Mr. President, it is to my disinterest personally, but I offer my services to you to take over as chief of staff and organize your White House and organize your cabinet for you."[33]

While this proposal appeared to be novel, in essence it merely repeated Rockefeller's December 16 argument that White House staff responsibilities should become centralized. The aspect of novelty lay in the suggestion that such centralization be focused on the vice president as White House chief of staff. However, for the president this new offer possessed no greater appeal than the vice president's proposals of December 16. Therefore, he declined further discussion of it.[34]

To repeat an earlier observation, it is tempting to accept Rockefeller's argument that Ford would have been better served by a centralized hierarchical system, with the executive office dominated organizationally by the Domestic Council on domestic-policy issues and by the National Security Council on national-security and foreign-policy matters. However, that temptation should be firmly resisted. Explicit in Rockefeller's analysis is an assumption that is by no means immediately apparent: that Rockefeller did indeed know what was in Ford's best interest as president.

Although it may seem rather evident, the question of what kind of White House structure serves best the interests of the incumbent of the oval office is one that turns on the background, experience, and personality of the particular president. To reiterate Neustadt's point here: a president's problem is to make the powers of his office work for *him*. In Ford's case, his assumption of the presidency came as the climax of a political career that had for twenty-five years totally immersed him in legislative politics. Prior to his selection for the vacant vice presidency by Richard Nixon in 1973, Ford's political world had been a Congressional world that emphasized a constant personal interplay involving competition, conflict, bargaining, and patronage. Consequently, on the face of it, what would work for Ford would appear to be a structure that reflected his own particular background and political style.[35]

When the White House organizational structure adopted by Ford is reconsidered in the light of his background as a legislator, it becomes immediately apparent how well that structure was tailored to his own political style. The flaws located by Rockefeller in the competition and conflict generated by the shared domestic-policy jurisdictions of the various units within the executive office of the president become virtues for Ford. The structure retained for the new president the necessary elements of compromise, bargaining, conflict, and competition that are so much the hallmarks of congressional politics.

The consequence of combining this competitive organizaiional structure with the management style attributed to Ford by Hartmann (as discussed earlier) was to produce a decision-making process that placed the president at the vital center. Commenting on this, Donald Rumsfeld observed in 1975 as White House coordinator that:

The Domestic Council, the National Security Council, the Economic Policy Board, and the Energy Resources Council . . . are attempts to take those different domestic or foreign forums, departments, and agencies and their views and bring them in toward the president in a way that is digestible and workable, so that he can make judgments in a timely fashion. . . . [The president provides] the connection between those different spokes as they come in because the decisions don't fit on any one spoke.[36]

In practice, this was precisely how the process of decision making worked as highlighted by the experiences of Rockefeller in developing proposals in the administration. Each of the cases discussed earlier (the domestic policy options package for the 1975 State of the Union Message, the Energy Independence Authority proposal, and the initiative leading to the establishment of the Office of Science and Technology Policy) evidenced the constant need to gain presidential clearance and approval to legitimate developments that were under challenge by competing or conflicting institutional actors.

The demands put upon the president by an organizational structure that promotes institutional competition and conflict clearly are extremely large. In particular, the competitive model of decision making would appear to require that the president:

• Constantly guards his own personal interests;

• Demands and is given complete information by the full range of institutional actors;

• Is able to manage conflict.

In the case of Gerald Ford, it is clear that the president was not always successful in meeting the demands placed upon him. In theory, the White House coordination system operated first by Rumsfeld and later by Richard Cheney was designed to insure that Gerald Ford received all relevant information. However, in practice the system did not have the integrity claimed for it, as was evidenced in the case of the budget ceiling decision made by the president in October, 1975. The meetings between Ford, Lynn, Greenspan, Rumsfeld, and Cheney that produced a presidential announcement on a federal budget ceiling of $395 billion for fiscal year 1977 were arranged to exclude other institutional actors from the opportunity of counseling the president on the wisdom of the proposal. Thus Ford made a critical presidential decision on the basis of limited advice.[37]

A further lesson may be drawn from Ford's budget ceiling decision: it suggests an inability on the president's part to guard adequately his own personal interests. Ford's own fiscal-conservative instincts were aroused in the fall of 1975 by the views of two of his senior economic and budget advisers, who expressed fears about the fiscal integrity of the nation as it faced a record federal deficit in 1976. Therefore, his action reflected a single concern: to reduce the size of that deficit. As noted earlier, the consequences of the decision were wide reaching. Immediately, it negated the domestic policy options package developed by the vice president for the 1976 State of the Union Message. Beyond that, it deprived Ford of a programmatic base for the 1976 presidential election and left him vulnerable to charges that he was a "do-nothing" president who lacked compassion about social needs. But these wider interests of the president were not the considerations of Lynn and Greenspan, who focused exclusively upon the size of the federal deficit.[38] Ford had personal stakes in protecting his own wider interest, but he failed to safeguard these in allowing the concerns of Lynn and Greenspan to prevail.[39]

The third primary area of concern to a president for successful operation of an organizational structure based on competition is the management of the ensuing conflict generated between competitors. However, as described by Robert Hartmann, President Ford's approach to conflict management presented a somewhat baffling appearance. According to Hartmann:

You never get a reaction from President Ford when you're criticizing someone else, except a slight annoyance and wish that you hurry up and get on to another subject. Now that doesn't mean that he isn't taking all this in, and that he may later on do something about it. But he isn't going to give you the satisfaction of telling you that you've prompted him to do that.

He pretends that he doesn't like this bickering. But the fact is that he does try to play off one against the other, which he thinks is administratively sound.[40]

Unfortunately, this present study provides an insufficient number of cases for fully assessing Ford's abilities as a conflict manager; therefore, no general statement here about these abilities is possible. However, the evidence of the relevant major case available for discussion here (the EIA proposal) does evidence a performance that was decidedly mixed. In that case, Ford intervened successfully to bring Zarb and Rockefeller together for the resolution of the outstanding points of disagreement between them.[41] Yet, on the other hand, Ford failed disastrously to generate general acceptance among his senior aides of his decision to designate the EIA proposal as an administration initiative. Even as Ford flew to San Francisco, to the Convention of the AFL-CIO Building and Construction Trade's Department on September 22 to unveil publicly the EIA proposal, opponents of the EIA attempted to get the president to reverse his decision. As Hartmann recalled Ford's reaction:

He was annoyed. They [Alan Greenspan and Roderick Hills] tried to kill [the EIA] out of the speech that we were going to make in San Francisco. They rode all the way till the 'plane was on the landing field trying to cut it out. Finally, he just put his foot down and said: "No. It is going to stay."[42]

In fact, although Ford announced the EIA initiative in his San Francisco speech, Hills and Greenspan prevailed in preventing the issuance of a fact sheet to the press. Moreover, they succeeded in having a number of issues reopened, which were promptly dealt with by Frank Zarb in a presidential options memorandum on September 24. But it was Zarb, and not the president, who took the necessary action to get final resolution of reopened issues. Zarb's memorandum of September 24 setting out the various options on the outstanding issues (with the individual recommendations of senior staff members indicated for each option) gave the president a decision-making vehicle for final resolution of these issues.

Accordingly, although the competitive organizational framework President Ford adopted for structuring his White House was well suited to his background and political style, his performance in the "vital center" of events appears to have been distinctly uneven. While his ability to operate that structure may present a questionable appearance, the structure was nonetheless quintessentially Gerald R. Ford. In contrast, the alternative framework offered by Rockefeller in his memorandum of December 16 proposed a structure that was decidedly alien to Ford. Besides, with its emphasis on a powerful Domestic Council dominating all of the domestic-policy units in the executive office, that structure bore too strong a resemblance to the White House of Richard M. Nixon to make it an acceptable approach to Nixon's successor.[43]

A DUAL ROLE: VICE PRESIDENT OF THE UNITED STATES AND STAFF ASSISTANT TO THE PRESIDENT

There was in the vice presidency of Rockefeller a tension created by roles that pulled him in different directions: on the one hand, he wanted to develop his portfolio with the Domestic Council vice chairmanship; on the other hand, he was determined to function as a generalist undertaking as vice president a variety of tasks as a "minister without portfolio."[44] But it was a creative tension wrought by a dynamic political actor who was utterly determined to play a major role in the Ford administration.

The ambiguity inherent in Rockefeller's situation in the Ford White House surfaced early in his vice presidency over the question of whether he should participate, as did the senior White House staff, in the process of reviewing decision papers and submitting personal recommendations for the president's considerations. As James Cannon has described the problem:

It was a very awkward situation. We had to settle this early, on whether he should comment on papers that went to the president on policy issues. Here he is, he wants to have this great influence. But the process was that you put [your views] all down on a piece of paper and you sent it to the president with everybody's views. And I wanted him, since the other views were seen by these people on my staff, I wanted him to express his point of view on paper to get it to the president. And nobody else would see it, I could have arranged that. [But] he didn't want to do it, he dismissed that idea.[45]

The point brought out by this decision is an important one. The gulf between the positions of Vice President of the United States and staff assistant to the president is really very wide. The essence of the model staff assistant is (according to Brownlow) "his passion for anonymity." Moreover, in the highly differentiated modern presidency, the role of the staff assistant has become increasingly narrowed into highly specialized fields of activity. In this respect, the Ford White House followed modern practice and featured a staff of specialists rather than generalists. The vice president, on the other hand, has had a role in the modern presidency that has encompassed a broad spectrum of activities including such disparate areas as public ceremonial and party activities. The essence of the position is its public face: a recognition of the fact that the vice president is a public official in a constitutional office.

While it may never have presented itself in any clear-cut fashion, Rockefeller's desire to serve as a presidential staff assistant to Ford raised the very interesting question of whether he was prepared to accept the restrictions that such a role implied. The answer was, of course, that he was not. But such an answer did not imply that he was not serious about his desire to play such a role: in his case, his willingness was impeded by the limits of his personal constitution. As Cannon has emphasized:

Rockefeller [was] incapable at his level of experience of being a staff assistant to anybody. He was an executive. He was a decision maker. For fifteen years he had been a governor, he had been the chief executive. You can't put that genie back in the bottle, where you have to be when you're the staff assistant.[46]

Cannon's assessment received wide support from most of Ford's senior White House staff members. Philip Buchen, as noted earlier, was outspoken in his view that Rockefeller was incapable of functioning merely as a staff assistant. James Lynn's opinion was that "Rockefeller is first among equals and then some. . . . On substantive issues he was like E. F. Hutton: 'When he speaks, everyone listens.' "[47] William Seidman conceded that "the vice president really tried to act like a staff man," and added "but he was different because he was Nelson Rockefeller."[48] In a similar vein, Richard Cheney noted: "Rockefeller portrayed himself publicly as a staffer, but acted differently in the administration and was perceived differently. When you add in *who* Nelson Rockefeller was, it was impossible to have him treated like a staff person."[49]

Nelson Rockefeller's inability to limit himself to the restricted sphere of a White House staff assistant guaranteed that he would play a wider, more encompassing role in the administration than would otherwise have been the case. The duality of Rockefeller's positions as a presidential staff assistant with a domestic-policy role and as vice president with a catholic political role enabled him to transcend the limitations normally associated with each individual position.

As a White House staff assistant, Rockefeller's policy role was widened considerably by the fact that he served in two distinctive capacities: as a presidential assistant with a specific jurisdictional brief as vice chairman of the Domestic Council; and as a roving "staff assistant to the president" as vice president.[50] The Domestic Council brief provided a craft in which he could push out into the turbulent mainstream of administration policy making. Consequently, unlike so many of his unfortunate predecessors in the vice presidency, he was not left stranded in political backwaters. At the same time, his use of the vice presidential office for a roving "staff assistant's" role enabled him to maintain control of policy development initiated under his Domestic Council brief that otherwise might have been lost by adherence to the narrower confines of the council within the Ford administration.[51]

As vice president, Rockefeller possessed significant advantages not enjoyed by other senior White House assistants—advantages that enabled him to push his policy proposals through several stages of development. Not only was he able, as a White House staff assistant, to formulate proposals and develop these within the administration to the point of presidential adoption of them as administration initiatives, but, as vice president, he was also able to combine his support for and advocacy of these beyond the administration into the legislative arena and into lobbying efforts with business, labor, and other groups to mobilize public support for them. Rockefeller's adroit use of these advantages is best exemplified in his success with the proposal to create an Office of Science and Technology Policy within the executive office of the president and with the initiative to create an Energy Independence Authority. Both endeavors testify eloquently to the vice president's ability to play private and public roles on policy proposals at all of the respective stages of their development.

While the duality of his situation afforded distinct benefits for Rockefeller concerning his participation in the policy work and politics of the administration, at the same time some significant costs were incurred by him. For one thing, the range and number of activities undertaken severely strained Rockefeller's ability to give adequate time and attention to each. In the first six months of his vice presidency, for example, according to his legal counsel, Peter Wallison, the Commission on CIA Domestic Activities occupied about 50 percent of his time.[52] These six months were extremely active months for Rockefeller, whose endeavors also included developing the proposal for a White House science advisory unit, establishing the nature of his Domestic Council responsibilities, developing domestic-policy options for the 1976 State of the Union Message, developing the proposal to create a federal energy and resources policy corporation, and participation as a member of the Murphy Commission. Even though Rockefeller was able to attract good staff people to assist him on this large range of activities, the fact is that he was compelled to extend himself extremely broadly.[53]

However, more significant were the conflict and controversy generated by Rockefeller's efforts to play a major role in the Ford White House. The plain fact is that Rockefeller was viewed as a threat by most of the senior staff in the White House. For some, the vice president posed a distinct threat to established positions. It is clear, for example, that the jurisdictions of the EPB, the ERC, the OMB, the CEA, and the treasury department were all challenged by Rockefeller's original ERFCO proposal. And, as a political actor undertaking major development of domestic program policy options, he presented a challenge to the tight budgetary positions of the OMB, the CEA, and the treasury department. With respect to the full range of domestic-policy components of the Ford administration, Rockefeller's policy development activism put him in a challenging and competing posture at the outset.

A major institutional conflict, which developed rather rapidly into a personal conflict, involved Rockefeller in an ongoing dispute with White House coordinator Donald Rumsfeld. The institutional aspect of the Rockefeller-Rumsfeld dispute concerned Rumsfeld's White House coordination system, which had been designed for the purpose of insuring that the president was provided with complete information and a range of views and options in all presidential decision papers.

Regarding the vice president's position vis-à-vis the White House coordination system, Rumsfeld adopted an assertive stance at the outset, making it clear that he would resist efforts by Rockefeller to bypass the system. Therefore, his opposition to Rockefeller's intention personally to operate the Domestic Council as a vehicle for coordinating domestic-policy matters was total and unyielding. Significantly, the first submission of a recommendation from Rockefeller to the president was seized upon by Rumsfeld as a test case to assert the applicability of the coordination system to the vice president. However, this test case proved to be disastrous for Rumsfeld, since it involved the recommendation on the creation of a White House science advisory unit which had been requested by Ford as a vice presidential recommendation from Rockefeller. Rumsfeld's assertion that the president did not want "an advocacy paper" was at odds with the fact of Ford's original request.

Rockefeller's early entanglements with Rumsfeld set the basic pattern for the remainder of their relationship in the course of the administration.[54] The treatment Rumsfeld had accorded his science advisory unit recommendations led Rockefeller to employ his regular weekly meetings with the president for the purpose of submitting proposals and recommendations directly to Ford, thus insuring that Rumsfeld would be bypassed. In a wider context, the vice president regarded Rumsfeld with total suspicion and in fact believed that Rumsfeld was deliberately attempting to undercut him. Sustaining this belief were some persuasive examples that ranged from the trivial to matters of substance. On the trivial side, Rockefeller has cited the opposition Rumsfeld made to an effort to change the Vice Presidential Seal. As Rockefeller recalled the situation:

The only favor I asked President Ford was to sign an executive order restoring the Vice Presidential Seal to the way it had been when it was under Roosevelt, and even on that Rumsfeld tried to stop that.

He tried to stop it by saying that the cost would be prohibitive to change all the seals. So I said, "That is fine, if you feel that way, which is perfectly absurd. All it is is on matches and on little trinkets." I said, "I just won't order any more. We will just use the old ones." And I said, "All I want is a flag and I will pay the cost of the flag."[55]

Ford supported Rockefeller and signed executive order 11884 on October 7, 1975, changing the Vice Presidential Seal.

More seriously, Ford's decision to hold his 1976 federal budget to a ceiling of $395 billion provides a substantive example of Rumsfeld's less than neutral role behind the scenes. As previously noted, this decision was taken by the president in an exclusive series of meetings with Greenspan, Lynn, Rumsfeld, and Cheney. According to William Seidman, the initiative for the meeting was "mutually a Rumsfeld-Greenspan initiative." And when the decision was presented at an EPB meeting, Seidman further recalled that it was "mainly argued by Rumsfeld" as a "great political boon" with a balance of tax cuts and spending cuts.[56]

Since the direct effect of the decision was the negation of Rockefeller's domestic program policy options package, Rumsfeld's role takes on a special significance. Moreover, the speech delivered by the president on October 6, 1975, announcing the budget ceiling, was written by David Gergen, a Rumsfeld choice later brought in as a White House speechwriter by Richard

Cheney in early December, 1975. Gergen's speech for Ford contained the following lines: "Sometimes when fancy new spending programs reach this desk, promising something for almost nothing and carrying appealing labels, I wonder who the supporters think they are kidding."[57] Since Rockefeller was the only administration figure engaged in developing major new program proposals, these lines clearly could be seen as having a special significance for him.

Finally, it should be noted here that Rumsfeld played a significant role in Rockefeller's withdrawal from consideration for the 1976 Republican vice presidential nomination.[58] While the full scope and detail of the Rockefeller-Rumsfeld relationship is incomplete, there is enough on the record to indicate its bitter acrimony. While their struggle began as a prima facie institutional clash, it developed more antagonistically into a highly charged, personal vendetta.[59]

Besides the institutional conflicts generated by Rockefeller's policy activism, there were ideological conflicts that flowed from the vice president's position as the liberal-in-residence in a basically conservative administration. Much of the controversy and bitter opposition attached to his EIA proposal, at all stages of its development, sprang from ideological passion about the role of government in the private sector. Both Alan Greenspan and Treasury Secretary Simon raised essentially conservative concerns about the expansion of the government role in the marketplace inherent in the EIA proposal.[60]

In a wider context, Rockefeller's liberalism became a political issue of some consequence in the spring and early summer of 1975. As the likelihood developed of a conservative challenge to President Ford from former California Governor Ronald Reagan for the 1976 Republican nomination, so too did the view develop of Rockefeller as an ideological liability for the president. Despite Ford's impressive conservative credentials, it was argued by some of the president's supporters that Rockefeller's presence as a potential 1976 running mate damaged Ford's prospects of beating out the Reagan challenge.[61] Ultimately, the problem of Rockefeller's "liability" status was resolved by his withdrawal on November 3 as an available candidate for the Republican vice presidential nomination.

In short, there were for Rockefeller both advantages and disadvantages to be gleaned from the dual pursuit of the distinctly different roles of staff assistant to the president, with a specific domestic-policy portfolio, and of vice president, as a generalist functioning as a "minister without portfolio." Combining both roles had the effect of enlarging his contribution to the policy and political goals of the administration, and this made possible his personal supervision of policy proposals from the formulative to the legislative stages of their development. However, the costs incurred were several and included conflicting and competing demands on Rockefeller's time and energies, and resistance to vice presidential proposals from individual and institutional actors who felt threatened by Rockefeller's ambitious pursuits.

THE VICE PRESIDENT AND THE PRESIDENT:
AN UNCERTAIN RELATIONSHIP

As previously discussed, the circumstances of Nelson Rockefeller's entry as vice president into the Ford administration in December, 1974, were highly inauspicious. For one thing, the position of Gerald Ford had changed considerably from the first few days of his presidency in mid-August when he and Rockefeller had discussed the vice presidential nomination. Since that time, Ford had begun to consolidate his position in the White House with the installation of his own presidential appointees and a reorganization of the White House organizational structure.

The effect of these changes on the vice presidential role in domestic policy as outlined by the president in August was significant and clearly demanded some redefinition. However, no such redefinition by the president was forthcoming, and the vice president's first six weeks in the administration were highlighted by acrimonious disputation with senior presidential advisers over the precise dimensions of his domestic-policy role with the Domestic Council. Significantly, throughout the dispute, Ford took no part. Only when Rockefeller threatened withdrawal from any active role with the Domestic Council did the president become involved in support of Rockefeller's compromise proposal that brought in Cannon and Dunham.

That experience taught Rockefeller a vitally important lesson about Ford—he was given to imprecision and could not always be relied upon to support his own previous decisions. Thereafter, in all of his dealings with the president, whenever Rockefeller sought approval of vice presidential actions, proposals, recommendations, or assignments, he always got Ford to sign or initial that approval on documents retained by Rockefeller. In this way, the vice president could protect himself against shifts in presidential positions or challenges to vice presidential actions from senior White House staff members. With signed presidential approval, every assignment undertaken by Rockefeller carried with it documented legitimation. In a White House in which the president was given to shifts in his positions and in which there were challenges to vice presidential actions from senior staff members, written presidential approval of his actions gave Rockefeller an important measure of self-protection.

As a veteran of White House politics in the Roosevelt, Truman, and Eisenhower administrations, Rockefeller understood well the vital importance of securing good lines of communication to the president. Accordingly, he moved to build into his vice presidency a further measure of self-protection by instituting a regular weekly meeting between himself and the president. Although its primary purpose was to insure for him regular access to the president, Rockefeller considered such regular meetings to have significant advantages for Ford—as his recollection of his discussion of the matter with the president makes clear:

Mr. President, I want to have an arrangement with you where we meet once a week alone no matter what else we do, and at those meetings I will tell you how I view the scene. I don't really even want you to answer because I want to be able to say things that maybe you won't want to comment on. And I may be totally wrong. Probably will be on many occasions, but I feel I owe it to you.

And I have been a survivor as a minority party leader for four terms in New York and it wasn't because I was naive. And, therefore, I am always sort of looking under stones and behind my back to see what is going on, and so I want to share that with you.[62]

Ford agreed to the proposal and throughout the course of his administration held regular weekly meetings with Rockefeller. The format of the meetings was left entirely in the vice president's hands: it was Rockefeller's responsibility to prepare the agenda for each meeting. To protect the privacy of these meetings with Ford, Rockefeller devised a system of double agendas: an open agenda that was submitted to Ford through White House channels (i.e., Rumsfeld's White House coordination process), and a private agenda that was hand carried by the vice president to each meeting. Although the private agenda contained items for private and personal discussion with Ford, in fulfillment of Rockefeller's responsibility to guard the president's interests, it was also clearly used by Rockefeller to bypass Rumsfeld's coordination system. It afforded the opportunity of taking up privately and directly with Ford vice presidential proposals and recommendations for which Rockefeller sought presidential clearance.[63] This proved to be of enormous advantage to the vice president in developing several of his proposals and was of critical importance in the formative stages of the domestic policy options review of 1975 and the EIA proposal.

Rockefeller's desire to buttress his position as vice president by various measures of self-protection also extended to an area that had proved to be troublesome for past vice presidents: the freedom to adopt positions not endorsed by the administration.[64] Early in his vice presidency, Rockefeller established an understanding with the president that in cases where he disagreed seriously with an administration position, he would feel free to speak out independently on the issues raised. However, at least until his withdrawal in November, 1975, from consideration for the 1976 vice presidential nomination, Rockefeller invoked his right to independence on only one issue: New York City's need for federal bond guarantees after state and city action to balance the municipal budget. While it became the subject of considerable press attention, the disagreement between the president and vice president on this issue (which both characterized as "minimal") did not achieve the status of a cause celebre. Later, in 1976, during the lame-duck period of his vice presidency, Rockefeller did speak out more widely in advocacy of policy positions not endorsed by the administration, including establishment of a national health insurance program and federal assumption of welfare programs administered by state government.[65]

While Nelson Rockefeller may have chaffed at the indecision and ambivalence of the president in dealing with roles and policy proposals, this apparently did nothing to affect adversely the warm and open relationship he developed with Gerald Ford. Publicly and privately, the two men gave every sign of mutual respect and support. Given this relationship, the forced withdrawal of Rockefeller from consideration as Ford's 1976 running mate presents itself as something of an enigma.

Certainly the basic facts surrounding this enigma are fairly straightforward. Ford's campaign for the 1976 Republican nomination was faced with a strong challenge from Ronald Reagan, a candidate more conservative than himself. Since the Republican Party was largely dominated by conservative elements, the president was required to emphasize his own basic conservatism to maintain his own appeal to these elements within the party. Accordingly, it was argued by some of Ford's intimate advisers that it would be advisable for him to disengage himself from Rockefeller, in his pursuit of the nomination, to avoid alienating conservative delegates who still harbored resentment against Rockefeller for his staunch liberal campaigns against Nixon in 1960 and Goldwater in 1964. Bowing to such political necessity, Ford agreed and announced that he and Rockefeller would separately seek their own delegates for the Kansas City convention in 1976.[66]

However, while the announced disengagement of candidate Ford from possible running-mate Rockefeller was seen as a political necessity and, as such, did not reflect adversely on Rockefeller, the subsequent public statements of Howard (Bo) Callaway, Ford's campaign manager, presented a different picture. Declaring on July 9 that he was "not going to alienate persons who don't want Rockefeller,"[67] Callaway proceeded to label Rockefeller three weeks later as the president's "number-one problem" in winning the Republican nomination. Although Callaway discussed Rockefeller as an ideological liability because of his liberalism, he added insult to injury by observing that Ford might prefer to have a younger running mate.[68]

Despite the fact that Rockefeller was being undercut politically by Callaway's publicly reported comments, Ford did nothing publicly to stop such criticism of his vice president. When asked in a televised interview on August 7 about speculation that Callaway's comments presaged action to "dump" Rockefeller from the ticket for 1976, the president responded: "I have read the various reports, and, frankly, I think it is a tempest in a teapot."[69]

But it was tempest that continued, and, despite his own denials to the contrary, Rockefeller acted much like a candidate for the vice presidential nomination. Following assertions by Callaway that southern opposition to the vice president was harmful to Ford's nomination prospect, Rockefeller gave several speeches in some southern states to rebut the charges that he was devoid of southern support.[70]

The controversy about Rockefeller's place on a Ford ticket was resolved decisively by Rockefeller's withdrawal on November 3. In a letter to the president, Rockefeller declared:

Regarding next year and my own situation, I have made clear to you and to the public that I was not a candidate for the vice presidency, that no one realistically can be such, and that the choice of a vice presidential running mate is, and must be, up to the presidential candidate to recommend to a national party convention.

After much thought, I have decided further that I do not wish my name to enter into your consideration for the upcoming Republican vice presidential nominee. I wish you to know this now for your own planning.[71]

Although Rockefeller's withdrawal clearly was occasioned by the controversy and speculation that his presence as an available running mate damaged Ford's prospects of defeating Reagan for the nomination, the president emphatically denied in a White House press conference that he had urged the withdrawal. He emphasized on the contrary that:

The decision by Vice President Rockefeller was a decision on his own. He made the decision and delivered to me personally the letter that has now been published.

The vice president has done a superb job and will continue to do so in the months ahead. But, under no circumstances was it a request by me. It was a decision by him.[72]

Despite Ford's denials at the time to the contrary, and despite the impression of voluntarism created by the manner of Rockefeller's withdrawal,[73] there is ample reason to believe that Rockefeller was requested to withdraw himself from consideration. Ford himself has undercut severely the notions of voluntarism in the account provided in his autobiography, *A Time to Heal*. According to the former president, he arranged a meeting with Rockefeller on October 28 to discuss the problems of a 1976 running mate. Indicating that "Nelson . . . would do anything I asked him to do," Ford notes that he raised the issue of growing conservative opposition and then said to Rockefeller: "There are serious problems, and, to be brutally frank, some of these difficulties might be eliminated if you were to indicate that you didn't want to be on the ticket in 1976. I'm not *asking* you to do that, I'm just stating the facts." In the face of these "facts," Rockefeller is reported by Ford as responding, "I understand. Well, it's probably better that I withdraw."[74]

Accounts from Ford and Rockefeller associates lend further support to the view that Rockefeller did not exit voluntarily but was "dumped." James Cannon, Rockefeller's long-time associate, has declared:

It is my strongest impression . . . from people who know, that Rockefeller was asked to take himself out of the race. And I believe that Ford was put up to that . . . it came at the same time as the firing of Schlesinger, and Kissinger as national security adviser. I think that whole series was set up by Rumsfeld and sold to Ford over a period of time very carefully by Rumsfeld.[75]

Melvin Laird similarly has declared that Rockefeller was asked to withdraw from consideration, though he offered a different perspective on the reasoning behind the request. According to Laird:

People close to Gerry [Ford] on this thing convinced him that if he would do this [i.e., request Rockefeller's withdrawal], there wouldn't be a challenge from Reagan at the convention. I didn't believe that [about Reagan], [but] I think perhaps that perhaps Barry Goldwater . . . Rummy, Callaway, and some of these people believed that.

There was no problem between Ford and Rockefeller. The only problem came as [the Ford people] got closer to those primaries . . . and closer to the convention, and they panicked.[76]

Rockefeller's view was that the Callaway campaign against him, while not authorized by Ford, nonetheless proceeded because the president "allowed it to happen . . . [and] because he didn't stop it."[77] Discussing this point in an interview given during the final days of his administration, President Ford admitted:

There may be some credence to that. It in no way undercuts my admiration and affection for Nelson Rockefeller. We were in a tight situation. In retrospect, I probably let it go further than I would if I were doing the same thing today. But I never told Bo Callaway to go out and make the statements. I can't believe Don Rumsfeld did either. But the statements were made and the momentum kind of let things get out of hand.[78]

It is a first lesson of the Constitution and the American political experience that the vice president is dependent on the president for his place in the executive branch of government. That lesson is amply demonstrated in the vice presidency of Nelson Rockefeller. The problems and vicissitudes he encountered in his efforts to play an active role as a policy maker in the Ford administration sprang in large measure from the ambivalence, indecision, and imprecision that characterized Ford's leadership style. Given the nature of his experiences in the Ford White House, it was perhaps altogether appropriate that the vice presidency of Rockefeller should ultimately be ended by the benign neglect of the president.

· 7 · THE ROCKEFELLER VICE PRESIDENCY: REFLECTIONS AND CONSIDERATIONS FOR THE FUTURE

As considered by this study, the vice presidency of Nelson Rockefeller presents a serious challenge to the view that vice presidents cannot successfully become substantively involved in the policy processes of the modern presidency. Despite the brevity of his incumbency (a mere twenty-five months),[1] Vice President Rockefeller was responsible for initiating and developing program policy proposals of far-reaching consequence for the administration and the nation. His achievement was impressive by most political standards and included development of the following proposals: the creation of a White House science advisory unit (which was accomplished by enactment of an administration-backed bill); the domestic program policy options for the 1976 State of the Union Message (these became a casualty of the president's 1976 federal budget ceiling decision); and the creation of a federal energy development finance corporation (which was adopted as the administration's Energy Independence Authority proposal, but which languished on Capitol Hill for lack of support in 1976). While his policy endeavors were frequently the subject of controversy and conflict within the administration, such controversy and conflict provided prima facie evidence that these endeavors were regarded seriously. Moreover, the energy thus generated by the vice president's proposals gave to the Ford White House a dynamism and sense of activity it otherwise might well have lacked.

There were, of course, some special if not unique aspects of Rockefeller's vice presidency that cast doubts on its usefulness as "the final test" sought by Arthur M. Schlesinger, Jr. However, it is reasonably clear that Rockefeller's experience did (to use Schlesinger's words) "demonstrate that the vice presidency can be more than a nonjob."[2] From the Rockefeller incumbency a number of considerations emerge to suggest that the vice presidential office has a meaningful future ahead.

THE ROCKEFELLER VICE PRESIDENCY:
SOME REFLECTIONS

At the outset, the most significant feature about Rockefeller's acceptance of the vice presidential nomination was the fact that he neither sought it nor especially wanted it. When Ford prevailed upon him to accept an office he had twice before rejected, Rockefeller did so under unique personal circumstances. In becoming vice president, he had essentially nothing to gain; his presidential ambitions had been all but extinguished when Ford's accession to the presidency in 1973 gave the Republican Party an incumbent to nominate in 1976.[3] By the same token, having little or nothing to gain he also had little to lose by his acceptance. Having no discernible political ambitions to further beyond the vice presidency, he risked virtually nothing by serving in an office that previous incumbents had bitterly scorned after leaving it. As Rockefeller has described his situation:

I went into this thing totally psychologically prepared having known all the vice presidents since Wallace, having turned it down twice, not wanting the job but feeling that this was a moment in national history, a constitutional crisis, a crisis of confidence in the executive branch. . . . If I could help President Ford in any way [to] reestablish confidence and respect and decency in the White House, I would do it.[4]

This is not to suggest that, as vice president, Rockefeller was not a highly ambitious political actor within the Ford administration. Indeed, to the contrary, his actions in office evidence a total commitment to success in all of the endeavors he initiated or was associated with. Rather, it is argued here that his vice presidential endeavors were unencumbered by the normally present, cautionary considerations of a political future. Rockefeller's ambitions were altogether focused on the political present that constituted his vice presidency.[5]

In addition to the realization that he had little to lose in vigorously pursuing vice presidential endeavors, Rockefeller enjoyed the advantage of knowing that his services were *needed* by the president. His nomination had been completely unconnected with the more usual considerations of a pressing political campaign, but rather was concerned with the domestic-policy needs of the administration.

The realization that his services were needed in the administration, combined with an awareness that his situation was virtually risk-free, gave a hard edge to his efforts to secure personal leadership of the Domestic Council. Thus, when his initial proposal to implement personal direction of the council's activities encountered serious opposition from senior members of the White House staff, he displayed little willingness to yield. His compromise plan, which was ostensibly designed to meet opponents' objections to his personal assumption of council leadership, relinquished such leadership only to the point of vesting it in council staff directors to be nominated by him. When this plan was also opposed, he took the matter immediately and directly to the president and in effect forced Ford to make a choice between support of the vice president or the senior White House staff. This choice was given a harder edge by Rockefeller's warning to the president that he would withdraw from *any* Domestic Council role unless his plan obtained presidential approval.[6]

The vice president's demanding stance on the issue of Domestic Council leadership had an importance that transcended the immediate issue in question. By acting with such firm resolve and forcing the president to such an extreme choice, Rockefeller served notice on Ford and the senior members of his White House staff that he meant to be taken seriously as a participant in White House politics. His action had the effect of shattering the preconceptions among the president's staff that his vice presidency would not be any different from that of previous vice presidents. For his subsequent policy initiatives and proposals, success in winning recognition as a serious actor on the White House stage was a vital accomplishment since it insured that these in turn would also receive serious attention.

The controversy and dispute over the nature of his Domestic Council role evidenced further that Rockefeller appreciated the importance of three interrelated aspects of the vice president's position: first, that the institutional base provided by the office of the vice president is, by itself, a poor vehicle for vice presidential policy making; second, that the vice president is highly dependent on the president for his role in the administration; and, third, that the vice president must actively take steps to safeguard his own position.

In the highly differentiated policy structure of the Ford White House, it was immediately apparent from the organization chart issued by the White House on December 18, 1974, that the office of the vice president had been assigned no policy functions. Consequently, as Rockefeller entered the administration it was vital that he obtain an institutional base that could support the major domestic policy role that he envisaged. The matter was resolved at the outset by the president's designation of the Domestic Council as an area of the vice president's responsibility—a designation that mooted the question of the adequacy of the vice presidential office to function as a policy vehicle. However, the serious opposition to the vice president's leadership of the council raised for Rockefeller the specter of exclusive reliance on the vice presidential office as an institutional base for policy endeavors within the administration. Accordingly, it is likely that at least a portion of his resolve not to relinquish control over the Domestic Council's activities sprang from concern about the adequacy of his vice presidential office.[7]

On the matter of the vice president's dependency upon the president for his role in the administration, Rockefeller's handling of the Domestic Council leadership dispute evidences his awareness of the realities of his situation. However, his efforts to secure decisive action from the president subsequently were not always so successful: Ford's imprecision and indecision proved to be extremely troublesome for Rockefeller. But the fact that these were troublesome aspects of the president's leadership style indicates that the president's leadership *mattered* to the vice president. Drawing on his own past White House background, and his early experiences with Ford's style, Rockefeller insured that all of his initiatives and proposals obtained the president's written clearance at their various stages of development.

The precaution of securing such written presidential approval of vice presidential endeavors was also a device to protect Rockefeller's position from possible attack within the administration. As a vice president committed to an active and energetic policy role, Rockefeller would be drawn inevitably into the conflicts and disputes of White House politics. In his case, that inevitability was confirmed quickly: the dispute over his leadership of the Domestic Council provided an object lesson in the vulnerability of the vice president to White House staff sniping. Accordingly, the device of legitimating all of his policy endeavors with the president's imprimatur provided a necessary measure of self-protection.

As an active participant in the policy work of the administration Rockefeller also displayed an impressive awareness of the traditional problem afflicting the vice president—that he is given too little to do. Instead of waiting for assignments to come to him, Rockefeller actively initiated several of his own. Thus the proposal to establish a federal energy development resources corporation and the review to develop domestic program policy options for the 1976 State of the Union Message were vice presidential activities he commenced on his own initiative. This sense of initiative extended itself additionally to assignments that had been given to him, with the effect of extending these far beyond the initial scope of the assigned tasks (as in the case of his recommendations on a White House science advisory unit). Therefore, by initiating policy endeavors of his own Rockefeller was able to avoid the paralysis of dependency traditionally associated with the vice presidential office.

The need for vice presidential initiatives was closely related to a further demand Rockefeller made of his vice presidency within the Ford administration—that he establish his own area of policy jurisdiction. Since his perception of the domestic-policy role that Ford had briefly outlined in August, 1974, was one that indicated a position of preeminence over the various domestic-policy actors within the White House organizational structure, it insured for him a place at the center of conflict and controversy. His sense of jurisdictional preeminence can best be observed in his proposal for the creation of a federal energy development finance corporation. In addition to the jurisdictional area of the Domestic Council, under whose auspices it was developed, the proposal embraced the jurisdictions of other executive office units, namely, the Energy Resources Council, the Economic Policy Board, the Office of Management and Budget, and the Council of Economic Advisers. The inevitable result was controversy and conflict, but from Rockefeller's standpoint such a result provided evidence that his proposal (and therefore his policy role in the administration) was held in serious regard. Moreover, it attested to his central place in the policy work of the Ford administration.

CONSIDERATIONS FOR THE FUTURE

Although it is evident that Rockefeller succeeded in fashioning a substantive policy role as vice president in the Ford administration, less evident is the extent to which his experience demands a reassessment of the vice presidency. It can be argued that much of Rockefeller's success was situational, the product of a unique set of circumstances that saw an appointed vice president succeed to the presidency and in turn appoint a successor.[8] As an "accidental" president, Ford lacked the qualities normally demanded of elected presidents, and thus needed to "compensate" for his deficiencies in the selection of a vice president and cabinet appointees. Therefore, the conditions for the success of Nelson Rockefeller's policy-making role were virtually ideal but unlikely to be repeated.

While there is much persuasive power in what may be termed "the situational argument," there are some useful insights to be drawn from the Rockefeller experience that offer elements for the consideration of future presidents and vice presidents. Chief among these is the question of what constitutes a valid vice presidential role. Here the needs of the president ought to be of paramount importance and employed in fashioning the vice presidential role within a particular administration. Second, and related to this point, is the necessity of communicating the precise nature of the vice presidential role in unambiguous terms to all administration personnel. This is a vital preliminary to the process of implementing the vice president's role. Third, the relationship between the president and the vice president deserves fuller attention, given the nature of the vice president's dependency on presidential support for his ongoing role in the administration. Fourth, consideration ought to be given to the extent to which the vice presidential office serves as an adequate vehicle for the vice president's administration role. Finally, the nature of the problems that tend to alienate vice presidents from senior presidential staff assistants deserves further attention.

While the question of what constitutes a valid vice presidential role is complex and necessarily transcends the limits of this present study, the major consideration must concern the personal needs of the president. In the absence of any statutory or constitutionally mandated specification of the vice president's role within the executive branch, presidents remain free to utilize their vice presidents as they choose. In Ford's case, he clearly sought to employ Rockefeller's experience and expertise as a policy-making executive to take charge of domestic policy within the new administration. But, while Rockefeller was given a clear statement of President Ford's intentions in their telephone discussion of August 17, the problem was that the president did not communicate these intentions regarding Rockefeller's vice presidential role to anyone else in the administration. Moreover, the White House organizational structure adopted by the president in December, 1974, was wholly at odds with the role he had outlined in August for the vice president.

Consequently, the most difficult problem encountered by Rockefeller concerned the nature of his vice presidential role. While Rockefeller supposed that he would enjoy unchallenged preeminence in domestic-policy matters, the reorganization of the Ford White House was devised, in contrary fashion, on the basis of lateral equality between competing domestic-policy units. The outcome was that Rockefeller's efforts to claim his expected preeminence in domestic affairs received rude treatment from a White House staff that was unaware of a prior Ford-Rockefeller arrangement.

However, it is instructive to reflect further on Rockefeller's situation and to consider what had happened in the four months Rockefeller was locked out of the administration by his lengthy confirmation hearings. In the first place, Ford had begun to adjust to the unfamiliar decision-making powers of the presidential office and found that he liked them. Therefore, it is possible that the nature of his needs had changed regarding the kind of role Rockefeller could play as vice president. In August, Ford indicated his need as president to have his vice president operate as a domestic policy director who could make some of the decisions for him. By December, Ford had endorsed a domestic-policy structure of relatively equal competing units that looked to him as president for decisions. Therefore, the inescapable conclusion appears to be that Ford's presidential needs changed. Meanwhile, he was committed to Rockefeller as a vice president whose role was now badly in need of revision. Ford failed to provide that revision; he remained silent about Rockefeller's situation and thus allowed an acrimonious dispute to develop between his senior staff and Rockefeller.

Consequently, it is a first lesson of Rockefeller's vice presidency that, before discussion of a vice presidential role, an inventory of presidential needs should be undertaken. It is only when a president has determined what his needs are that he can begin to assess the potential of his vice president in meeting some of these needs.[9] Second, when the vice president's role in the administration is discussed and defined, this should be done in unambiguous terms that set out clearly the ways in which presidential needs will be met by the vice president's endeavors.[10] Third, these terms should be communicated fully to all senior administration personnel by the president personally, to underscore his own commitment to them. Finally, some arrangement should be discussed by president and vice president concerning periodic review and revision of the vice presidential role as the administration matures and presidential needs change over time.[11]

Although the difficulties concerning the nature of his vice presidential role proved to be the most troubling of Rockefeller's problems, the most enigmatic problem he encountered concerned his relationship with Ford. At least initially, Ford and Rockefeller had established a relationship that was open and trusting. How trusting can be gauged from the agreement Rockefeller had with Ford concerning his freedom to disagree publicly with administration policy if there were strong vice presidential disagreement. More generally, Rockefeller built into his relationship with the president a number of impressive safeguards designed to nurture and protect a close and warm relationship between the two. Thus the vice president had a regularly scheduled weekly meeting in private with the president, which was conducted on the basis of an agenda Rockefeller prepared. Moreover, all of the vice president's policy proposals and initiatives were punctiliously cleared by Rockefeller with the president to secure his written approval at their various stages of development. In these respects, Rockefeller created admirable mechanisms that reflected vice presidential dependency on presidential support.

However, the fact is that Rockefeller was in effect "fired" in November, 1975, by the president, through the device of a forced letter of withdrawal from consideration as a candidate for the 1976 Republican vice presidential nomination. The point here is that mechanisms by themselves are not sufficient providers of secure relationships. It is not entirely clear that Rockefeller employed his weekly meetings to their fullest advantage in the Callaway situation. The interviews John Osborne conducted with Rockefeller and Ford point unerringly to a communications gap between the two men concerning Callaway's biting criticisms of the vice president.[12] And the outcome of the continued repetition of these led inevitably to a decision to have Rockefeller withdraw as a 1976 running mate.

Therefore, the "Callaway affair" is a useful case for future presidents and vice presidents to consider, as they discuss their own relationships and order these on the basis of the commendable mechanisms pioneered by Rockefeller.

A major area of concern that is not fully addressed by the Rockefeller experience concerns the extent to which the office of the vice president provides an adequate vehicle for substantive vice presidential involvement in the administration. Because of the estrangement that developed between Rockefeller and his primary domestic-policy vehicle, the Domestic Council, he employed his vice presidential office to develop major policy proposals. The domestic programs policy review of 1975 was conducted from the vice president's office by John Veneman, counselor to the vice president. And, similarly, work on the proposals to create a federal energy development corporation and a White House science advisory unit was also undertaken within the vice presidential office.

However, Rockefeller found it necessary to have these ongoing projects formally designated as review group endeavors under the auspices of the Domestic Council. Here it is difficult to separate the various reasons for such a step. Clearly, there was a desire on Rockefeller's part to obtain legitimacy for the proposals by associating them with the Domestic Council and having them identified as *administration* rather than as *vice presidential* endeavors. Beyond that consideration, it was also possible to tap the resources of the council staff and to obtain additional staff on detail from various agencies for council review group endeavors.[13]

The question of the adequacy of vice presidential office resources clearly relates directly to the nature of the vice presidential role. In Rockefeller's case, the office of vice president evidently was not designed to accommodate the needs of a political actor who saw as his mission to operate as the preeminent domestic policy maker.[14] Again, this is a question that ought to be explored carefully in developing the vice president's role in the administration. No political actor should be deprived of adequate resources necessary to carry out his mission.

Finally, the problem of the hostility and bitterness that develops between vice presidents and presidential staff assistants ought to be more fully explored. Rockefeller's own situation might be accounted for by his delayed entry into the administration and by the sweeping nature of the policy role he was determined to assert for himself, and such an explanation may well be accurate. But the fact of the matter is that Rockefeller's bitter feud with key senior White House staff members (and principally with Donald Rumsfeld) provides no different a picture from those presented by all vice presidencies over the past two decades.[15]

It is difficult to account fully for the gulf that appears constantly to divide vice presidents from presidential assistants. Two unrelated possibilities suggest themselves: first, the relative lateness of a vice president's arrival into the president's inner circle; and, second, the special status of the vice president as a nationally elected figure in the administration. Taking first the relatively late appearance on the scene of the vice president, this reflects the hard realities of the convention nomination system. Whereas the presidential candidate has had his staff working on his nomination campaign for the several months of the primary election season,[16] his consideration of a vice presidential nominee is a decision that is typically made at, or immediately prior to, the nominating convention. Moreover, after the convention, the presidential and vice presidential candidates run separate campaigns to obtain maximum national exposure of their ticket. Thus, the vice president on Election Day presents himself as a stranger to a closely knit presidential staff that has been with the president constantly over the past year.

Second, it is difficult after the election for the staff and the vice president to bridge the gulf that separates them because his status as a nationally elected public official presents an obstruction to such a bridge-building effort. It has become almost de rigueur for presidential staff to regard such vice presidential status as prima facie proof of intent to share or steal presidential limelight. Accordingly, vice presidential activities that even remotely suggest an upstaging of the president are immediately quashed.

Presidential attitudes concerning the vice president are, of course, the principal signals noted by protective staff assistants. But in Ford's case, at least until his benign neglect of Rockefeller during Callaway's attacks upon him, there were no presidential signals that the vice president was persona non grata. In Rockefeller's situation, the problem lay with the view that the staff members themselves held of the vice president. The fact was that the Ford staff saw Rockefeller not as a threat to the president's position, but rather as a threat to their own position. As a vice president who loudly proclaimed his self-styled status as "staff assistant" to the president, Rockefeller was jealously viewed as a "first among equals." Specifically, in the case of Rockefeller's most bitter White House adversary, Donald Rumsfeld, the vice president directly threatened Rumsfeld's carefully constructed power base as White House coordinator.

Proposals to remedy the traditionally disastrous relationship between vice presidents and senior presidential staff assistants do not immediately present themselves. However, the president can do much to influence the attitudes of his staff members by bearing in mind that his own attitudes do constitute signals for the staff.

POSTSCRIPT ON THE MONDALE VICE PRESIDENCY

On November 5, 1976, three days after the presidential election, Vice President Nelson A. Rockefeller submitted a memorandum to the president-elect and the vice president-elect, outlining "matters that relate to an effective working relationship between the president and the vice president." Discussing the vice president's role in the executive branch, Rockefeller counseled:

The single most important responsibility of the vice president is to be prepared to assume on a moment's notice the duties of the presidency.

The single most important element in accomplishing this is a close and intimate working relationship with the president.

Essential to achieving this are:

1. Direct access to the president, at any time, either by phone or in person.
2. Regular weekly meetings alone with the president, from half an hour to an hour each time, with an agenda prepared by the vice president. This is essential because of the press of events.

Regular meetings are also important as they enable the president to use the vice president as a special source of informed, confidential, and independent advice.

To effect a working relationship between the president and vice president, Rockefeller suggested that the president communicate the following instructions to his staff:

That the vice president be notified of and invited to all important meetings, such as: the cabinet; the National Security Council; the Domestic Council; congressional leaders' meetings; presidential-level advisory groups in important policy areas such as energy, economics, and science and technology.

That the vice president's staff representative always attend the daily White House staff meetings.

That the vice president's staff be kept informed of any significant developments.

That all White House staff, all executive office elements and all executive branch departments and agencies give full cooperation to the vice president and his staff.

That the Office of Management and Budget provide adequate funds and office space to finance and house an appropriate vice presidential staff.[17]

Rockefeller's memorandum is of interest here on two grounds: first, it conveys some sense of the problems and inadequacies that he encountered during his two years in the vice presidential office; and, second, because it is useful to consider, however briefly, the extent to which an incoming vice president makes use of the counsel of his predecessor.

At the outset, the most striking feature about Mondale's vice presidency concerned the impressive efforts by Carter and Mondale to provide a good foundation for its future development. These efforts began with the imaginative selection process employed by Jimmy Carter in choosing his running mate in 1976. Carter took the highly novel step of interviewing seven candidates on a publicly announced short list,[18] making his final selection of Mondale on the basis of the selection criteria rank-ordered as follows: competence to succeed to the presidency; personal and political compatibility; and balance of the national ticket. Some indication of Carter's presidential needs were evidenced by the fact that all of the short-listed candidates were members of Congress. He acknowledged in the course of the selection process that: "I feel a need to know more about the Washington political procedure. This is an aspect of my own experience that is missing."[19]

Having selected his running mate, Carter approached the question of his vice president's role with admirable caution, noting on the day of Mondale's selection:

I have to be frank in telling you that the relative duties that would be accepted by me and by Senator Mondale if we are elected will have to be evolved as we get to know one another better and as we discern each other's particular strengths and weaknesses and particular interests in matters of public importance.

I am determined, beyond what has ever been done in this country, to put major responsibilities on the vice president if I'm elected president.

I can't give you now any better analysis than that, but I have discussed it enough with him to know that he and I will be searching for a way to let the vice president be completely involved in our nation's affairs.[20]

Conscious of the dangers inherent in separation during the campaign and the postelection period, Carter and Mondale worked closely together to build their relationship. As a first step Mondale's staff joined Carter's staff in Atlanta, Georgia, for the period of the presidential campaign. After the campaign, Mondale was involved heavily in the preinauguration transition work on issues and personnel selection.[21]

As vice president, Mondale developed an apparently warm and close relationship with the president. Promoting that relationship was the provision of an office for Mondale in the west wing of the White House, which insured for the vice president an important physical presence close to the president. Moreover, applying some of Rockefeller's advice, Carter and Mondale held private weekly meetings (patterned, perhaps, on Rockefeller's recommendation), and the vice president was a regular participant in all important senior White House staff meetings.[22]

Mondale's role from the outset was that of a "minister without portfolio," functioning as a general adviser and troubleshooter for the president. Outlining this role in the early days of the Carter administration, Mondale noted: "I sit in on the cabinet, I sit in on the National Security Council, I sit in on the economic policy group, I can go and work on anything I want to. I've already been given a significant international diplomatic assignment. I've done quite a bit of troubleshooting and it just couldn't be better."[23]

In developing his role as vice president, Mondale self-consciously chose to reject advice received from the late former Vice President and Senator Hubert H. Humphrey, his long-time political mentor, that he involve himself in a specific ongoing area of responsibility. Rather, he proposed in a memorandum to Carter on December 9, 1976, that he serve as a presidential adviser on a wide range of issues: as a "troubleshooter"; as a presidential representative in selected foreign policy matters; and as the political advocate for the administration. Discussing his reasons for avoiding operational responsibility as vice president in the early spring of 1978, Mondale explained that

. . . by staying away from direct line functions, I think you avoid the jealousies and competition that might otherwise develop and affect your role as adviser. Secondly, I don't have the staff to run a major line function. Nor should I. It takes a lot of time away from your advisory role. The way it is now, I don't have to defend a bureaucratic office. And that's good. I can spend my time elsewhere. . . . I can, more or less, be where the president needs me most, with not having the continuing responsibility of a staff nature, which is really a misuse of my time.[24]

In his vice presidential role of "minister without portfolio," Mondale undertook a wide variety of tasks. He made a number of foreign trips, including one to the People's Republic of China in August, 1979, another to Panama for the ceremonies implementing the Panama Canal Treaty in September, 1979, and finally to represent the United States at the funeral of Marshal Tito in Yugoslavia in May, 1980. More substantively, in foreign affairs, the vice president stood in for President Carter to deliver a major speech on disarmament to the General Assembly of the United Nations on May 24, 1978. On the domestic front, Mondale was involved with proposals to provide full federal electoral representation for the District of Columbia, the proposal that led to the creation of the Department of Education in 1979, the expansion of federal child welfare services, and the Carter administration's efforts to provide financial assistance for Chrysler Corporation (in which the vice president's role was to persuade the United Auto Workers Union to moderate wage demands in support of the Carter assistance plan). More broadly, Mondale functioned as an administration spokesman reaching out to groups with whom he had long-established liberal connections, including black groups, labor unions, Jewish groups, Catholics, and Democratic Party regulars.

There are, of course, dangers in the vice presidential role of generalist. In the first place, much of Mondale's time was taken up in meetings with President Carter. In a memorandum to the president on September 6, 1977, which analyzed the vice president's working time in the first six months of the administration, Mondale disclosed that "a considerable portion of each week is spent with the president. The highest percentage to date has been in July, when 48 percent of total hours was spent . . . with the president."[25] The problem with so much time spent with the president is, of course, that there is little left to spend on other kinds of activity. Rockefeller was highly skeptical about Mondale's situation, observing that "[Because] he is pulled into these meetings, while his staff is over at the executive office building, he has no contact with them. . . . This is the way you can isolate a vice president, or you can pull him in so close he can't do anything and suffocate him, either one."[26]

Second, the nature of the activities undertaken by Mondale does not suggest that he was involved as a principal in matters of great import for the administration. Indeed, they appear rather to come within the scope of what David S. Broder has termed "the great tradition of American vice presidents, who are expected to busy themselves with a variety of projects and stay out of the hair of the men who are running the government."[27]

It would be unfair (not to say premature) to draw any definite conclusions about Mondale's vice presidential role at this stage. His area of exclusive competence and ability in the Carter administration was largely focused on his expertise and experience as a Washington "insider." As a consequence, his role as adviser to a president and White House staff who were for the most part "outsiders" was largely hidden from view and cannot, at present, be adequately assessed. However, it should be noted that this particular area of exclusive competence has a limited life: in Washington politics, "outsiders" quickly become "insiders." This point was nicely put by Arthur M. Schlesinger, Jr., who warned early in 1978:

Undoubtedly Carter is making a serious effort to use [Mondale]. But I would guess his influence varies in reverse ratio to the extent that the Carter team doesn't know the Washington terrain. When they feel they have things in hand, Mondale is in retreat; when they get in trouble, he gets a new lease of life. But invariably, they will become Washingtonians and will need him less.[28]

The closing months of the first term of an administration would appear to present an appropriate point for the president and vice president to conduct a review of the vice presidential role. As suggested in the preceding section, such a review ought to focus on the changing nature of the administration and the extent to which presidential needs have altered. In Mondale's case, such a review would have provided timely assessment of the extent to which his area of exclusive competence as an "insider" had shrunk with the accommodation of members of the Carter White House to the political "folk ways" of Washington, D.C.

In any event, the prospects inherent in a second Carter-Mondale term were moved into the realm of academic speculation by Reagan's spectacular victory. However, in the short term, there was clear evidence of development of a new area of exclusive vice presidential competence to meet presidential needs in the 1980 election campaign. As Jimmy Carter became a voluntary "hostage" in the 1980 primary elections while the U.S. Embassy staff were held hostage in Iran, Vice President Mondale operated as the principal Carter surrogate carrying the president's campaign against Democratic rivals through most of the presidential primaries. Mondale's new short-term role on the campaign trail was affirmed by the inclusion of his name in the title of the president's reelection campaign committee—the Carter-Mondale Committee. This unusual campaign committee title provided a useful presage for the vice president's prospects in a second Carter administration, prospects that vanished with the Carter-Mondale defeat.

* * *

That renowned wit among past vice presidents, Thomas B. Marshall, made a statement of profound importance concerning consideration of the vice president's administration role, when he observed of his own experience: "I soon ascertained that I was of no importance to the administration beyond the duty of being loyal to it and ready, at any time, to act as a sort of pinch hitter; that is, when everybody else on the team had failed, I was given a chance."[29] Marshall's point is clear: if the vice president is to be part of the team on the field, he needs to develop himself as a position player with particular contributions to make throughout the game. In other words, unless the vice president possesses, or develops, an exclusive area of ability or competence that is needed by the president in furtherance of the work of the administration, he will remain as Rockefeller once described him—"standby equipment."

Finally, concerning the future of the vice presidency, there is an appropriate symbolic aspect to Rockefeller's determined effort to change the Vice Presidential Seal of the United States. Whereas the old seal depicted the bald eagle with drooping wings, the new Vice Presidential Seal presents the wings of the eagle upraised and ready for flight.

NOTES

INTRODUCTION

1. Quoted in Michael Harwood, *In the Shadow of Presidents* (Philadelphia: J. B. Lippincott Co., 1966), p. 157.

2. Quoted in Institute of Politics, *Report of the Study Group on Vice Presidential Selection*, John F. Kennedy School of Government (Cambridge: Harvard University, 1976), p. 66.

3. The most recent call for abolition of the vice presidency has come from Arthur Schlesinger, Jr. See Schlesinger, "Is the Vice Presidency Necessary," *Atlantic* 233 (May 1974): 37-44, and Schlesinger, "On Presidential Succession," *Political Science Quarterly* 89, no. 3 (Fall 1974): 475-505. See also earlier abolitionist studies by Lucius Wildermung, Jr., "The Vice Presidency," *Political Science Quarterly* 68 (March 1953): 17-41, and Earl D. Ross, "The National Spare Tire," *The North American Review* 239 (March 1935): 275-79.

4. Joseph F. Menez, "Needed: A New Concept of the Vice Presidency," *Social Science* 30 (June 1953): 143-49. Other notable reformist proposals for upgrading the vice presidential office include the following: James M. Burns, "A New Look at the Vice Presidency," *New York Times Magazine*, October 9, 1955; G. Homer Durham, "The Vice Presidency," *Western Political Quarterly* 1 (1948): 311-15, and Clinton Rossiter, "The Reform of the Vice Presidency," *Political Science Quarterly* (September 1948): 383-403.

5. James Bryce, *The American Commonwealth*, 2 vols. (New York: Commonwealth Publishing Co., 1908), 1: 327.

6. Schlesinger, "Is the Vice Presidency Necessary," p. 39. Schlesinger's view that vice presidential candidates seldom make a difference to the outcome of presidential elections is supported by an interesting study which concluded that the home state advantage supplied by such candidates was at best "minimal." See Carl D. Tubbessing, "Vice Presidential Candidates and the Home State Advantage: Or, 'Tom Who?' Was Tom Eagleton in Missouri," *Western Political Quarterly* 26, no. 4 (December 1973): 702-16.

7. However, given the hasty and often ill-considered (from the standpoint of the needs of the future administration) basis upon which selection is made, this is not terribly surprising. The question of vice presidential selection was addressed by the

Harvard University Study Group. See Institute of Politics, *Vice Presidential Selection*. This question is taken up again in Chapter 1.

8. This is, of course, a proposition that underlies many of the reformist school's proposals for upgrading the vice presidency.

9. Although Gerald Ford was himself the first person appointed to the vice presidency under the Twenty-fifth Amendment, it has never seriously been suggested that his selection by Nixon was based on an assessment of his potential to contribute substantively to the administration.

10. Commenting on the "compensatory theory" of cabinet selection, Richard Fenno, Jr., has aptly observed of Warren Harding's case that

> the "best minds" concept required that someone integrate the diverse contributions of the group: firm principles and clear policy direction were required of the president. Warren Harding could furnish neither. The lack of a consistently thought-out program, the dearth of general constructive principles on which to base action, the personal qualities which produced poor appointments—all of these were Harding's own weaknesses. They were fatal, and no cabinet could compensate for them. Under these circumstances, the "best minds" idea was in its consummation a dream-wish, a mythical conception of a superstructure which well-qualified builders might construct on a perilously shaky foundation. A president who aspires to be only the simple sum of his cabinet advisers will be hardly anything at all.

Richard F. Fenno, Jr., *The President's Cabinet* (New York: Vintage Books, 1959), pp. 30-31. Fenno's words have a particular applicability to Gerald Ford, as will be evident from the later chapters of this present study.

11. Interview with Nelson A. Rockefeller, Rockefeller Center, New York, December 21, 1977.

12. Presidential News Conference, August 28, 1974. Quoted in *Congressional Quarterly* 32, no. 35 (August 31, 1974): 2349.

13. U.S. Congress, Senate, Subcommittee on Constitutional Amendments of the Committee on the Judiciary, *Examination of the First Implementation of Section Two of the Twenty-fifth Amendment*, 94th Cong., 1st Sess., February 26, 1975, p. 116.

CHAPTER 1

1. See James Madison, *Notes of Debates in the Federal Convention of 1787*, with an introduction by Adrienne Koch (Athens: Ohio University Press, 1966), p. 569.

2. Ibid., pp. 574-75.

3. Ibid., p. 138.

4. Ibid., p. 576.

5. Ibid., p. 596.

6. Ibid.

7. Ibid.

8. Ibid.

9. Ibid.

10. Ibid., p. 597.

11. *The Federalist Papers*, with an introduction by Clinton Rossiter (New York: New American Library, 1961), p. 415.

12. Quoted in Clinton Rossiter, "The Reform of the Vice Presidency," *Political Science Quarterly* 63 (September 1948): 384.

13. Woodrow Wilson, *Congressional Government*, 13th ed. (Boston: Houghton Mifflin, 1893), pp. 240-41.

14. Quoted in Rossiter, "The Reform of the Vice Presidency," p. 385.

15. John Adams holds the record with twenty-nine tie-breaking votes, while John Calhoun is second with twenty-eight.

16. For an informative discussion of the vice president's role in the Senate, see Irving G. Williams, "Senators, Rules and Vice Presidents," *Thought Patterns* 5 (1957): 21-35.

17. Jefferson asserted that the office of vice president was "constitutionally confined to legislative functions, and that I could not take part whatever in executive consultations, even were it proposed." (Cited in Charles O. Paullin, "The Vice President and the Cabinet," *American Historical Review* 29 (April 1924): 496-500). The view that the office of vice president lay solely within the legislative branch was widely held until the end of the nineteenth century. Even midway through the twentieth century this view continued to have champions: for example, see Marshall E. Dimock, *American Government in Action* (New York: Rhinehart, 1946). Dimock argues, on page 577, "Unless the Constitution is amended, the vice president is disqualified for the post of general manager because he must preside over the Senate." However, no constitutional challenge has seriously been mounted against the modern practice of investing the office of vice president with executive branch duties. Therefore, it must be considered doubtful that any such constitutional barrier exists.

18. Edgar Waugh makes the sensible point that, by itself, the Twelfth Amendment was not to blame, but rather the guilt here properly belonged to the political party practice of nominating one candidate for the presidency and another for the vice presidency. As Waugh aptly observed: "Being a posterior ratification of a fait accompli, the amendment merely added pavement to the road already chartered for presidential decline." See Waugh's excellent discussion in his book, *Second Consul* (New York: Bobbs-Merrill Company, Inc., 1956), pp. 50-58.

19. Of the twenty-two vice presidents who served in the nineteenth century, most held public office prior to election as vice president: nine held office as governor, fourteen served in the U.S. House of Representatives, while eleven served in the U.S. Senate (the totals exceed twenty-two since several vice presidents held two or more of these offices).

20. James Q. Wilson points out that by the time of Grover Cleveland's inauguration in 1881 there were only 95,000 appointed civilian officials in the executive branch. Within forty years, this number grew to nearly half a million and continued to grow, reaching a total in excess of two million at the present time. Wilson goes on to disclose that the growth of the executive branch in the first half of the nineteenth century "was almost entirely the result of the increase in the size of the post office. From 1816 to 1861, federal civilian employment in the executive branch increased nearly eightfold (from 4,834 to 36,672), but 86 percent of this growth was the result of additions to the post office." See Wilson, "The Rise of the Bureaucratic State," *The Public Interest* (Fall 1975), 77-103.

21. James Bryce, *The American Commonwealth*, 2 vols. (New York: Commonwealth Publishing Company, 1908), 1: 326-37.

22. The major pieces of regulatory legislation enacted included:

The Interstate Commerce Act of 1887 (this established the Interstate Commerce Commission)

The Sherman Antitrust Act of 1890

The Pure Food and Drug Act of 1906

The Meat Inspection Act of 1906

The Federal Trade Commission Act of 1914

The Clayton Antitrust Act of 1914

23. Theodore Roosevelt, *An Autobiography* (New York: Macmillan Company, 1921), p. 395.

24. In addition to his vigorous antitrust prosecutions, Taft proposed to the Congress a constitutional amendment to make possible a federal system of income tax, and this subsequently was ratified in 1913 as the Sixteenth Amendment. Moreover, it was Taft's Commission on Economy and Efficiency that, in 1912, proposed establishment of a national budget system. Taft's views on the scope of presidential powers are expressed in his *Our Chief Magistrate and His Powers* (New York: Columbia University Press, 1916).

25. Initially, the executive office of the president comprised three units: the White House Office, the Bureau of the Budget, and the National Resources Planning Board.

26. See the discussion of what Edward S. Corwin has termed the "institutionalized presidency" in *The President: Office and Powers*, 4th rev. ed. (New York: New York University Press, 1957), pp. 299-305.

27. Perhaps because he was overly self-conscious of the groundbreaking nature of the occasion, Marshall read the following statement at the first such cabinet meeting:

In assuming the chair and presiding over what is known as a meeting of the cabinet, I deem it proper to make a brief statement so that my conduct may not be misunderstood nor misinterpreted. I am here and am acting in obedience to a request preferred by the president upon the eve of his departure and also at your request. But I am here informally and personally. I am not undertaking to exercise any official duty or function. I shall preside in an unofficial and informal way over your meetings out of deference to your desires and those of the President. (Quoted in Paullin, "The Vice President and the Cabinet," p. 499.)

28. A brief, but useful, account of Garner's vice presidency is provided in Donald Young, *America Roulette: The History and Dilemma of the Vice Presidency*, rev. ed. (New York: Holt Rhinehart and Winston, 1972), pp. 163-73.

29. The fullest account of Wallace's activities as BEW board chairman is to be found in his diary of the period. See John Morton Blum, ed., *The Price of Vision: Diary of Henry A. Wallace, 1942-1946* (Boston: Houghton Mifflin Company, 1973), pp. 53-229.

30. In his political autobiography, *Six Crises*, Nixon claimed that Eisenhower called him on the phone and "expressed chagrin at the way this exchange had been handled by the press. He pointed out that he was simply being facetious and yet they played it straight and wrote it seriously." However, in Nixon's account of the press' question and answer he omits the last three words of Ike's response, which were, "I don't remember." These would appear to undercut any claim that the basic statement was "facetious." See Richard M. Nixon, *Six Crises* (Garden City: Doubleday & Co.,

1962), p. 339. Nixon himself appeared to acknowledge Eisenhower's point in his own assessment of the vice presidency as a "hollow shell . . . the most ill-conceived, poorly defined position in the American political system." Quoted in Joseph Albright, *What Makes Spiro Run* (New York: Dodd Mead & Co., 1972), p. 246.

31. A useful account of Johnson's vice presidency is given in Rowland Evans and Robert Novak, *Lyndon B. Johnson: The Exercise of Power* (New York: New American Library, 1966), pp. 323-53.

32. Humphrey provided his own account of his vice presidential years in his autobiography, *The Education of a Public Man* (Garden City: Doubleday & Co., 1976), pp. 313-429. The enormous frustrations Humphrey experienced in the vice presidency are captured nicely in the following paragraphs:

> When I was frozen out, the symptoms were everywhere. The staff took their cues from the boss. It meant sitting outside Joe Califano's office, while he, pretentiously, went about his work inside at his own pace. Or Marvin Watson instructed to cancel the use of a boat on the Potomac just before my guests were to arrive.

> Sometimes I wasn't frozen, just forgotten. If I said something of interest in the course of work with the Space Council, the Youth Opportunity Program, in work on oceanography, trade, or travel, the president not only frustrated ordinary human desire for praise or recognition, he openly clamped down. I continued to work and tried to do my best.

33. Accounts of Agnew's vice presidency are found in Albright, *What Makes Spiro Run*, pp. 246-91, and Jim Lucas, *Agnew: Profile in Power* (New York: Scribners, 1970), pp. 100-152. The definitive account of Agnew's fall from power is that of Richard M. Cohen and Jules Witcover, *A Heartbeat Away: The Investigation and Resignation of Vice President Spiro T. Agnew* (New York: Bantam Books, 1974).

34. As vice president, Gerald Ford provided a discussion of the vice presidential office in *Atlantic Monthly* (July 1974): 63-65.

35. The other three vice presidents were Theodore Roosevelt, Calvin Coolidge, and Harry S. Truman.

36. Institute of Politics, *Vice-Presidential Selection*.

37. For a firsthand account of Truman being informed about the development of the atomic bomb, see Harry S. Truman, *Memoirs*, 2 vols. (New York: Doubleday & Co., 1956), 1: 10-11.

38. Theodore Roosevelt, "The Three Vice-Presidential Candidates and What They Represent," *The Review of Reviews* 14 (September 1896): 291.

39. Walter Clark, "The Vice-President: What to Do with Him?" *Green Bag* 8 (October 1896): 427.

40. Albert J. Beveridge, "The Fifth Wheel in Our Government," *The Century Magazine* 79 (December 1909): 213.

41. Franklin D. Roosevelt, "Can the Vice President Be Useful?" *Saturday Evening Post* 193 (October 16, 1920): 8.

42. G. Homer Durham, "The Vice-Presidency," *Western Political Quarterly* 1 (1948): 314.

43. Rossiter, "The Reform of the Vice Presidency," pp. 383-403.

44. Ibid., pp. 397-99.

45. Joseph E. Menez, "Needed: A New Concept of the Vice-Presidency," *Social Science* 30 (June 1955): 148-49.

46. James McGregor Burns, "A New Look at the Vice Presidency," *New York Times Magazine*, October 9, 1955, p. 11.

47. U.S. Congress, Senate, Committee on Government Operations, *Administrative Vice President, Hearings before the Subcommittee on Reorganization*, 84th Cong., 2nd Sess., 1956.

48. Memorandum for the president from Nelson A. Rockefeller, chairman, President's Advisory Committee on Government Organization, dated March 21, 1956.

49. Senate Committee on Government Operations, *Administrative Vice President, Hearings*.

50. Recent examples would include John F. Kennedy, Lyndon B. Johnson, and Richard M. Nixon.

51. See Blum, *Wallace Diary, 1942-1946.*

52. Blum, *Wallace Diary, 1942-1946*, pp. 226-27.

53. For example, see Paul T. David, "The Vice Presidency: Its Institutional Evolution and Contemporary Status," *Journal of Politics* 29 (November 1967): 725. David writes:

> Wallace was dismissed from his chairmanship and the board was reorganized. The experience tended to suggest that any president should avoid putting his vice president into a position directly competitive with an antagonistic and politically powerful member of the cabinet.

54. The case of Garner and Roosevelt is illustrative. Garner's nomination as vice presidential candidate came about as the product of a deal that swung the Texas delegation behind Roosevelt at a moment when the 1932 Democratic Convention appeared to be deadlocked on the presidential nomination. Thus Roosevelt had little or no choice on selection of his running mate. As vice president, Garner proved himself to be surprisingly supportive of Roosevelt's New Deal programs during the president's first term. And, as indicated earlier, Roosevelt employed Garner's legislative skills to assist in the passage of these programs on Capitol Hill. However, in Roosevelt's second term, Garner grew increasingly disaffected with the president's liberalism and reached a point of total estrangement from the administration. He became an embarrassment at cabinet meetings, openly displayed his opposition to Roosevelt's programs on the Hill, and, finally, campaigned actively against Roosevelt's bid for a third term. See the account of Garner's vice presidential nomination in Young, *American Roulette*, pp. 164-67.

55. Institute of Politics, *Vice Presidential Selection*, p. 7.

56. It was Henry Wallace's view that:

> No president should be burdened with a vice president he does not respect and in whose ideas he does not believe.

> It is all-important today that the voters should chastise severely any party which runs for vice president a man who disagrees on matters of policy with the president. My battle cry would be, "No more deals—no more balancing of the ticket." Let's warn both parties that we, the voters, hold them accountable for presenting men who like each other and who believe earnestly in the same policies.

Henry A. Wallace, "How a Vice President Is Picked," *U.S. News and World Report*, April 6, 1956, p. 89.

57. Rossiter, "Reform of the Vice Presidency," p. 400.

CHAPTER 2

1. *Christian Science Monitor*, August 7, 1974, p. 1.
2. *New York Times*, August 8, 1974, p. 1.
3. Ibid., and *Newsweek*, August 19, 1974, p. 32.
4. Interview with Melvin R. Laird, Washington, D.C., February 1, 1978.
5. Ibid.
6. *Milwaukee Journal*, August 13, 1974, as quoted in the *New York Times*, August 14, 1974, p. 16.
7. Laird interview.
8. Ibid.
9. Interview with Hugh Morrow, assistant to Nelson A. Rockefeller, Rockefeller Center, New York, December 21, 1977.
10. Laird interview.
11. Morrow interview.
12. *Newsweek*, August 26, 1974, p. 18.
13. *New York Times*, August 18, 1974, p. 1.
14. The other members of the transition team were Interior Secretary Rogers Morton, who was the liaison with the cabinet; John O. Marsh, Jr. (a Ford staffer and former congressman), who was liaison with the Congress; and former Governor William Scranton of Pennsylvania, who was responsible for recruitment of new personnel. Rumsfeld had the role of coordinator of the entire transition effort, as well as liaison with the White House staff.
15. Cited in Richard Reeves, *A Ford not a Lincoln* (New York: Harcourt Brace Jovanovich, 1975), p. 125.
16. See *Newsweek*, August 19, 1974, p. 19. In fact, Rumsfeld was eventually selected to replace Alexander Haig as White House coordinator.
17. Laird interview.
18. Interview with John O. Marsh, Jr., former counselor to President Ford, Washington, D.C., February 8, 1978.
19. Morrow interview.
20. Ibid.
21. Rockefeller's son, Nelson, Jr., had told Arthur Goldberg that he hoped he would win the 1970 New York gubernatorial campaign so that "Daddy could stay home more." Cited in Alvin Moscow, *The Rockefeller Inheritance* (Garden City: Doubleday & Co., 1977), p. 367.
22. Morrow interview.
23. *Newsweek*, September 2, 1974, p. 16.
24. *New York Times*, August 9, 1974, p. 4.
25. *New York Times*, August 11, 1974, p. 43.
26. *Newsweek*, September 2, 1974, p. 16. Melvin Laird has confirmed that he was the "close associate" quoted in the *Newsweek* account (Laird interview).
27. Morrow interview.

28. John D. Rockefeller Jr.'s credo is set out in full, carved in a granite memorial erected by all of his sons in front of Rockefeller Center, New York City. The ten points of the credo are listed below:

I believe in the supreme worth of the individual and in his right to life, liberty, and happiness.

I believe that every right implies a responsibility; every opportunity, an obligation; every possession, a duty.

I believe that the law was made for man and not man for the law; that government is the servant of the people and not their master.

I believe in the dignity of labor, whether with the head or hand; that the world owes no man a living but that it owes every man the opportunity to make a living.

I believe that thrift is essential to well-ordered living and that economy is a prime requisite of sound financial structure, whether in government, business, or personal affairs.

I believe that truth and justice are fundamental to an enduring social order.

I believe in the sacredness of a promise, that a man's word should be as good as his bond; that character—not wealth or power or position—is of supreme worth.

I believe that the rendering of useful service is the common duty of mankind and that only in the purifying fire of sacrifice is the dross of selfishness consumed and the greatness of the human soul set free.

I believe in an all-wise and all-loving God, named by whatever name, and that the individual's highest fulfillment, greatest happiness, and widest usefulness are to be found in living in harmony with His will.

I believe that love is the greatest thing in the world; that it alone can overcome hate; that right can and will triumph over might.

29. Nelson A. Rockefeller, quoted in Moscow, *The Rockefeller Inheritance*, p. 366.

30. Senator Charles Percy also recognized that the prospects of an openly contested presidential nomination had disappeared: he announced in the week following Nixon's resignation that his campaign was being placed "in deep freeze."

31. This assumption, of course, predated Ronald Reagan's 1980 success in overcoming any "age barrier" to presidential ambitions. However, Reagan's triumph in 1980 came while he was sixty-nine years old and not quite a septuagenarian.

32. U.S. Congress, Senate, Committee on Rules and Administration, *Hearings on the Nomination of Nelson A. Rockefeller of New York to Be Vice President of the United States*, 93rd Cong., 2d Sess., pp. 8-9. (Referred to hereafter as Senate Confirmation Hearings.)

33. Reasons of space do not permit a discussion of Nelson Rockefeller's fascinating childhood. As the son of a millionaire he was raised to understand the value of money—not as an end in itself, but as a means to pursue desired ends. For an interesting account of his childhood, see Moscow, *The Rockefeller Inheritance*, pp. 34-61, 109-22.

34. More accurately, it should be noted that it was Rockefeller who asked Eisenhower for the position.

35. Rockefeller clashed notably with Secretary of State John Foster Dulles. Rockefeller did score a notable victory when he persuaded Eisenhower, over Dulles's objections, to announce an "open skies" proposal at the 1955 Geneva summit conference for exchange of military blueprints with the Soviets, linked to an aerial inspection of missile sites.

36. See "Statement of Nelson A. Rockefeller, Nominee for Vice President of the United States," Senate Confirmation Hearings, p. 67.

37. The full list of the topics covered by the study reports is set out below:

1. "The Mid-Century Challenge to U.S. Foreign Policy"

2. "International Security: The Military Aspect"

3. "Foreign Economic Policy for the Twentieth Century"

4. "The Challenge to America: Its Economic and Social Aspects"

5. "The Pursuit of Excellence: Education and the Future of America"

6. "The Power of the Democratic Idea"

38. John F. Kennedy borrowed freely from the Rockefeller study reports in his 1960 presidential campaign. In particular, he skillfully exploited allegations of a "missile gap" with the Soviets.

39. For a full analysis of the record compiled by Nelson Rockefeller in his fifteen years as governor of New York, see Robert H. Connery and Gerald Benjamin, eds., *Governing New York State: The Rockefeller Years* (New York: Academy of Political Science, 1974). See also the penetrating analysis provided by Connery and Benjamin in their more recent study, *Rockefeller of New York: Executive Power in the State House* (Ithaca, New York: Cornell University Press, 1979).

40. A brief but good account of Rockefeller's 1960 challenge is found in Theodore H. White, *The Making of the President, 1960* (New York: Atheneum, 1961), pp. 72-84, 197-225.

41. For an account of Rockefeller's contest with Goldwater, see Theodore H. White, *The Making of the President, 1964* (New York: Atheneum, 1965), passim.

42. A good discussion of Rockefeller's "stop-go" efforts in 1968 is found in Lewis Chester, Godfrey Hodgson, and Bruce Page, *An American Melodrama: The Presidential Campaign of 1968* (London: Andrew Deutsch, 1969).

43. The panel studies were issued by the Commission on Critical Choices and published as a fourteen-volume work by Lexington Books in 1976 and 1977. The fourteen volumes issued were as follows:

1   *Vital Resources*

2   *The Americans*

3   *How Others See Us*

4   *Power and Security*

5   *Trade, Inflation, and Ethics*

6   *Values of Growth*

7   *Qualities of Life*

8   *Western Europe: The Trials of Partnership*

9   *The Soviet Empire: Expansion and Detente*

10   *The Middle East: Oil, Conflict, and Hope*

11   *Africa: From Mystery to Maze*

44. Nelson A. Rockefeller, Transcript of Press Conference No. 1, Seal Harbor, Maine, August 23, 1974.

45. William V. Shannon, *New York Times*, August 25, 1974, p. E 19.

46. Senate Confirmation Hearings, p. 20.

47. Ibid.

48. *New York Times*, September 25, 1974, p. 1.

49. *New York Times*, September 20, 1974, p. 21.

50. The taxes were due because the IRS had disallowed deductions for investment expenses. As Rockefeller told the committee: "With respect to the recent audit, I am advised by my tax counsel, that is the audit and the taxes, the issues raised involve legal questions on which tax attorneys and the IRS can and do differ." See Senate Confirmation Hearings, 1974, p. 505.

51. Senate Confirmation Hearings, pp. 500, 503.

52. Ibid., p. 472.

53. By granting only loans during the time that Ronan and the other public-service employees were on a public payroll, Rockefeller avoided infractions of the state's antibribery statutes. In fairness to Rockefeller, it should be pointed out that his aim was to secure the employment of highly competent staff who could obtain much better salaries in the private sector. Rockefeller's assistance was a kind of bonus for remaining in the public sector.

54. This was the conclusion the committee came to when it issued its report on the confirmation hearings. See U.S. Congress, Senate, Committee on Rules and Administration, *Report on Hearings on the Nomination of Nelson A. Rockefeller of New York to be Vice President of the United States*, 93d Cong., 2d Sess., 1974, p. 180.

55. Senate Confirmation Hearings, 1974, p. 617.

56. Nelson A. Rockefeller, Address to the U.S. Senate, December 19, 1974.

57. Senate Confirmation Hearings, p. 164.

58. Laird interview.

59. Interview with Nelson A. Rockefeller, Rockefeller Center, New York, December 21, 1977.

60. Marsh interview.

61. Rockefeller interview.

62. In attendance at the December 21 meeting were, on the president's staff, Donald Rumsfeld, White House coordinator; John O. Marsh, Jr., counselor to the president; and Brent Scowcroft, deputy assistant for National Security Affairs. On the vice president's staff were Robert Douglas, an adviser brought in to assist in the vice presidential transition; Ann Whitman, vice presidential chief of staff; and James Cannon, vice presidential adviser (later named executive director of the Domestic Council).

63. In fact, the vice president's membership in the NSC is mandated by statute.

64. Vice presidential membership in the Domestic Council is also mandated by statute.

65. Rockefeller had expressed a special interest in this assignment.

66. Rockefeller was Ford's replacement for Anne Armstrong, who had just resigned her commission membership.

67. For this "rescue mission," Rockefeller brought in General Andrew Goodpaster, who was just retiring from NATO, to work for him as his assistant on the Murphy Commission.

68. Ultimately, however, Rockefeller's efforts in this endeavor (as in other areas) were almost totally frustrated: few of his appointment recommendations received positive action in the Ford White House.

69. It was as executive director of the Domestic Council that John Ehrlichman had become a figure of real power in the Nixon administration. A good discussion of Ehrlichman's rise to power is found in Dan Rather and Paul Gates, *The Palace Guard* (New York: Harper and Row, 1974), passim.

70. Kenneth Cole had replaced Ehrlichman, following Ehrlichman's fall from power in April 1973.

71. President Gerald R. Ford, quoted in U.S. Office of the Federal Register, *Weekly Compilation of Presidential Documents* 10, no. 52 (December 27, 1974): 1599.

CHAPTER 3

1. Memorandum to President Nixon from Roy Ash, dated August 20, 1969, quoted in Larry Berman, "The Office of Management and Budget That Almost Wasn't," *Political Science Quarterly* 92, no. 1 (1977): 298.

2. Message of President Nixon transmitting Reorganization Plan No. 2 of 1970 to the Congress, March 12, 1970. Reprinted in *Congressional Quarterly* 28, no. 11 (March 13, 1970): 825.

3. Ibid.

4. For a detailed discussion of the activities and operations of the Domestic Council staff during Ehrlichman's tenure as executive director, see John H. Kessel, *The Domestic Presidency: Decision-Making in the White House* (North Scituate: Duxbury Press, 1975). A briefer discussion of the council's staff work by a former staff member is provided by Raymond J. Waldman, "The Domestic Council: Innovation in Presidential Government," *Public Administration Review*, 36 (May/ June 1976): 260-68. For a contemporaneous report of the Domestic Council staff's role within the Nixon administration, see Dom Bonafede, "White House Report/Ehrlichman Acts as Policy Broker in Nixon's Formalized Domestic Council," *National Journal* 3, no. 24 (June 12, 1971): 1235-44.

5. The subject matter areas were constantly changed and regrouped. For example, Kessel, *The Domestic Presidency*, outlined the following seven areas: environment, energy, agriculture; labor, welfare; civil rights, housing; tax policy; long-range plans, budget, revenue sharing; crime, transportation, government organization; and health.

6. John Ehrlichman, "How It All Began," *National Journal* 7, no. 50 (December 13, 1975): 1690.

7. An interesting interpretation of Nixon's creation of "super-secretaries" and accompanying reorganization maneuvers is provided in Richard P. Nathan, *The Plot That Failed: Nixon and the Administrative Presidency* (New York: John Wiley & Sons, 1975).

8. For a wider discussion of these changes, see Dom Bonafede, "White House Report/End of Counselor System Enlarges Policy-Forming Role of the Cabinet," *National Journal* 5, no. 20 (May 19, 1973): 726-29.

9. The White House changes effected in the wake of the Haldeman and Ehrlichman resignations were chronicled in detail by Dom Bonafede, "White House Report/Haldeman, Ehrlichman Departures to Bring Major Changes in Administration," *National Journal* 5, no. 18 (May 5, 1973) 633-36; "White House Report/Staff, Style Changes Slow in Coming Despite President's Post-Watergate Reforms," *National Journal* 5, no. 29 (July 21, 1973): 1057-62; and "White House Report/Executive Office in Transitional Stage, According to President's Senior Aides," *National Journal* 5, no. 34 (August 25, 1973): 1239-44.

10. Kenneth Cole, Jr., quoted in Bonafede, "White House Report/Haldeman, Ehrlichman Departures," p. 635.

11. Kenneth Cole, Jr., undated memorandum for the president.

12. Gerald R. Ford, as quoted by Nelson A. Rockefeller. Interview with Nelson A. Rockefeller, Rockefeller Center, New York, December 21, 1977.

13. Rockefeller interview.

14. Peter J. Wallison, memorandum to Nelson A. Rockefeller, dated December 9, 1974.

15. U.S. Office of the Federal Register, *United States Government Manual*, rev. ed., May 1, 1975, p. 644.

16. Ibid., p. 94.

17. Rockefeller interview.

18. Ibid.

19. Interview with Philip W. Buchen, Washington, D.C., February 8, 1977.

20. Ibid.

21. Rockefeller interview.

22. Ibid.

23. According to Richard Cheney, deputy to Rumsfeld and his successor as White House coordinator, Rumsfeld's perception of the role of the Domestic Council staff was that the work was almost exclusively comprised of routinized and day-to-day operations dealing with agency disputes, bill analysis, veto recommendations, etc. Therefore, it followed that Ford needed someone who had previous White House experience for the position of executive director. Interview with Richard B. Cheney, Washington, D.C., July 27, 1977.

24. Buchen interview.

25. John Osborne described Areeda as "one of the very few people at the Ford White House who had some claim to distinction before coming here." See John Osborne, "White House Watch: Ford's Image Machine," *New Republic*, March 1, 1975.

26. Buchen interview.

27. Rockefeller interview.

28. Ibid.

29. Memorandum of meeting, dated February 7, 1975, prepared by L. William Seidman, EPB executive director.

30. Memorandum to members of the Domestic Council from the president, dated February 13, 1977.

31. Interview with James M. Cannon, Washington, D.C., February 23, 1977.

32. Ibid.

33. Ibid.

34. Ibid.

35. Cannon has indicated his astonishment on discovering that the staff of the Domestic Council had responsibility for these messages. He had previously assumed that they were prepared by the White House speechwriters. Cannon interview.

36. Cannon interview.

37. At the end of December, 1974, Rumsfeld gave Kenneth Cole six weeks to find another job. At that point, Cole effectively vacated the executive director's position, and Cavanaugh as Cole's deputy moved into the executive director's office and assumed the direction of the council's staff operations. Cannon interview.

38. Rockefeller interview.

39. Ibid.

40. Ibid.

41. Cannon interview.

42. Rockefeller interview.

43. Ibid.

44. Cannon interview.

45. Rockefeller interview. The project that Rockefeller had discussed with Ford concerned a review of federal social programs, which would include public hearings, for the purpose of developing policy options for the 1976 State of the Union Message. It had been Rockefeller's intention to focus the planning side of the staff operations of the Domestic Council on this review. However, having concluded that the council was no longer a secure and reliable vehicle for him, he decided to operate the review from the office of the vice president. See the following section of this present chapter for a full discussion of the development of this review.

46. Cannon interview.

47. Interview with Richard L. Dunham, Washington, D.C., February 21, 1977.

48. Memorandum for the vice president from William J. Ronan, dated January 8, 1975.

49. Ibid.

50. Memorandum for the president from the vice chairman of the Domestic Council, dated February 20, 1975. Interestingly, this was the only memorandum for the president in which Rockefeller styled himself as vice chairman of the Domestic Council. After his decision to do policy development outside the council from the vice presidential suite, he styled himself in memos to Ford as "vice president."

51. Interview with G. Richard Allison, assistant to the vice president, Washington, D.C., December 17, 1976.

52. Memorandum on the Domestic Council Meeting of June 10, 1975, for the vice president from G. Richard Allison, dated June 10, 1975.

53. Dunham interview.

54. Veneman was one of the first counselors to the vice president in the history of the vice presidency. The other counselor appointed was Raymond Shafer, former governor of Pennsylvania, who was brought in by Rockefeller to work on federal-states relationships.

55. Memorandum for the vice president from James Cannon, dated April 17, 1975.

56. Memorandum for the vice president from John Veneman, dated May 8, 1975.

57. Ibid.

58. Memorandum for the president from the vice president, dated May 15, 1975, enclosing a copy of Cannon's memorandum for the president of April 17, 1975.

59. The problem of inadequate staff resources was taken up with the president in a memorandum for the president from James Cannon, dated July 17, 1975. Ford approved the addition of twenty-nine Domestic Council staff positions (twenty-three professional, six clerical).

60. Memorandum for James Cannon, Richard Dunham, and James Cavanaugh from John Veneman, dated May 22, 1975.

61. The formal membership of the Domestic Council Review Group comprised: the vice president; the secretaries of the treasury, HEW, labor, agriculture, and HUD; the director of the OMB; the chairman of the Council of Economic Advisers; and the executive director of the EPB. However, formal members played virtually no role in the policy development work of the review group staff directed by Veneman. As noted above, the review group was formally established as a Domestic Council for reasons of legitimacy and provision of resources.

62. Domestic Council Social Program Review, Overview Options Memorandum, dated June, 1975, enclosed with memorandum to the vice president from John Veneman, dated June 16, 1975. The Overview Options Memorandum was prepared by the Washington-based consultant firm, ICF, Inc. ICF, Inc., was operated by two former Veneman HEW associates: James Edwards (former deputy assistant HEW secretary for welfare legislation) and Richard Darman (former special assistant to HEW Secretary Elliot Richardson).

63. Memorandum for the vice president from John Veneman, dated July 10, 1975.

64. Memorandum for the vice president from John Veneman, dated July 14, 1975.

65. Memorandum for James Cannon from John Veneman, dated July 22, 1975.

66. Cannon had asked Veneman whether there were other groups, such as the Brookings Institution, RAND Corporation, and Stanford Research Institute, which had the capacity to develop the options papers as well as ICF, Inc. Veneman's response presented an interesting comment on academia:

> My general experience has been that the scholarly orientation of policy institutes, such as Brookings, etc., often produces papers which are academic; which are rarely decision-oriented; and very seldom integrate sensible political analysis. They often take months to produce, and, in many cases, take off from biased ideological viewpoints which are often far afield from the president's. (Veneman memorandum, July 22, 1975.)

67. Memorandum for the vice president from the president, dated July 24, 1975.

68. Memorandum for James Cannon from John Veneman, dated August 7, 1975.

69. Memorandum for the vice president from John Veneman, dated August 7, 1975.

70. *Congressional Quarterly*, "Ford Plans Restructuring of Social Programs" 33, no. 30 (July 26, 1975): 1613-17.

71. *Washington Post*, August 13, 1975.

72. Memorandum for the vice president from John Veneman, dated August 13, 1975.

73. Memorandum for the president from the vice president, dated August 26, 1975.

74. Some changes were made to the final list of locations and dates. The revised schedule that was finally adopted is shown below:

October   21—Denver, Colorado

October   29—Tampa, Florida

November 11—Austin, Texas

November 18—Philadelphia, Pennsylvania

November 25—Indianapolis, Indiana

December   9—Los Angeles, California

75. Memorandum for the president from the vice president, dated September 10, 1975.

76. However, neither the manner nor the timing of this announcement was in accordance with Cannon's recommendation. In actual fact, the announcement of the forums came in a routinely distributed presidential announcement handed out by the White House Press Office: there was no joint presidential-vice presidential appearance, and no vice presidential briefing on forum details.

77. Presidential Announcement, September 29, 1975, in U.S. Office of the Federal Register, *Weekly Compilation of Presidential Documents* 11, no. 40 (October 6, 1975): 1081-82.

78. Memorandum for the vice president from John Veneman and Arthur Quern, dated September 25, 1975.

79. Presidential Address to the Nation, October 6, 1975, in U.S. Office of the Federal Register, *Weekly Compilation of Presidential Documents* 11, no. 41 (October 13, 1975): 1127.

80. In fact, Ford's proposal appeared to promise greater tax cuts than was actually the case. His proposal involved the addition of $11 billion in new permanent income tax reductions to $17 billion in tax reductions already passed by the Congress in March, 1975.

81. Presidential address, October 6, 1975, pp. 1127-28.

82. Interview with John G. Veneman, Washington, D.C., August 15, 1978. Cannon considered resigning over the circumstances surrounding Ford's decision, which had been made by the president on the exclusive advice of CEA Chairman Alan Greenspan, OMB Director Lynn, Rumsfeld, and his deputy, Richard Cheney. Cannon felt that this was the single most important domestic-policy decision made in 1975, and, therefore, as the presidential assistant for Domestic Affairs he ought to have been consulted (Cannon interview). The political dimensions of the $395 billion budget decision will be discussed in chapter 6.

83. Cannon interview.

84. Memorandum for the vice president from John Veneman and Arthur Quern, dated October 24, 1975.

85. Although Callaway's attacks on Rockefeller as a political liability to Ford's prospects of capturing the nomination against the conservative challenge of former California Governor Ronald Reagan were widely reported by the news media, there is no evidence that these had any effect on the work on the domestic policy options prior to November 3. The circumstances surrounding Rockefeller's withdrawal have not been definitively established. Although Ford denied that Rockefeller was forced

to withdraw, sources close to both Ford and Rockefeller have indicated otherwise. This will be discussed further in Chapter 6.

86. Memorandum for the president from the vice president, dated November 6, 1975.

87. It is unclear why Ford allowed Rockefeller to pursue this domestic policy options endeavor when it clearly had been negated by Ford's budget ceiling decision of October 6.

88. Memorandum for the vice president from John Veneman and Arthur Quern, dated November 17, 1975.

89. Memorandum for the president from the vice president, enclosing the vice president's "Suggestions for the State of the Union Message," dated December 15, 1975.

90. The vice president delivered his report on the Domestic Council Public Forums to the president on December 15, 1975. This report and edited transcripts of the forums' hearings were published by the Domestic Council. See *White House Public Forums on Domestic Policy*, Domestic Council, Executive Office of the President, Washington, D.C., December 1975.

91. Of the nineteen initiatives proposed by Rockefeller, only the following were (to varying degrees) included in Ford's State of the Union Message:

   3. Achieving energy independence (complete inclusion)

   8. Modernizing the regulatory system (partial inclusion)

   10. Encouraging continued private ownership of small farms and businesses (complete inclusion)

   11. Encouraging small business development (partial inclusion)

   14. Increasing financing for housing and initiating research to reduce housing costs (minimal inclusion)

   15. Revitalizing the federal system (complete inclusion)

CHAPTER 4

1. Presidential Address to the Nation, January 13, 1975, in U.S. Office of the Federal Register, *Weekly Compilation of Presidential Documents* 11, no. 3 (January 20, 1975): 40.

2. A good discussion of energy supply changes in the United States is provided by James W. McKie, "The United States," in *The Oil Crisis: In Perspective*, Proceedings of the American Academy of Arts and Sciences 104, no. 4 (Fall 1975): 73-90. See also Joel Darmstadter and Hans H. Landsberg, "The Economic Background," in *The Oil Crisis: In Perspective*, pp. 15-38. An excellent collection of articles exploring the nature of the energy crisis is found in *The Energy Crisis: Reality or Myth*, Annals of the American Academy of Political and Social Science 410 (November, 1973).

3. The Organization of Petroleum Exporting Countries (OPEC) was formed in 1960 by five major oil-exporting countries—Iraq, Kuwait, Saudi Arabia, Iran, and Venezuela—to protect the common interests of member nations regarding oil prices and export revenues. Over a period of thirteen years, dissatisfaction grew over the prices and revenues established by the multinational oil companies that owned and controlled the oil wells and production facilities within the various host nations. In

1973, OPEC members took over direct control of wells and production facilities and established their own prices and revenue levels. The resultant increases in crude oil prices were spectacular: within a twelve-month period the cost of a barrel of Arabian light crude rose from $2.59 in January, 1973, to $11.65 in January, 1974.

4. Following the outbreak of the Arab-Israeli conflict on June 6, 1973, the Arab members of OPEC decided to employ oil as a weapon against nations providing assistance to Israel. As the principal supplier of arms and aid to Israel, the United States became a prime target of the oil embargo, which was imposed from October 20, 1973, until March 17, 1974. The cutoff in Arab oil supplies caused severe energy shortages in the eastern part of the United States and underscored the extent of American dependence on foreign oil supplies.

5. The Presidential State of the Union Address, January 15, 1975, in U.S. Office of the Federal Register, *Weekly Compilation of Presidential Documents* 11, no. 3 (January 20, 1975): 45-53.

6. Presidential Message to Congress on the Energy Crisis, November 8, 1973, reprinted in *Congressional Quarterly* 31, no. 46 (November 17, 1973).

7. Two commission study volumes emerged from the work of the energy panel. Published in 1976 by Lexington Books (Lexington, Mass.) for the Commission on Critical Choices, these volumes were 4: *Power and Security* and 10: *The Middle East: Oil, Conflict, and Hope.*

8. Two studies, in particular, considered the application of technology for the development of domestic energy resources. See Hans Mark, "Technology Development in the National Purpose," and Edward Teller, "Energy—A Plan for Action," both in Edward Teller et al., *Power and Security* (Critical Choices for Americans, vol. 4, Lexington Books, Lexington, Mass., 1976), pp. 1-138.

9. Interview with Peter Wallison, Washington, D.C., August 17, 1977. Wallison indicated that although Rockefeller was not consulted on the State of the Union package, he did discuss briefly aspects of the energy components with the president. Wallison credits Ford's reference to FDR's call for action on military plane production to a conversation the president had with Rockefeller, who constantly invoked FDR's "can do" spirit.

10. Draft proposal for the vice president prepared by Peter Wallison, dated December 26, 1974.

11. Memorandum for the vice president from Alan Greenspan, dated January 22, 1975.

12. The concern to bring down the level of unemployment was a constant preoccupation of members of the Ford administration. However, concerning the merits of the proposal there were other considerations. For Rockefeller, whose political base in New York State had included labor unions (notably construction industry labor unions), the political benefits to be derived from an accelerated energy program for Ford's 1976 campaign appeared to be self-evident.

13. Memorandum for the vice president from Richard Kaufman, dated February 7, 1975.

14. Created at a time when the capital markets and industry were in a state of collapse and disarray in the depression of the 1930s, the RFC functioned to extend credit to agriculture, commerce, and industry by means of secured self-liquidating loans to banks and other financial institutions, insurance companies, and agricultural credit agencies. The RFC's initial functions were broadened to allow it

to purchase the capital stock of financial institutions and to make direct loans to business enterprises. Begun with an initial treasury department capitalization of $500 million, the RFC had issued some $54 billion in credits and loans by the time it was liquidated in 1953.

15. Memorandum for the vice president from Richard Parsons, dated February 27, 1975.

16. To illustrate how massive the proposed RPFC's financing was, its total of $205 billion was almost two-thirds of the federal budget proposed by President Ford, whose f.y. 1976 budget was $349.4 billion.

17. Parsons memorandum, February 27, 1975.

18. Memorandum for the vice president from Peter Wallison, dated March 6, 1975.

19. Disclosed in memorandum for the president from the vice president, dated May 3, 1975.

20. Memorandum for the vice president from Richard Dunham, dated March 25, 1975.

21. Dunham's memorandum of March 25 had discussed the suitability of recommending to Ford the vehicle of a "fireside chat" broadcast as early as April 2 for announcing the RPFC initiative to the nation.

22. Memorandum for the president from the vice president, dated May 2, 1975.

23. The agenda for the May 5 meeting listed the following examples for consideration by the review group:
- one billion barrel oil storage capacity

- 100 atomic energy plants

- conversion of electricity plants from oil to coal

- low-sulphur coal surface mining

- gas (including R & D)

- roadbed repair and new railroad cars to transport coal

- suspension-transmission of liquefied coal

- purchase and maintenance of rights-of-way

- mining technology

- coal liquefaction and gasification (in situ)

- production of aluminum from sand and clay

- conversion of idle plants to make equipment in short supply

- oil pipe and new connection pipelines

- long-term projects (e.g., solar energy); venture capital

- subsidiary corporations

24. Memorandum for the vice president from Richard Allison, dated May 3, 1975. The brisk pace of the RPFC timetable reflected Rockefeller's normally fast work pace. In the case of the energy corporation, he insisted on a fast timetable because of the need to move quickly to deal with a real energy crisis. However, Wallison has indicated that Cannon, Dunham, and Allison thought that the timetable was unrealistic. (Wallison interview.)

25. Memorandum for Members of the Domestic Council Review Group: Energy and Resource Policy and Finance, from the vice president, dated May 5, 1975.

26. Memorandum for the vice president from Peter Wallison, dated May 9, 1975.

27. Thus, by May 14, 1975, the full membership of the review group comprised the following: the vice president, the secretary of the treasury, the secretary of the treasury as chairman of the Economic Policy Board, the secretary of commerce, the secretary of commerce as chairman of the Energy Resources Council, the secretary of labor, the secretary of transportation, the director of the Office of Management and Budget, the chairman of the Federal Reserve Board, the administrator of the Federal Energy Administration, the administrator of the Energy Resources and Development Administration, the chairman of the Council of Economic Advisers, and the assistant to the president for Economic Affairs.

28. Memorandum for the vice president from Richard Allison, dated May 12, 1975.

29. As related by Hugh Morrow. Interview with Hugh Morrow, Rockefeller Center, New York, March 15, 1978.

30. The proposal to streamline the regulatory processes for energy projects had strong appeal for an "antiregulatory" energy industry.

31. Memorandum for the president from the vice president, undated (it was in fact hand delivered by Rockefeller on May 21).

32. Disclosed by Rockefeller to Zarb in their meeting of May 29, 1975. Memorandum for the vice president from Richard Allison, dated May 30, 1975, enclosing transcript of meeting of May 29, 1975.

33. Allison transcript of ERFCO meeting of May 23, 1975, enclosed with covering memorandum for the vice president dated May 24, 1975.

34. Quoted in Allison transcript of May 29, 1975.

35. Allison transcript.

36. Notes taken by Susan Herter at meeting of the vice president, Arthur Burns, and Richard Dunham on May 28, 1975.

37. Allison transcript of May 29, 1975. The agreement with Zarb reflects the extent to which Rockefeller was concerned about the survival of the ERFCO proposal. Only three weeks earlier he had steadfastly refused the ERC's request for joint sponsorship of the review group. Now he ceded to Zarb responsibility for revising the proposal as an options paper for the president, and, moreover, he accepted a further scaling down of ERFCO borrowing authority to the $60 billion level.

38. Memorandum for the vice president from the secretary of commerce and the administrator of the Federal Energy Administration, dated June 4, 1975.

39. Memorandum for the vice president from William Ronan, dated June 4, 1975.

40. At the outset of his vice presidency, Rockefeller arranged to have regular weekly meetings in private with the president on the basis of an agenda prepared by the vice president. These meetings with Ford insured for Rockefeller easy access to the president, thus avoiding the problems of isolation encountered by past vice presidents. However, Rockefeller's use of his weekly meetings with the president to lobby for vice presidential ideas and initiatives was resented by some members of the administration who saw such meetings as a vehicle for "end-running established White House staff procedures." See Roger B. Porter, *Presidential Decision Making: The Economic Policy Board* (Cambridge: Cambridge University Press, 1980), pp. 206-7, for critical comment on the vice president's use of his weekly meeting with the

president to press for adoption of the proposal to create a federal energy corporation.

41. Disclosed in a memorandum for the president from James Connor, dated July 30, 1975.

42. Ibid.

43. Ibid.

44. Disclosed in memorandum for the president from the vice president, dated July 31, 1975.

45. Memorandum for the vice president from Rogers Morton and Frank Zarb, undated (this was the memorandum Connor identified in the chronology he reported to the president as having been submitted to Rockefeller by Morton and Zarb on July 9).

46. President Ford planned to attend a summit meeting at Helsinki concerning the Conference on Security and Cooperation in Europe. Ford's European trip would include visits to West Germany, Rumania, and Yugoslavia. He would depart for Europe on July 26 and return home on August 4.

47. Memorandum for the president from the vice president, dated July 31, 1975. In fact, although the president did discuss the general problems of unemployment and the economy at a Labor Day speech at the Maine AFL-CIO Field Day Program, his remarks contained no reference to ERFCO.

48. Federal Energy Administration, "A Brief Description of the Energy Resources Finance Corporation (ERFCO)," undated.

49. Memorandum for the president from the vice president, dated August 6, 1975.

50. Memorandum for the president from the vice president (on the "Political Considerations of ERFCO"), dated August 6, 1975.

51. Memorandum for the president from the vice president, dated August 26, 1975.

52. Memorandum for Frank Zarb from William Simon, dated August 28, 1975.

53. Memorandum for Eric Zausner, FEA, from Alan Greenspan, dated August 28, 1975.

54. Memorandum for the president from James Lynn, dated August 29, 1975.

55. Memorandum for the president from Rogers Morton, dated August 29, 1975.

56. Zarb advised that the necessary legislation and supporting material could be ready for congressional submission within two weeks (or sooner if required) of a presidential decision.

57. Memorandum for the president from Frank Zarb, dated August 30, 1975. Without explanation Zarb changed the name of the ERFCO to the Energy Finance Corporation (EFC), but this proposed name change passed unnoticed and was not taken up.

58. This is an interesting claim in the light of Rockefeller's previous willingness in his meeting with Frank Zarb on May 29 to accept an ERFCO borrowing authority limit of "about $60 billion."

59. Memorandum for the president from the vice president, dated September 3, 1975.

60. On September 2, in an article by David Burnham on Ford's imminent decision on ERFCO, the *New York Times* discussed a bill (S.740) authored by Senator Henry Jackson (D-Wash.) proposing the creation of a National Energy Mobilization Board. Although much smaller in scale and scope than the ERFCO proposal, this board would have a similar objective in promoting accelerated development of energy resources to achieve energy self-sufficiency by 1985. Spurred, no doubt, by the *Times* piece, Jackson wrote to the president on September 4, pointing out the

broad similarity between his proposed board and ERFCO and suggesting that the Congress and executive work together in developing a common proposal.

61. The week of August 31 was a critical one in the deteriorating financial situation of New York City. It was widely reported at the time that the city could go into bankruptcy during the week. Rockefeller advised Ford on September 3 that "the New York City situation is going to drag on, one way or another, in all probability throughout this session of Congress." Therefore, it was imperative in Rockefeller's view that the EIA become an adopted presidential program before the city's financial crisis dominated the attentions of Congress, the administration, and the public.

62. Memorandum for the president from the vice president (on the "Energy Independence Authority"), dated September 3, 1975. Concerning the change of name for ERFCO, James Cannon had prepared the following list of possible names:

Full Name	Abbreviation
Energy Resources Authority	ERA
Energy Independence Agency	EIA
Energy Resources Investment Corporation	ERIC
Energy Production Corporation	EPC
Consumers Energy Corporation	CEP
American Energy Corporation	AEC
1985, Inc.	1985, Inc.
United States Energy Authority	USEA
Energy Resources Corporation	ERC
Future Energy Development Corporation	FEDCO
Energy Independence Corporation	EIC
Energy Independence Authority	EIA

63. Questionnaire for the vice president's staff from Richard Cheney, dated September 4, 1975.

64. Interview with Frank Zarb, Washington, D.C., July 28, 1977.

65. Rockefeller and Zarb continued to be troubled by press leaks about the disagreement within the administration over the proposal.

66. Memorandum for the president from the vice president and Frank Zarb, dated September 15, 1975.

67. Although the memorandum of September 15 had indicated a resolution of the points of disagreement, Rockefeller's emphasis on two particular points at his weekly meeting with the president suggested some residual disputation: first, he stressed to Ford that EIA functions include assistance for some conventional technologies; second, he reassured Ford about "the exclusion of ordinary private sector projects from the EIA."

68. Presidential Address to the AFL-CIO Building and Trades Department's Annual Convention, September 22, 1975, in U.S. Office of the Federal Register, *Weekly Compilation of Presidential Documents* 11, no. 39 (September 29, 1975): 1052-54.

69. According to Zarb, an EIA fact sheet had been prepared but was withdrawn at the last minute. Zarb interview.

70. Memorandum for the president (via Rogers Morton) from Frank Zarb, dated September 24, 1975.

71. In addition to discussing the reopened issues, Rockefeller took up consideration of mobilizing support for the EIA by means of an administration strategy aimed at three major constituencies: labor, business, and environmentalists.

72. At the same time, the White House Press Office released the delayed EIA fact sheet.

73. In the submission of the original ERFCO proposal to the president on May 21, Rockefeller had cautioned that serious delay in adopting the proposal would weaken its legislative prospects the closer 1976 approached.

74. Remarks of the vice president at "Energy Conference with Business Executives," Washington, D.C., October 6, 1975.

75. Rockefeller's resolve to play a major role in building support for passage of the EIA in Congress was based on his strong belief in the merits of the proposal, the need for it, and the following considerations: first, the fact that few members of the Ford administration displayed any enthusiasm for the EIA, thus making his own contribution more vital; second, the fact that he was already widely identified in the news media as the author of the proposal.

76. Notably from Peter Peterson, chairman of the board, Lehman Brothers, who subsequently testified in favor of the EIA at hearings held by the Senate Banking, Housing, and Urban Affairs Committee in mid-April, 1976.

77. For example, Wallison reported to Rockefeller in mid-January, 1976, that not one of thirty members of the Natural Resources Committee of the U.S. Chamber of Commerce was willing to support the EIA. Wallison indicated that "the argument which seemed most persuasive to the group was that the removal of government regulations would provide all the incentive that was necessary to bring about substantial domestic energy production." Memorandum for the vice president from Peter Wallison, dated January 14, 1975.

78. AFL-CIO press release of November 14, 1975. The AFL-CIO reservations alluded to by Meany concerned the EIA's discretionary funding powers: the AFL-CIO favored giving priority to projects not sponsored by major oil corporations.

79. Memorandum for the vice president from Peter Wallison, dated October 20, 1975.

80. Memorandum for the vice president from Peter Wallison, dated November 20, 1975.

81. Memorandum for the vice president from John Veneman, dated January 27, 1975.

82. The three previous instances when vice presidents testified as witnesses before congressional committees were as follows:

    1. Thomas R. Marshall, on January 17, 1921, appeared before the Senate Committee on the District of Columbia to testify in favor of a bill he had drafted to create a District of Columbia public welfare department.

    2. John Nance Garner, on June 27, 1935, appeared before the Senate Committee on Appropriations to testify in favor of a $3 million appropriation for the Texas Centennial celebration.

    3. Richard M. Nixon, on April 27, 1955, appeared before the Senate Committee on Appropriations to testify in favor of restoring $10 million in funds cut from the International Educational Exchange Program.

See Congressional Research Service Brief, April 11, 1975, Library of Congress, Washington, D.C.

In addition to his testimony as a witness before the Senate Banking Committee, Rockefeller appeared before the following congressional committees:

- On June 20, 1975, before the House Committee on Science and Technology, on a bill to create a White House science advisory unit.

- On February 6, 1976, before the Senate Committee on Government Operations, at a committee symposium entitled "Our Third Century: Directions."

- On March 18, 1976, before the Joint Economic Committee, at a conference on full employment.

83. U.S. Congress, Senate Committee on Banking, Housing, and Urban Affairs, *Hearings on the Energy Independence Authority Act of 1975*, 94th Cong., 2nd Sess., April 12, 13, 14, and May 10, 1976. The opposition of Commoner, Nader, and Browder provided a clear measure of the antipathy of the environmental lobby to the EIA proposal.

84. Although the EIA met with no success as an administration proposal in 1976, Rockefeller insisted on and got inclusion of the EIA proposal in Ford's 1977 State of the Union Message.

In the fall of 1977, Rockefeller testified on the merits of his EIA proposal to the Senate Committee on Finance. The committee chairman, Senator Russell Long, expressed some interest in the proposal during the committee's hearings on the Carter administration's 1977 energy tax bill.

In the following year, Rockefeller disclosed to the New York *Daily News* on March 29, 1978, that he was involved in negotiations with the government of Saudi Arabia to establish a New York City-based development corporation which would invest Arab petro-dollars into energy and food projects. Essentially, what Rockefeller was discussing was a private sector version of his original ERFCO proposal. His American partners in the enterprise were reported to be George Woods, former president of the World Bank (and original inspiration for the kernel of the ERFCO concept), and Arthur Taylor, former president of CBS (who had been helpful in private sector lobbying for the EIA bill in 1975 and 1976). However, this project failed to move much beyond the discussion stage by the time of Rockefeller's death on January 26, 1979.

Rockefeller's concept of employing a federal energy corporation to develop energy production and to speed up the regulatory process where it adversely affected construction of new energy projects was revived by the Carter administration in the summer of 1979. On July 15, 1979, President Carter announced a program to reduce American dependence on foreign energy sources. His proposals included the creation of two new federal energy agencies: an Energy Security Corporation to be funded over ten years at a level of $88 billion to produce an additional 2.5 million barrels daily of oil substitutes, and an Energy Mobilization Board to be given power to issue exemption permits for energy project construction where the regulatory processes at local, state, or federal levels caused undue delays.

Carter succeeded in getting congressional approval of his Energy Security Corporation proposal with passage of the Energy Security Act, 1980. This legislation created the Synthetic Fuels Corporation, with an initial funding of $20 billion to stimulate commercial production of synthetic fuels. However, his proposal to create an Energy Mobilization Board to speed up energy projects, was defeated on the House floor in June, 1979. For details of the Carter proposals, see *Congressional Quarterly* 37, no. 29: 1433-41.

CHAPTER 5

1. The position of White House science adviser had originated with Eisenhower's appointment of a special assistant to the president for science and technology following the Soviet launch of *Sputnik I* in 1957. This position was consolidated in 1962 by Kennedy, who established the Office of Science and Technology in the executive office of the president. However, friction developed between the science adviser and the president in the next two administrations: in the Johnson presidency, there were disagreements about the Vietnam war; in the Nixon presidency, the disagreements were over proposals for an ABM system and an American-built SST airplane. In January, 1973, Nixon abolished both the position of presidential science adviser and the Office of Science and Technology, declaring that he could get necessary scientific advice from the director of the National Science Foundation.

2. Vice Presidential Assignments, in U.S. Office of the Federal Register, *Weekly Compilation of Presidential Documents* 10, no. 52 (December 27, 1975): 1599. The president's interest in expeditious action reflected growing pressures from the nation's scientific community for restoration of a visible and active science presence in the White House. These same pressures had produced congressional action in the fall, 1974, with Senate passage of a bill introduced by Senator Edward Kennedy (D-Mass.), to create a Council of Science Advisers in the executive office of the president. Although the House did not act on a similar measure before it, there were indications that this would be given serious consideration early in the 94th Congress.

3. Advising the vice president were Dr. Edward Teller, Livermore Laboratory, University of California; Dr. Hans Mark, director, Ames Research Center, NASA; William O. Baker, president, Bell Telephone Laboratories, Inc.; Dr. John S. Foster, Jr., TRW, Inc.; and Dr. Carol L. Wilson, Sloan Management School, MIT. All of these individuals, except Teller and Mark, were full members of the commission. Teller and Mark were working members of the commission's panel on energy. Also consulted about the science advisory unit were Dr. Guy Stever, director, National Science Foundation, and Dr. Edward David, who had been the last White House science adviser. Neither man was associated with the commission.

4. Memorandum for the vice president from Henry L. Diamond, dated January 3, 1975.

5. The reference to the "revitalization of the Domestic Council" reflected the ongoing dispute at the time between Rockefeller and Ford's senior staff (particularly Rumsfeld and Buchen) regarding the nature of the vice president's oversight of the council (see the discussion provided earlier in Chapter 3). Memorandum for the president from the vice president, dated January 31, 1975.

6. Recommendation for the president on "Science, Technology, and the President" from the vice president, dated February 5, 1975.

7. As Richard Cheney has explained the situation, Rumsfeld saw his mission on behalf of the president as one that required compilation of all of the information and all of the arguments, pro and con, on any given decision topic. To do this adequately, it was Rumsfeld's position that the president should have a range of options that had been cleared with the senior White House staff for comments and recommendations. Therefore, the problems with the vice president's recommendations were that they had not gone through this process, contained no options, and had no other staff member's recommendations for presidential consideration. Interview with Richard B. Cheney, Washington, D.C., July 27, 1977.

8. Memorandum for the president from James Cavanaugh, dated February 12, 1975. Rockefeller has commented on Cavanaugh's "options" memorandum as follows:

> And this paper floated through the Domestic Council which came back with three options [sic]. My proposal to the president was identified in the paper as being the Kennedy plan which was designed to kill it, of course. Then they came up with one other alternative which was an absurdity, and then something which they wanted. (Interview with Nelson A. Rockefeller, Rockefeller Center, New York, December 21, 1977).

In fact, Kennedy's bill proposed the creation of a three-member White House Council of Advisers on Science and Technology and, therefore, bore little relation to the vice president's OTS proposal.

9. Rockefeller interview.

10. Memorandum for the vice president from Oscar Reubhausen, dated February 19, 1975.

11. Memorandum for the president from the vice president, dated March 3, 1975. Although Rockefeller presented "weighted" options, only one of which he recommended, the arguments marshaled to "weight" each option had considerably more integrity than those accompanying the options presented by Cavanaugh in his memorandum of February 12.

12. Interview with James M. Cannon, Washington, D.C., February 23, 1978.

13. For Cannon, this response gave some insight about Gerald Ford. As he explained:

> It was very interesting to me that nobody had thought of it up to that time—not Rockefeller, not Cavanaugh, not Rumsfeld, not anybody else. It was my first insight of any consequence into the way Ford worked and thought. For as long as I was there, he would ask the most simple common sense questions. "What did they actually accomplish?"—it hadn't been addressed in the paper. (Cannon interview.)

14. In a memorandum to President Ford on April 18, outlining the contributions of the various science advisers to past presidents, Cannon noted:

> The fifteen-year record of the office indicates that when a presidential science adviser supported the president's goals, broadened his range of solutions, and kept his ego and ambitions in check, he made great contributions to government and was a major political asset.

15. Although Cannon's memorandum to the president indicated his own recommendation for acceptance of Option 2 (the vice president's option), he had at first discussed with Ford his preference about not submitting a personal recommendation. As Cannon has explained his position:

> I told the president that under the special circumstances—it was the first option paper of any consequence done under my regime . . . and I understood that the Domestic Council was supposed to make a recommendation—on this one I would prefer not to recommend any option. I would want to be able to say to Rockefeller that I had taken this responsibility and was not going to take any sides. (Cannon interview.)

The fact that Cannon ended up supporting Rockefeller's option made such caution unnecessary.

16. Cannon interview. Ford's concern about the size of the OTS reflected concerns of two of his close associates, Buchen and Seidman. Recalling this issue,

Buchen indicated: "Everybody that talked to me on the subject had been scared of creating another big scientific bureaucracy in the White House." (Interview with Philip W. Buchen, Washington, D.C., February 8, 1978.)

17. Memorandum for the president from James Cannon, dated May 14, 1975. Ford's meeting with congressional supporters of a science advisory unit was scheduled for May 22. Invited from the House were two members of the Committee on Science and Technology: Rep. Olin Teague (D-Tex.), committee chairman; and Rep. Charles Mosher (R-Ohio), ranking minority member. On March 6, Teague and Mosher had introduced their own proposal to create a White House Council of science advisers (H.R.4661). From the Senate, Ford invited Senators John Tunney (D-Cal.) and Glenn Beall (R-Md.), respectively chairman and ranking minority member of the Subcommittee on Science, Technology, and Commerce. In addition, Senator Kennedy was invited as the sponsor of S.32.

18. Ford's decision to yield on the issue of the OTS staff size reflected the concern of congressional sponsors of the proposals to create a Council of Science Advisers who wanted a much larger White House science unit than Rockefeller had recommended.

19. The committee hearing was not a hearing in the technical sense. The committee agreed to employ the format of a "Special Conference with the Vice President" for Rockefeller's portion of testimony on the OTS. This had been urged on the committee by Rockefeller, who was attempting to meet objections from senior White House staff members who argued that he could not testify as vice president on an administration proposal because of constitutional reasons relating to "separation of powers." See U.S. Congress, House of Representatives, Committee on Science and Technology, *Special Conference with the Vice President on Science Policy*, 94th Cong., 2nd Sess., June 10, 1975.

20. As discussed in memorandum for the president from the vice president, dated September 16, 1975.

21. Vice president's memorandum of September 16, 1975.

22. Presidential Announcement in U.S. Office of the Federal Register, *Weekly Compilation of Presidential Documents* 11, no. 46 (November 17, 1975): 1271-72.

23. The vice president wrote to Senator Kennedy to urge approval of H.R. 10230, which had administration support. However, Kennedy wanted language in the bill that more clearly defined the science adviser's responsibilities in the areas of budget and national security.

24. On May 1, Rockefeller had recommended that the president exercise his discretion to make the OSTP director, in addition, a member of the Economic Policy Board, the Energy Resources Council, and a participating member of the daily (8:00 A.M.) White House senior staff meeting. With the exception of EPB membership, Ford approved these recommendations. Memorandum for the president from the vice president, dated May 1, 1975.

25. Ford's firm stance against federal aid to assist New York City was ultimately modified, but only after the city's mayor and council adopted an austerity budget making draconian cuts in the city's personnel and services, and after the state had agreed to provide assistance of its own for the city.

26. Transcript of vice presidential press conference aboard *Air Force II*, en route to the funeral of Chiang Kaishek, Republic of China, April 14-15, 1975.

27. An excellent discussion of the various factors involved in the New York City

fiscal crisis is provided in U.S. Congress, Congressional Budget Office, *New York City's Fiscal Problem: Its Origins, Potential Repercussions, and Some Alternative Policy Responses*, October 1975.

28. Transcript of vice presidential press conference at the Business Council Meeting, Hot Springs, West Virginia, May 9, 1975.

29. Nelson A. Rockefeller, quoted in John Osborne, "Rocky Digs In," *New Republic*, May 31, 1975.

30. Governor Hugh Carey, as quoted by Nelson A. Rockefeller at the National Republican Heritage Group's Council Luncheon, Washington, D.C., May 16, 1975.

31. Although Rockefeller had close ties to the banking community of New York City through his relationships as a member of the Rockefeller family (especially his brother David, who headed the Chase Manhattan Bank), he clearly was not acting to advance the interests of this community in taking a hard line against federal assistance for the city. On the other hand, the fact that both Carey and Beame were Democrats suggests that Rockefeller's advice to the president may not have been entirely objective.

32. Letter from the president to the Mayor Abraham D. Beame, dated May 14, 1975, in U.S. Office of the Federal Register, *Weekly Compilation of Presidential Documents* 2, no. 20 (May 19, 1975): 512.

33. Transcript of vice presidential remarks at the National Republican Heritage Group's Council Luncheon, Washington, D.C., May 16, 1975.

34. Memorandum for the president from the vice president, dated June 3, 1975. The legislation to which Rockefeller referred was introduced by Senator Jacob Javits (R-N.Y.) on May 22. The Javits bill (S.1833) provided federal guarantees of emergency loans to cities of more than 100,000 population facing financial crises. In some respects, Javits's bill was similar to legislation passed by Congress in 1971 to guarantee loans to the financially distressed Lockheed Aircraft Corporation.

35. Rockefeller's was also a neglected voice: he was not consulted on the New York City crisis until September, 1975. At the same time, it should be noted that Rockefeller made no attempt on his own initiative to raise the issue at his weekly meetings with the president throughout the months of July and August.

36. As reported in *Congressional Quarterly* 33, no. 26 (June 28, 1975): 1358.

37. Transcript of vice presidential remarks at meeting with White House summer interns, August 5, 1975. Although this transcript was made available to the press, the vice president's comments on federal guarantee of municipal obligations failed to attract the attention of the news media.

38. Memorandum for the vice president, from Richard Dunham, dated September 2, 1975.

39. Hand-delivered draft proposal for the president from the vice president, dated September 3, 1975.

40. Transcript of vice presidential press conference, Rochester, New York, September 5, 1975.

41. As quoted in *Congressional Quarterly* 33, no. 39 (September 27, 1975): 2056.

42. Standard and Poor's, which rates municipal bonds, warned New York State that additional state assistance for New York City would compromise its own fiscal integrity and would damage the state's credit rating. Reported in CBO study, *New York's Fiscal Problem* (October 1975), p. 3.

43. *Congressional Quarterly* 33, no. 39, p. 2060.

44. Hand-delivered draft proposal for the president from the vice president, dated October 2, 1975.

45. John Osborne reported that Rockefeller informed Ford at their meeting on October 2 that he intended to advocate his position publicly. Osborne then noted:

> Mr. Ford immediately told Simon, Greenspan, Lynn, Chairman Arthur Burns of the Federal Reserve Board, and other fiscal advisers that Rockefeller was about to jump the ship. Most of the advisers urged the president to stick to his past and deeply held view that nothing but steadfast federal refusal to promise help would force New York, city and state, to do what was necessary to restore solvency and confidence. (John Osborne, "Hard Times," *New Republic,* November 1, 1975.)

46. Transcript of vice presidential remarks at Luncheon for Local Editors and Publishers, Portland, Oregon, October 3, 1975.

47. As quoted in *Congressional Quarterly* 33, no. 41 (October 11, 1975): 2180.

48. Presidential Press Conference, October 9, 1975, in U.S. Office of the Federal Register, *Weekly Compilation of Presidential Documents* 11, no. 41 (October 13, 1975): 1149.

49. Transcript of vice presidential remarks at the Annual Columbus Day Dinner, New York, October 11, 1975.

50. Transcript of vice presidential press conference, Columbus, Ohio, October 15, 1975.

51. Presidential Address to the National Press Club, October 29, 1975, in U.S. Office of the Federal Register, *Weekly Compilation of Presidential Documents* 11, no. 44 (November 3, 1975): 1201-04. The headline that greeted Ford's announcement the following morning in the New York *Daily News* was "Ford to New York: 'Drop Dead.' " This headline, while a crude exaggeration of Ford's position, dogged the president in the 1976 campaign.

52. Transcript of vice presidential press conference, Tampa, Florida, October 29, 1975.

53. Transcript of vice presidential press conference, Washington, D.C., November 6, 1975. In the event, Ford did lose New York State to Jimmy Carter in the 1976 presidential election, trailing Carter by some 289,000 votes out of a total of 6,489,000 cast for the two major candidates.

54. The Republican opposition, which had firmly supported the president's stance against such assistance, began to weaken. House Minority Leader John Rhodes (R-Ariz.) announced on November 11 that under certain conditions he could support federal guarantees aimed at preventing a New York City default. His conditions were threefold: implementation of a workable plan to balance the city's budget; extension of the city's short-term debt; and alterations in the municipal pension plans. Essentially Rhodes was supporting the vice president's position. Reported in *Congressional Quarterly* 33, no. 44 (November 15, 1975): 2445.

55. A good discussion of the Carey package, with analysis of the entire crisis, is provided in Daniel J. Baltz, "Economic Report/There's No End in Sight for New York's Money Problems," *National Journal* 7, no. 48 (November 29, 1975): 1627-31.

56. Presidential Statement, November 19, 1975, in U.S. Office of the Federal Register, *Weekly Compilation of Presidential Documents* 11, no. 47 (November 24, 1975): 1300-01.

57. Presidential News Conference, November 26, 1975, in U.S. Office of the Federal Register, *Weekly Compilation of Presidential Documents* 11, no. 48 (December 1, 1975): 1318-20.

58. Ford's signing the assistance measure into law was done without the usual White House signing ceremony.

59. Memorandum for the vice presidential record from G. Richard Allison, dated January 13, 1975.

60. Nelson Rockefeller represented the president at the following state funerals on the deaths of foreign leaders:

- On March 25, 1975, to Saudi Arabia on the death of King Faisal.

- On April 16, 1975, to Taiwan, Republic of China, on the death of Chiang Kaishek.

- On November 22, 1975, to Spain on the death of Generalissimo Francisco Franco.

61. In fact, the modern practice began with President Kennedy and has been continued by subsequent presidents.
Below is a listing of vice presidential council or commission assignments of Rockefeller's predecessors, beginning with Vice President Lyndon B. Johnson:

Lyndon B. Johnson (1961-1963)	Chairman, National Aeronautics and Space Council Chairman, President's Committee on Equal Employment Opportunities
Hubert H. Humphrey (1965-1969)	Chairman, National Aeronautics and Space Council Chairman, Peace Corps Advisory Council Chairman, Antipoverty Program Advisory Council
Spiro T. Agnew (1969-1973)	Chairman, Cabinet Committee on Economic Policy Chairman, National Aeronautics and Space Council Chairman, National Council on Indian Opportunity

62. Rockefeller interview.

63. Quoted in Sanford Ungar, "Having Fun in the EOB," *Atlantic Monthly*, May 1976, p. 6.

64. Commission on the Organization of Government for the Conduct of Foreign Policy, *Report to the President and Congress*, June 27, 1975.

65. In particular, a *New York Times* article published on December 22, 1974, which reported the existence of a massive CIA domestic surveillance operation aimed at U.S. citizens at the height of the Vietnam war in the late 1960s.

66. According to John Osborne, Rockefeller was not even the first choice for commission chairman. As Osborne discussed the situation:

It's said at the White House that Federal Judge Henry Friendly of New York first agreed and then declined to serve as a member (not chairman) because of possible conflict with his judicial responsibilities. Erwin Griswold . . . tentatively accepted the chairmanship and suggested that the president and his assistants had better consider whether the possibility that he might have to testify in cases involving an ITT antitrust settlement disqualified him. Mr. Ford decided that this prospect ruled Griswold out as chairman but not as a member of the commission. (John Osborne, "Rocky at Work," *New Republic*, January 25, 1975.)

67. Belin, a lawyer from Des Moines, Iowa, had worked with Ford on the Warren Commission. At that time, Belin was a commission staff member while Congressman Ford was a commission member. Rockefeller described the situation regarding Belin's appointment as executive director as follows: "And I was really handed Dave Belin, but that was all right. We 'supplemented' him and had good rapport." (Rockefeller interview.)

68. Rockefeller interview. Although he was unhappy about the situation, Rockefeller did undertake an investigation of the assassination plots, but this was done on a confidential basis and was not a part of the commission report issued on June 6, 1975. Rockefeller, in fact, disclosed that he reported as follows to Ford on this investigation:

> We have not got conclusive evidence that would warrant a public report. Therefore, I am turning over all of this information to you to give to the Congress, which is doing the investigation also, and they can then follow these leads.

Of this approach to concluding matters, Rockefeller observed: "It got the president off the hook, got me off the hook, [and] got it right where it belonged in the Congress." (Rockefeller interview.)

69. After the submission of the commission's report to Ford, Rockefeller recommended to the president in a memorandum on June 19, 1975, that early followup action be taken on the commission recommendations. To assist Ford in this effort, he made the following categories for action:

1. Recommendations requiring presidential submission of legislation to Congress

2. Recommendations requiring executive orders

3. Recommendations requiring presidential directives

4. Recommendations which do not require presidential action but which might be endorsed explicitly by the president

However, Ford failed to adopt the suggestion of early action. In September, 1975, Rumsfeld established a White House Intelligence Reorganization Group, under the direction of John Marsh, to consider the various recommendations of the Murphy Commission, the CIA Commission, and other reports. Final action by the president was not taken until February, 1976, when he issued an executive order reorganizing the various components of the intelligence community.

70. The commission was not quite terminated on November 28. For the purposes of submitting a report to the president and Congress, the commission was treated as an ongoing entity. The report was issued on December 31, 1975. See National Center for Productivity and Quality of Working Life, *Report on Activities and Plans to the President and Congress*, December 31, 1975.

71. See President's Panel on Federal Compensation, *Report to the President*, December 2, 1975.

72. See National Commission on Water Quality, *Report to the Congress*, March 18, 1976.

CHAPTER 6

1. Rockefeller has disclosed that, at one point during the House confirmation hearings, he indicated to Representative Jack Brooks (D-Tex.) that demands by

House members for the full disclosure of financial holdings by individual members of the Rockefeller family went beyond reasonable bounds. Accordingly he informed the congressman:

"Look, Jack, I want to serve my country if I can be useful in this but I am not going to do it by destroying my family. I have got a responsibility to the family. And I have given you all the information and you know all the holdings of the family. We have given everything. Which one owns how much is totally irrelevant and therefore if that is demanded by the committee I withdraw my acceptance of this nomination."

The demands were not pressed and the hearings moved on toward confirmation. Interview with Nelson A. Rockefeller, Rockefeller Center, New York, December 21, 1977.

2. Richard E. Neustadt, *Presidential Power*, 2nd ed. (New York: John Wiley & Sons, Inc., 1976), preface to the original edition.

3. Rockefeller interview.

4. The members of the team included Donald Rumsfeld, U.S. ambassador to NATO; Interior Secretary Rogers Morton; former Governor W. William Scranton of Pennsylvania; and John O. Marsh, Jr., counselor to the president. According to Richard Cheney, Ford made it clear to the transition team that there should be no examination of the national security apparatus, that this was an "off limits area." Interview with Richard Cheney, Washington, D.C., July 27, 1977.

5. For an excellent discussion of the early work of the Ford transition team, see David S. Broder, "Ford Team Seeks Small, Open Staff," *Washington Post*, August 17, 1974.

6. Quoted in *Congressional Quarterly* 32, no. 34 (August 24, 1974): 2348.

7. Press Office Announcement, December 18, 1974, in U.S. Office of the Federal Register, *Weekly Compilation of Presidential Documents* 10, no. 51 (December 23, 1974): 1592. Ford's acceptance of a highly differentiated staff system underscored the modern trend in White House staffing toward functional assignment areas, thus consigning the "generalist" to an earlier age. Moreover, the listing of the "nine key staff directors" confirms Thomas Cronin's observation that

with rare exceptions, presidential aides can be identified as members of one of the following staff units: (1) domestic policy and legislative program, (2) budget and economic policy, (3) national security and foreign policy, (4) congressional relations, and (5) administrative and public relations.

See Thomas Cronin, " 'Everybody Believes in Democracy until They Get to the White House . . . :' An Examination of White House Department Relations," in Norman C. Thomas and Hans W. Baade, eds., *The Institutionalized Presidency* (Dobbs Ferry, N.Y.: Oceana Publications, Inc., 1972), p. 169.

8. Interview with Philip W. Buchen, Washington, D.C., February 8, 1977.

9. Interview with Peter J. Wallison, Washington, D.C., August 17, 1977. Concurring in Wallison's assessment were Frank Zarb and Richard Dunham.

10. Quoted in Richard Reeves, *A Ford not a Lincoln* (New York: Harcourt Brace Jovanovich, 1975), p. 187.

11. Interview with James M. Cannon, Washington, D.C., February 25, 1978.

12. Ibid. Rockefeller's expectations suggested a view of Ford shared by James David Barber in September 1974. Then, Barber had voiced concern about Ford's "compliant streak, a certain geniality . . . that might lead us into drift." However, by April, 1975, Barber was discussing Ford's "openness, flexibility, personal growth

in the office . . . " and was prepared to rate him as "an active-positive president, along with Franklin Roosevelt, Harry Truman, and John Kennedy." See Barber, *The Presidential Character: Predicting Performance in the White House*, 2d ed. (Englewood Cliffs: Prentice-Hall, Inc., 1977), pp. 486-87.

13. Interview with Robert T. Hartmann, Washington, D.C., April 20, 1978. In Hartmann's case, his responsibilities over presidential speechwriting came about in a somewhat opportunistic manner. As he recalled the situation: "To some extent, I staked out control of the president's words on my own. I just did it and nobody gave me too much of an argument, and Rumsfeld came along and codified it. But it was not that the president gave me a piece of paper saying: 'Here, you are delegated responsibility for this area.' It didn't work that way with him."

14. Hartmann interview.

15. According to John Marsh, Ford had instructed the transition team not to deal with Rockefeller's vice presidential role in its deliberations concerning reorganization of White House staffing and structure. Interview with John O. Marsh, Jr., Washington, D.C., February 8, 1978.

16. Buchen interview.

17. Hartmann interview.

18. Marsh interview.

19. Buchen interview.

20. Hartmann interview. The evident hostility toward Kissinger in this quotation is reflective of the widespread antipathy shown by the Ford staff toward Kissinger, especially during the first year of Ford's presidency. For an illustration, see John Osborne, "Kissinger and Ford," *New Republic*, April 26, 1975. It should be remembered, of course, that Kissinger and Rockefeller had enjoyed a long and close association. When Rockefeller flew off to the Caribbean for a vacation immediately following his confirmation as vice president, his vacation guest was Kissinger. Therefore, Ford's senior staff was understandably nervous about the possibility of a White House (and a president) operated under the joint direction of two such close allies.

21. Buchen interview.

22. Cannon became so much a part of the White House circle that Philip Buchen concluded that "Cannon worked as though the vice president wasn't involved. By default he became a Ford man: I don't think Rockefeller paid any attention." Buchen interview.

23. A withdrawal made almost total after Cannon's retention of Cavanaugh and Rockefeller's related decision to develop domestic policy options from the vice presidential office under the direction of John Veneman.

24. Rockefeller's proposed Office of Executive Management would comprise five bureaus: Bureau of the Budget, Bureau of Legislative Clearance and Coordination, Bureau of Program and Planning, Bureau of Organization and Management, Bureau of Personnel Management. To supervise the activities of the OEM, Rockefeller proposed an OEM director who would also serve as executive director to the president for the purpose of "assisting in planning and management in domestic affairs." See Nelson A. Rockefeller, "The Executive Office of the President," in Senator Henry M. Jackson, ed., *The National Security Council: Jackson Subcommittee Papers on Policy Making at the Presidential Level* (New York: Praeger, 1965), pp. 167-89.

25. Memorandum for the president from the vice president, dated December 16, 1975.

26. The budget ceiling decision was made by Ford in the course of a series of meetings with Greenspan, Lynn, Rumsfeld, and Cheney that had been arranged by Rumsfeld and Cheney. It should be noted that in arranging these decision meetings, Rumsfeld and Cheney broke the cardinal rule of the White House coordinator's system, which held that every major presidential decision had to be cleared with all senior staff members for recommendations for the president's consideration. Cheney has stressed in a personal interview the importance of maintaining the integrity of the coordinator's system to insure: "that the president has all of the information he needs, that all people with advice have given it, that all pros and cons have been stated, that nothing has been held back, and that no one has been suppressed from expressing his viewpoint." Cheney interview.

27. James Cannon felt so strongly about his exclusion from a decision that had such a major effect on domestic policy that he considered resignation in protest. Cannon interview.

28. Memorandum for the president from the vice president, dated December 16, 1975.

29. Ibid.

30. This is, of course, a well-known phenomenon. For a good discussion of what he terms "the inflexibility of the established web," see David B. Truman, *The Governmental Process* (New York: Alfred A. Knopf, Inc., 1951), Chapters 17 and 18.

31. The opposition was not solely institutional in nature. While the EPB, the CEA, the OMB, and the ERC opposed Rockefeller's initiative on the basis of their institutional briefs, some of the political actors who provided the leadership for these institutional units had opposition that transcended these briefs. Treasury Secretary Simon and CEA Chairman Alan Greenspan not only spoke out in opposition based on their respective treasury/EPB and CEA briefs, but also injected considerable ideological fervor into that opposition. Both opposed ERFCO/EIA on classical liberal grounds: it represented an unwarranted intrusion by the government into the free market economic system. OMB Director James Lynn and ERC Executor Director Frank Zarb essentially presented opposition based on organizational briefs.

It also should be noted here that it is difficult to extract the admission from individual political actors that disputes over particular policy proposals reflect the struggle to protect institutional jurisdictions. The case of Frank Zarb is instructive on this point. At the outset, Zarb was, at best, lukewarm about Rockefeller's proposal. He had requested that the ERC be given joint sponsorship with the Domestic Council of the ERFCO review group (a request based on the ERC's jurisdictional area). This request was rejected by Rockefeller, who was committed to retention of complete control over the proposal. However, when Rockefeller was met by a total impasse on developing the proposal further, he coopted Zarb by turning over to him responsibility for ERFCO's further advancement. It was at this point that Zarb became an ERFCO proponent. Yet, when asked directly about the ERC-Domestic Council jurisdictional dispute over sponsorship of ERFCO, Zarb dismissed this as "not important." Interview with Frank Zarb, Washington, D.C., July 28, 1977.

32. Theodore C. Sorensen, *Decision-Making in the White House* (New York: Columbia University Press, 1963), p. 3. Sorensen, like many of the Kennedy circle,

was not especially concerned about the procedures and machinery of government. Rather, he was interested in the dynamic forces and factors shaping the actions of the man at the vital center of politics: the president.

33. Rockefeller interview. The disclosure about his offer to take on the role of White House chief of staff was made to the author by Nelson Rockefeller on an "off the record" basis.

34. The indication given to the author is that Rockefeller's offer also was made in the context of some speculation that perhaps the president would do better to put the vice president back on the ticket for the 1976 campaign. In any event, Ford concluded that his needs as president, in terms of the administration and of the election campaign, would not be served by acceptance of Rockefeller's offer.

35. Discussing his personnel changes of November 3, 1975, in the NBC interview program "Meet the Press," on November 9, 1975, Ford told David S. Broder: " . . . for me to do the job as well as I possibly can, I need a feeling of comfort within an organization . . . " "Meet the Press Interview," in U.S. Office of the Federal Register, *Weekly Compilation of Presidential Documents* 11, no. 46 (November 17, 1975): 1257.

36. Quoted in James T. Barron, "Advising the President," *Princeton Alumni Weekly*, November 24, 1975, p. 10. Interestingly (and somewhat perplexingly), Ford cites Rumsfeld in his autobiography, *A Time to Heal*, on the *impracticability* of such a concept. In their discussion about White House organizational structure before Rumsfeld took on the post of White House coordinator, Ford quotes Rumsfeld as saying: "Mr. President, as I understand it, you're still running this place on the concept of the spokes of the wheel. You're the hub of the wheel; each member of your senior staff is a single spoke; and each is supposed to have equal access to you. In theory, that sounds fine. . . . In practice, however, it won't work." See Gerald R. Ford, *A Time to Heal* (London: W. H. Allen, 1979), p. 186. Presumably, Rumsfeld would claim that the reorganization of the White House undertaken under his guidance enabled the "spokes of the wheel" concept to work in practice.

37. Cheney has argued that it was the president who made the decision, that "staff skewing cannot be blamed," and that "the president decides who he wants to listen to." All of these statements may well be correct, but the fact remains that the coordination system was designed to protect the president from the narrow advocacy views of one or two staff people. At least, that was Rumsfeld's reasoning when he had Rockefeller's science adviser recommendations to the president "re-done" in January 1975. Cheney interview.

38. James Lynn has since recanted somewhat. He has indicated his opinion that:

> Nelson (Rockefeller) may have been right. The president never did articulate the detailed reasons of what he was doing regarding the $395 billion decision, with $28 billion in spending cuts and $28 billion in taxation cuts. The key to assisting the poor was a healthy economy . . . employing a larger pie approach. This was never well articulated by the president or those around him. We did not start out with a statement of compassion . . . that we care.
>
> Where the vice president was right was that a programs approach would have presented the president as a man of compassion. (Interview with James T. Lynn, Washington, D.C., July 29, 1977.)

39. Ford's case almost exactly parallels that of Eisenhower, who allowed his

treasury secretary's views to overshadow his own in cutting back the federal budget in the spring of 1957. As Neustadt has described Eisenhower's situation:

> The President in . . . [this] case failed to make [his] choice serve [his] influence. [He] failed because [he] did not reckon [his] own risks because [he] saw the issue through the eyes of [his] advisers. What Eisenhower saw around his cabinet table in January 1957 was gloom upon the faces of the men he most respected in the spheres of economics and finance and *party* politics. The choice before him featured fiscal policy; accordingly he took those spheres of expertise as relevant, and worried as he watched the experts worrying. (Neustadt, *Presidential Power*, p. 216.)

40. Hartmann interview.

41. An intervention for which Zarb gave Ford high marks. Zarb interview.

42. Hartmann interview. According to Hartmann, Hills was on *Air Force I* acting as Rumsfeld's agent to kill the EIA.

43. The two structural models presented in this discussion are discussed at length by Richard Johnson in his useful study, *Managing the White House*. Johnson discusses three models: the formalistic, the competitive, and the collegial. Using his terminology, Rockefeller's model can be said to employ the formalistic approach while Ford's White House structure appropriately describes the competitive approach. Categorizing several administrations according to these patterns, Johnson views the formalistic approach as predominant in the Eisenhower and Nixon presidencies. The competitive pattern he associates with Franklin D. Roosevelt, Truman, and Lyndon Johnson. Finally, the collegial approach is considered only within the Kennedy administration. See Richard T. Johnson, *Managing the White House* (New York: Harper and Row, 1974).

A different approach is embodied in the recent study by Roger Porter, *Presidential Decision Making*, which examines three organizational models of White House organization: adhocracy, centralized management, and multiple advocacy. In Porter's view, adhocracy tends to spurn employment of regular institutionalized channels, relying instead on having problems individually dealt with by different groups of advisers, sometimes on a virtually random basis. Franklin Roosevelt's approach is considered to be the epitome of adhocracy. Porter's second model, centralized management, is virtually identical to the approach advocated by Rockefeller. The third model, multiple advocacy, is characterized by Porter as a "managed process within a delineated policy area relying on an honest broker to insure that interested parties are represented and that policy debate is structured and balanced." Porter's study focuses on the Economic Policy Board as a useful exemplar of this model.

Stressing that the three models are not mutually exclusive (presidents have made use of a mix of all three approaches), Porter advocates the multiple advocacy model and advances a proposal to organize the White House on the basis of a fourfold division of discrete policy areas: budget, national security, economic policy, and social policy. Retaining the Office of Management and Budget and the National Security Council, he proposes the creation of two new executive office units, an Economic Policy Council and a Social Policy Council, thus providing an institutionalized policy process to be operated by a broker (not an advocate) for each of the four delineated policy areas.

However, while it is the case that the Ford White House employed elements of Porter's favored approach, the central feature of multiple advocacy—management of a policy unit by a broker rather than an advocate—was essentially absent in an administration of conspicuous advocates. See Roger B. Porter, *Presidential Decision Making: The Economic Policy Board* (New York: Cambridge University Press, 1980).

44. The position of "minister without portfolio" is, of course, a traditional one for generalists in the British cabinet.

45. Cannon interview.

46. Ibid.

47. Lynn interview.

48. Interview with L. William Seidman, Washington, D.C., August 29, 1977.

49. Cheney interview.

50. Rockefeller constantly described his White House role as that of being "a staff assistant to the president." See, for example, his discussion of his vice presidential role in "Rockefeller Talks about His Job and Future," *U.S. News and World Report*, October 13, 1975, pp. 50-56.

51. Confines assured by the use of the Domestic Council staff to perform many time-consuming service functions for the president. Ironically, while Rockefeller's withdrawal from active involvement with the operational side of the council's work was based on his conclusion that he could not control such operations with Cavanaugh (a Rumsfeld ally) as the deputy director with operations oversight, this had a beneficial result. It had the effect of liberating Rockefeller from oversight of such relatively mundane matters.

52. Wallison interview.

53. While it is not possible to assess how damaging this extension was to particular activities Rockefeller was engaged in, Wallison had indicated that in his judgment there was some adverse impact on the development of the EIA proposal. Wallison interview.

54. The fact was, of course, that Rumsfeld also saw Rockefeller as a political rival for power and influence in the Ford White House: Rumsfeld had already lost out to Rockefeller for the vice presidential nomination in 1974. He was not anxious to see the lines of power established by virtue of his central position as White House coordinator eroded by an active and challenging vice president. Virtually all of the senior White House staff members interviewed for this study testified to the strength of Rumsfeld's political ambitions and indicated that this was a large element in his disputes and conflicts with Rockefeller.

55. Rockefeller interview.

56. Seidman interview.

57. Presidential Address to the Nation, October 6, 1975, in U.S. Office of the Federal Register, *Weekly Compilation of Presidential Documents* 11, no. 40 (October 6, 1975).

58. This is discussed at length later in this chapter.

59. Rockefeller regarded himself as the victim of Rumsfeld's political ambitions. He has claimed that he attempted to avoid political in-fighting as vice president in the Ford administration and was, consequently, more vulnerable to attack than he otherwise might have been. This view is endorsed by Seidman and Hartmann, who both thought that Rumsfeld understood Rockefeller's intention to avoid conflicts and took advantage of it. (Rockefeller, Seidman, and Hartmann interviews). For a

complete account of the political in-fighting within the Ford White House, we must await the published memoirs of all the various participants. An interesting early account of such struggles is provided by John Casserly, a former Ford speechwriter who has published his political diary of 1975. See John J. Casserly, *The Ford White House* (Boulder: Colorado University Press, 1977).

60. While the $395 billion budget ceiling issue was one that could be discussed purely in economic terms, William Seidman has indicated that for CEA Chairman Alan Greenspan the question came down to a "purity argument," that the goal of balancing the budget (which has considerable ideological overtones for conservative economists) overruled all other considerations as a matter of principle. Seidman interview.

61. A view most notably argued by Senator Barry Goldwater and Howard Callaway, who was appointed as Ford's campaign manager. Callaway's position on Rockefeller as a political liability will be dealt with more fully later in the chapter.

62. Rockefeller interview.

63. As previously noted, Rockefeller's ability to deal directly in this way with the president was extremely irksome to Rumsfeld. According to John Osborne, who interviewed Rumsfeld in the final months of the Ford administration:

> Rumsfeld blamed much of his difficulty with Rockefeller, and Rockefeller's dislike of him, upon what seemed to Rumsfeld to be the president's neglect or refusal to require adequate coordination between the vice president's activities and statements and those of others in the president's service.

John Osborne, *White House Watch: The Ford Years* (Washington: D.C., New Republic Books, 1977), p. xxxiii.

64. The case of Hubert Humphrey is particularly illuminating on this point. Not only was he expected to deliver speeches written for him by the president's speechwriters, but, more significantly, Humphrey's inability to adopt an independent position on the Vietnam War proved to be a major factor in his defeat by Nixon in the 1968 presidential election. It was Humphrey's conviction:

> That a vice president regardless of talent and the president's personality, has a choice between two relationships: acquiescence and hostility. The vice president simply cannot move without the president's seal of approval.

See Hubert H. Humphrey, *The Education of a Public Man* (Garden City: Doubleday and Co., 1976), p. 367.

65. These and other issues were addressed in a series of bicentennial speeches given by Rockefeller which were published as a collected set under the title, *The Future of Freedom: Vice President Nelson A. Rockefeller Speaks Out on Issues Confronting Americans in Bicentennial, 1976.* However, here, as in all other vice presidential endeavors, Rockefeller first secured presidential approval of the speech series. As he discussed the situation:

> Now, by this time I was running out of activities so I decided to do a series, or to ask him if he would mind if I did a series, of speeches on key issues. And this is typical of him, he said, "Of course. I think it would be very valuable." But I said, "I might in some cases differ from the administration's position." He said, "I don't think there is anything wrong with that. I think that is very healthy." And he said, "All I ask is that after you have made the speech you give me a copy." Now, how can you ask for anything more from any man than that? That has to be the most extraordinarily open, big, generous position. (Rockefeller interview.)

66. Rockefeller accepted with equanimity the general proposition that custom decreed that Ford avoid public commitment to a vice presidential running mate until he had obtained the nomination. However, he was less gracious about his own responsibilities inherent in the proposition that he separately seek his own delegates for the vice presidential nomination. He declared to reporters in Atlanta, Georgia, on July 9: "I'm not a candidate. Have you ever heard of anyone running for vice president?" Quoted in *Congressional Quarterly* 33, no. 28 (July 12, 1975): 1513.

67. Quoted in *Congressional Quarterly* 33, no. 28, p. 1513.

68. Reported in *Congressional Quarterly* 33, no. 31 (August 2, 1975): 1711. However, the question of Rockefeller's age was also on Ford's mind at this time. Commenting on his concerns about his vice president and the problem of a 1976 running mate, Ford notes in his autobiography: "Yet I recognized that he was nearly seventy years old." Ford, *A Time to Heal*, p. 328.

69. Interview on PBS television, August 9, 1975, reported in U.S. Office of the Federal Register, *Weekly Compilation of Presidential Documents* 11, no. 32 (August 11, 1975): 846.

70. His efforts to demonstrate that he shared the concerns of fiscal conservatives were so successful that Governor James Edwards of South Carolina declared to reporters that the vice president's remarks on welfare and social programs sounded a lot like comments he would expect southern conservatives to make, including himself, Governor Wallace of Alabama, and Senator Strom Thurmond of South Carolina. Transcript of vice presidential news conference, Columbia, South Carolina, August 27, 1965.

71. Letter to the president from the vice president, dated November 3, 1975.

72. Presidential News Conference, November 6, 1975, in U.S. Office of the Federal Register, *Weekly Compilation of Presidential Documents* 11, no. 45 (November 10, 1975): 1236.

73. The account given by Alvin Moscow in his study of the Rockefellers, *The Rockefeller Family*, indicates nicely the scenario played out by Nelson Rockefeller in giving his withdrawal letter to Ford. As Moscow relates it,

> . . . in November of 1975, with the political pressures far outweighing the rewards of the office, Nelson carried his letter of future resignation into the oval office, while one of his aides released the text to the wire services. There would be no turning back. The letter asked the president not to consider him, Nelson Rockefeller, as a possible nominee for vice president in 1976. He was stepping aside, freeing the president to win over the conservatives who objected to Rockefeller. The president accepted his vice president's decision with a puff on his pipe, an expression of regret, and an attitude of neutrality on what was seen as the practicalities of politics.

Alvin Moscow, *The Rockefeller Inheritance* (Garden City: Doubleday and Co., 1977), p. 375.

74. See Ford, *A Time to Heal*, pp. 227-328.

75. As Cannon has elaborated on the situation, the series of forced resignations was sold,

> . . . with the appeal to Ford: You've got to be a strong man and assert yourself. This is the way to do it!" That appealed to Ford's sense of macho: "People think I'm weak, I'll show them."

Cannon indicated: "I have a whole lot of reasons without going in to details [to believe] this is how Rumsfeld sold it to him." Cannon interview.

76. Interview with Melvin R. Laird, Washington, D.C., February 1, 1978.

77. Quoted in Osborne, *White House Watch*, pp. xxii-xxiii.

78. Osborne, *White House Watch*, pp. xxxiii-xxxiv. Subsequently, Ford has gone much further in expressing regret. In his autobiography he reveals: "I was angry with myself for showing cowardice in not saying to the ultra conservatives, 'It's going to be Ford and Rockefeller, whatever the consequences.' " See Ford, *A Time to Heal*, p. 328.

CHAPTER 7

1. Although Rockefeller's vice presidency lasted a total of twenty-five months, December 19, 1974, through January 20, 1977, the productive period of his incumbency was of even shorter duration. After his withdrawal on November 3, 1975, as an available Ford running mate in 1976, he undertook no new initiatives of any significance.

2. Schlesinger testimony. See U.S. Congress, Senate, Subcommittee on Constitutional Amendments of the Committee on the Judiciary, *Examination of the First Implementation of Section Two of the Twenty-fifth Amendment*, 94th Cong., 1st Sess., February 26, 1975, p. 116.

3. While Rockefeller appeared vigorous and healthy, the fact was that by 1980, he would be seventy-two years old and thus too old to mount a successful campaign. It is true that notions of an "age barrier" were dented by Ronald Reagan in 1980, but the fact is that Reagan was still not seventy when elected.

4. Interview with Nelson A. Rockefeller, Rockefeller Center, New York, December 21, 1977.

5. It can be objected, of course, that in the past—both in the Eisenhower administration and as governor of New York—Rockefeller had not shown himself to have been at all encumbered by the "normally . . . cautionary considerations of a political future." While true, there are other examples of similarly "unencumbered" politicians whose political style changed dramatically once in the vice presidency. The case of Lyndon Johnson is particularly instructive on this point, as indeed is that of his successor in the vice presidential office, Hubert Humphrey.

6. Rockefeller's determination to have his vice presidency established on acceptable terms may be contrasted with Lyndon Johnson's situation in the Kennedy White House. According to Doris Kearns:

> Shortly after the inauguration, he sent an unusual executive order to the oval office for President Kennedy's signature. Outlining a wide range of issues over which the new vice president would have "general supervision," it put all the departments and agencies on notice that Lyndon Johnson was to receive all reports, information, and policy plans that were generally sent to the president himself. It led to remarks in the White House that compared Johnson to William Seward, Abraham Lincoln's secretary of state, who had sent his president an equally preposterous memo on how the government should be conducted and how he, Seward, should be the lead conductor. Kennedy's response was similar to Lincoln's; in both cases the memos were diplomatically shelved.

See Doris Kearns, *Lyndon Johnson and the American Dream* (New York: Harper and Row, 1976), p. 165.

7. As it turned out, Rockefeller was compelled to employ the vice presidential office as a policy vehicle following his withdrawal from the council after Cannon's

retention of Cavanaugh. But because the vice president retained the appearance of Domestic Council linkage through the device of council review groups, he managed to avoid exclusive reliance on the resources of the vice presidential office.

8. For a useful discussion of these unique circumstances, see Allan P. Sindler, *Unchosen Presidents: The Vice President and Other Frustrations of Presidential Succession* (Berkeley: University of California Press, 1976).

9. Of course, there may be cases where a president will decide that it is in fact not in his own best interest to give any kind of substantive role to the vice president. However, such cases are in the main likely to arise only when a presidential nominee has had his vice president "thrust upon him." What is argued here, however, is that given his own choice of a running mate a president who selects that running mate on the basis of the selection criteria proposed in 1976 by the Institute of Politics, Harvard University (and discussed earlier in Chapter 1), will have an interest as an elected president in employing the vice president in a substantive way.

10. The Reagan-Ford negotiations at Detroit in July, 1980, which sought to bring in the former president as the running mate on a Reagan-Ford ticket (the so-called "dream ticket") are particularly instructive on this point. Presidential nominee Reagan sought to restructure the vice presidential role for Ford in a manner consistent with his own perceived needs as an elected president. His operational style while a two-term governor of California, of a presider rather than a manager, led Ronald Reagan to conclude that his presidential needs could best be served by a Vice President Ford to whom major management functions could be delegated. Ford's vice presidential role was conceived to be that of White House operations director, supervising the work of the various units within the executive office of the president, and, as such, closely resembled the vice presidential role of chief of staff broached privately by Rockefeller with Ford as president in the spring of 1976. Ford's own desire for specificity in discussions of a possible vice presidential role evidences the extent to which he had learned from Rockefeller's experience with ambiguity on delineation of the vice president's role. However, the "dream ticket" negotiations were terminated by Reagan when Ford sought to expand the vice president's status to that of "co-presidency." The Reagan-Ford negotiations are discussed further in Michael Turner, "Reagan and the Vice Presidency," *Politics* 1, no. 1 (April 1981): 29-35.

11. Certainly in the spring of 1976, Rockefeller took up with Ford the proposal that his vice presidential role be recast to encompass White House management functions as chief of staff. However, this proposal may be regarded more as a late effort by Rockefeller to patch together a Ford-Rockefeller ticket for the presidential election rather than a deliberative discussion between president and vice president to review the vice president's role.

12. See John Osborne, *White House Watch: The Ford Years* (Washington, D.C.: New Republic Books, 1977), pp. xxii-xxiv.

13. It is interesting to ask here why it was not legitimate for the vice president's own office to obtain itself such additional resources, especially since all of the projects already carried presidential approval. The answer is, of course, that such a request would have been strenuously opposed by senior White House staff members (notably Rumsfeld).

14. According to information supplied to the author by Rockefeller's vice presidential staff in the summer of 1976, his vice presidential office had a total staff

of seventy-five (of whom thirty were professional staff) and an annual budget for f.y. 1977 of $1,900,700 (of which $654,700 represented the Senate budget and $1,246,000 the executive office budget).

15. Rockefeller himself acknowledged this in an interview with *U.S. News and World Report* in October, 1975:

> Q. "Do you feel you've been the target of unfair backbiting by the White House staff?"
>
> A. "Well—after all—what's new about that sort of thing?"

See "Rockefeller Talks about His Job and Future," *U.S. News and World Report*, October 13, 1975, p. 51.

16. In the case of Carter's 1976 campaign, the campaign season extended for two full years.

17. Memorandum for the president-elect and the vice president-elect from the vice president, dated November 5, 1976.

18. The seven on Carter's short list were, in addition to Mondale, Senators Frank Church (D-Idaho), John H. Glenn (D-Ohio), Henry M. Jackson (D-Wash.)., Edmund S. Muskie (D-Maine), Adlai E. Stevenson (D-Ill.), and Representative Peter W. Rodino, Jr. (D-New Jersey).

19. Carter news conference, New York City, July 12, 1976, in U.S. Congress, House of Representatives, Committee on House Administration, *The Presidential Campaign, 1976, Vol. I, Part I, Jimmy Carter*, 95th Cong., 2nd Sess., 1978, p. 317.

20. Carter news conference, New York City, July 15, 1976, quoted in House Administration Committee, *The Presidential Campaign*, p. 325.

21. Mondale was widely credited with promoting the appointment of Secretary of Agriculture Bob S. Bergland and Secretary of HEW Joseph Califano, Jr., and of Charles L. Schultze as CEA chairman. However, Califano was one of the principal victims in Carter's cabinet purge in July, 1979.

22. The following articles provide a useful overview of Mondale's developing vice presidency: John Osborne, "Mondale at Work," *New Republic*, April 23, 1977; Brock Brower, "The Remaking of the Vice Presidency," *New York Times Magazine*, June 5, 1977; David S. Broder, "The Veep," *Washington Post*, June 12, 1977; Martin Tolchin, "The Mondales: Making the Most of Being Number 2," *New York Times Magazine*, February 26, 1978; and Dom Bonafede, "Vice President Mondale—Carter's Partner with Portfolio," *National Journal* 10, no. 10 (March 11, 1978): 376-84.

23. Quoted in *Washington Star*, February 27, 1977.

24. Quoted in Bonafede, "Vice President Mondale," p. 379.

25. In a notation in the margin of Mondale's memorandum, signed "Jimmy," the president wrote: "Fritz, I'm pleased." Quoted in *Washington Post*, September 27, 1977.

26. Rockefeller interview.

27. Concerning vice presidential projects, Broder arrived at the following set of conclusions based upon his researches on four administrations:

1. If the project is of major importance to the president, you may be sure the vice president's role in it will be minor.

2. If the vice president's role is major, you can be almost certain that the president attaches minor importance to the project.

3. In those rare instances where the vice president's role is major and the project is obviously of importance, it is a safe bet that the president regards the project as one that is sure to fail.

See David S. Broder, "Vice President's Mission to Minot," *Washington Post*, October 1, 1970.

28. Quoted in Bonafede, "Vice President Mondale," p. 381.

29. Quoted in Michael Harwood, *In the Shadow of Presidents* (Philadelphia: J. B. Lippincott Co., 1966), p. 157.

SELECTED BIBLIOGRAPHY

PUBLIC DOCUMENTS

U.S. Congress. House. Committee on House Administration. *The Presidential Campaign, 1976: Vol. 1, Part 1, Jimmy Carter.* 95th Cong., 2nd Sess., 1978.
_____. Committee on Science and Technology. *Special Conference with the Vice President on Science Policy.* 94th Cong., 2nd Sess., June 10, 1975.
_____. Committee on the Judiciary. *Report on the Confirmation of Nelson A. Rockefeller as Vice President of the United States.* 93rd Cong., 2nd Sess., December 17, 1974.
_____. Committee on the Judiciary. *Hearings on the Nomination of Nelson A. Rockefeller to Be Vice President of the United States.* 93rd Cong., 2nd Sess., 1974.
_____. Committee on the Judiciary. *Application of the Twenty-fifth Amendment to Vacancies in the Office of Vice President: Legislative History.* 93rd Cong., 1st Sess., 1973.
U.S. Congress. Senate. Committee on Banking, Housing, and Urban Affairs. *Hearings on the Energy Independence Act of 1975.* 94th Cong., 2nd Sess., 1976.
_____. Subcommittee on Constitutional Amendments of the Committee on the Judiciary. *Examination of the First Implementation of Section Two of the Twenty-fifth Amendment.* 94th Cong., 1st Sess., 1975.
_____. Committee on Rules and Administration. *Report on Hearings on the Nomination of Nelson A. Rockefeller of New York to Be Vice President of the United States.* 93rd Cong., 2nd Sess., 1974.
_____. Committee on Rules and Administration. *Hearings on the Nomination of Nelson A. Rockefeller to Be Vice President of the United States.* 93rd Cong., 2nd Sess., 1974.
_____. Subcommittee on Constitutional Amendments of the Committee on the Judiciary. *Selected Materials on the Twenty-fifth Amendment.* 93rd Cong., 1st Sess., 1973.
_____. Subcommittee on Reorganization of the Committee on Government Operations. *Report on Hearings on a Proposal to Create an Administrative Vice President.* 84th Cong., 2nd Sess., 1956.

_____. Subcommittee on Reorganization of the Committee on Government Operations. *Hearings on a Proposal to Create an Administrative Vice President.* 84th Cong., 2nd Sess., 1956.

U.S. Congress. Congressional Budget Office. *New York's Fiscal Problem: Its Origins, Potential Repercussions, and Some Alternative Policy Responses.* Background Paper No. 1. Washington, D.C.: Government Printing Office, 1975.

Office of the Vice President. *The Future of Freedom: Vice President Nelson A. Rockefeller Speaks Out on Issues Confronting Americans in Bicentennial 1976.* Washington, D.C.: Government Printing Office, 1976.

Executive Office of the President. Domestic Council. *White House Public Forums on Domestic Policy.* Washington, D.C.: Government Printing Office, 1975.

BOOKS

Albright, Joseph. *What Makes Spiro Run.* New York: Dodd Mead and Company, 1972.

Bayh, Birch. *One Heartbeat Away: Presidential Disability and Succession.* Indianapolis: The Bobbs-Merril Co., 1968.

Barber, James D. *The Presidential Character: Predicting Performance in the White House.* 2nd ed. Englewood Cliffs: Prentice-Hall, Inc., 1977.

Blum, John M., ed. *The Price of Vision: Diary of Henry A. Wallace, 1942-1946.* Boston: Houghton Mifflin Company, 1973.

Casserly, John J. *The Ford White House.* Boulder: Colorado University Press, 1977.

Chester, Lewis; Hodgson, Godfrey; and Page, Bruce. *An American Melodrama: The Presidential Campaign of 1968.* London: Andre Deutsch, 1969.

Cohen, Richard M., and Witcover, Jules. *A Heartbeat Away: The Investigation and Resignation of Vice President Spiro T. Agnew.* New York: Bantam Books, 1974.

Collier, Peter M., and Horowitz, David. *The Rockefellers: An American Dynasty.* New York: Holt, Rinehart and Winston, 1976.

Connery, Robert H., and Benjamin, Gerald. *Rockefeller of New York: Executive Power in the State House.* Ithaca: Cornell University Press, 1979.

_____, eds. *Governing New York State: The Rockefeller Years.* New York: Academy of Political Science, 1974.

Corwin, Edward S. *The President: Office and Powers.* 4th rev. ed. New York: New York University Press, 1957.

Cronin, Thomas E. *The State of the Presidency.* 2nd ed. Boston: Little, Brown and Company, 1980.

Desmond, James. *Nelson Rockefeller: A Political Biography.* New York: The MacMillan Company, 1964.

DiSalle, Michael V. *Second Choice.* New York: Hawthorn Books, 1966.

Dorman, Michael. *The Second Man: The Changing Role of the Vice President.* New York: Delacorte Press, 1968.

Evans, Rowland, and Novak, Robert. *Lyndon B. Johnson: The Exercise of Power.* New York: New American Library, 1966.

Feerick, John D. *The Twenty-fifth Amendment: Its Complete History and Earliest Applications.* New York: Fordham University Press, 1976.

_____. *From Failing Hands: The Story of Presidential Succession*. New York: Fordham University Press, 1965.

Ford, Gerald R. *A Time to Heal*. London: W. H. Allen, 1979.

Hamilton, Alexander; Madison, James; and Jay, John. *The Federalist Papers*. With an introduction by Clinton Rossiter. New York: New American Library, 1961.

Harwood, Michael. *In the Shadow of Presidents*. Philadelphia: J. B. Lippincott Company, 1966.

Hatch, Louis C. *A History of the Vice Presidency of the United States*. Revised and edited by Earl L. Shoup. New York: American Historical Society, 1934.

Humphrey, Hubert H. *The Education of a Public Man*. Garden City: Doubleday and Company, 1976.

Johnson, Richard T. *Managing the White House*. New York: Harper and Row, 1974.

Kessel, John H. *The Domestic Presidency: Decision Making in the White House*. North Scituate: Duxbury Press, 1975.

Kramer, Michael, and Roberts, Sam. *"I Never Wanted to Be Vice President of Anything!": An Investigative Biography of Nelson Rockefeller*. New York: Basic Books, 1976.

Levin, Peter R. *Seven by Chance: The Accidental Vice Presidents*. New York: Farrar, Strauss, 1948.

Lucas, Jim. *Agnew: Profile in Power*. New York: Scribners, 1970.

Madison, James. *Notes of Debates in the Federal Convention of 1787*, With an introduction by Adrienne Koch. Athens: Ohio University Press, 1966.

Morris, Joe A. *Nelson Rockefeller: A Biography*. New York: Harper and Row, 1960.

Moscow, Alvin. *The Rockefeller Inheritance*. Garden City: Doubleday and Company, 1977.

Nathan, Richard P. *The Plot That Failed: Nixon and the Administrative Presidency*. New York: John Wiley and Sons, 1975.

Neustadt, Richard E. *Presidential Power: With Reflections on Nixon and Johnson*. 2nd ed. New York: John Wiley and Sons, 1976.

Nixon, Richard M. *Six Crises*. Garden City: Doubleday and Company, 1962.

Osborne, John. *White House Watch: The Ford Years*. Washington, D.C.: New Republic Books, 1977.

Porter, Roger B. *Presidential Decision Making: The Economic Policy Board*. New York: Cambridge University Press, 1980.

Rather, Dan, and Gates, Paul. *The Palace Guard*. New York: Harper and Row, 1974.

Reeves, Richard. *A Ford not a Lincoln*. New York: Harcourt Brace Jovanovich, 1975.

Rockefeller, Nelson A. *Our Environment Can Be Saved*. Garden City: Doubleday and Company, Inc., 1970.

_____. *The Rockefeller Report on the Americas*. Chicago: Quadrangle Books, 1969.

_____. *Unity, Freedom, and Peace: A Blueprint for Tomorrow*. New York: Vintage Books, 1968.

_____. *The Future of Federalism*. New York: Atheneum, 1964.

Sindler, Allan P. *Unchosen Presidents: The Vice President and Other Frustrations of Presidential Succession*. Berkeley: University of California Press, 1976.

Sorensen, Theodore C. *Decision Making in the White House*. New York: Columbia University Press, 1963.

Teller, Edward; Mark, Hans M.; and Foster, John S. *Power and Security*. Critical Choices for Americans, vol. 4. Lexington: Lexington Books, 1976.

ter Horst, Jerald F. *Gerald Ford and the Future of the Presidency*. New York: The Third Press, 1974.

Thomas, Norman C., and Baade, Hans W., eds. *The Institutionalized Presidency*. Dobbs Ferry: Oceana Publications, Inc., 1972.

Truman, David B. *The Governmental Process*. New York: Alfred A. Knopf, 1951.

Waugh, Edgar W. *Second Consul, the Vice Presidency: Our Greatest Political Problem*. Indianapolis: Bobbs-Merrill, 1956.

White, Theodore H. *The Making of the President, 1964*. New York: Atheneum, 1965.

_____. *The Making of the President, 1960*. New York: Atheneum, 1961.

Williams, Irving G. *The American Vice Presidency: New Look*. Garden City: Doubleday and Company, 1954.

Young, Donald. *American Roulette: The History and Dilemma of the Vice Presidency*. Rev. ed. New York: Holt, Rinehart and Winston, 1972.

REPORTS

Commission on CIA Activities within the United States. *Report to the President*. Washington, D.C.: Government Printing Office, 1975.

Commission on the Organization of Government for the Conduct of Foreign Policy. *Report to the President and Congress*. Washington, D.C.: Government Printing Office, 1975.

Institute of Politics, *Report of the Study Group on Vice Presidential Selection*. John F. Kennedy School of Government. Cambridge: Harvard University, 1976.

National Center for Productivity and Quality of Working Life. *Report on Activities and Plans to the President and Congress*. Washington, D.C.: Government Printing Office, 1975.

National Commission on Water Quality. *Report to the Congress*. Washington, D.C.: Government Printing Office, 1976.

President's Panel on Federal Compensation, *Report to the President*. Washington, D.C.: Government Printing Office, 1975.

PROCEEDINGS

American Academy of Arts and Sciences. Proceedings, Fall 1975. *The Oil Crisis: In Perspective*. Vol. 104, no. 4. Cambridge: Harvard University, 1975.

American Academy of Political and Social Science. Annals, November, 1973. *The Energy Crisis: Reality or Myth*. Vol. 410. Lancaster, Penn.: American Academy of Political and Social Science, 1973.

ARTICLES

Baltz, Daniel J. "Economic Report/There's No End in Sight for New York's Money Problems." *National Journal*. Vol. 7, no. 48 (November 29, 1975): 1627-31.

Bendiner, Robert. "The Changing Role of the Vice President." *Colliers* 137 (February 17, 1956): 48-51.

Berman, Larry. "The Office of Management and Budget That Almost Wasn't." *Political Science Quarterly.* Vol. 92, no. 1 (1977): 281-303.

Beveridge, Albert J. "The Fifth Wheel in Our Government." *The Century Magazine* (December 1909): 208-14.

Bonafede, Dom. "Vice President Mondale—Carter's Partner with Portfolio." *National Journal.* Vol. 10, no. 10 (March 11, 1978): 376-84.

_____. "The Veep: A Heartbeat Away or Only as Close as the Polling Place?" *National Journal.* Vol. 8, no. 28 (July 10, 1976): 968-72.

_____. "What Me Worry? The Disappearance of Nelson Rockefeller." *Washingtonian.* May 1976, pp. 103-6.

_____. "White House Report/Domestic Council Tries to Match Early Promise." *National Journal.* Vol. 7, no. 50 (December 13, 1975): 1687-96.

Broder, David S. "The Veep." *Washington Post.* June 12, 1977.

Brower, Brock. "The Remaking of the Vice Presidency." *New York Times Magazine.* June 5, 1977, pp. 38ff.

Burns, James M. "A New Look at the Vice Presidency." *New York Times Magazine.* October 9, 1955, pp. 11ff.

Cameron, Juan. "Nelson Rockefeller's Metamorphosis as Vice President." *Fortune.* October, 1975, pp. 119-207.

Clark, Walter. "The Vice President: What to Do with Him?" *Green Bag.* Vol. 8 (October 1896): 427ff.

David, Paul T. "The Vice Presidency: Its Institutional Evolution and Contemporary Status." *Journal of Politics.* Vol. 29 (November 1967): 721-48.

Durham, G. Homer. "The Vice Presidency." *Western Political Quarterly.* Vol. 1 (1948): 311-15.

Ford, Gerald R. "On the Threshold of the White House." *Atlantic.* Vol. 234 (July 1974): 63-65.

Garner, John Nance. "This Job of Mine." *American Magazine.* Vol. 118 (July 1934): 23ff.

Graham, Donald. "The Vice Presidency: From Cigar Store Indian to Crown Prince." *Washington Monthly.* Vol. 6 (April 1974): 41-44.

Humphrey, Hubert H. "Changes in the Vice Presidency." *Current History.* Vol. 67 (August 1974): 58-59, 89-90.

Hyman, Sidney. "New Focus on the Vice Presidency." *New York Times Magazine.* March 27, 1960, pp. 23ff.

_____. "Between Throttlebottom and Jefferson." *New York Times Magazine.* March 28, 1954, pp. 12ff.

Learned, Henry B. "Casting Votes of the Vice Presidents, 1789-1915." *American Historical Review.* Vol. 20 (April 1915): 571-76.

Menez, Joseph F. "Needed: A New Concept of the Vice Presidency." *Social Science.* Vol. 30 (June 1955): 143-49.

Osborne, John. "Mondale at Work." *New Republic.* November 1, 1977, pp. 10-13.

Packman, Martin. "Vice Presidency." *Editorial Research Reports.* Vol. 1, no. 13 (April 4, 1956): 239-55.

Paullin, Charles O. "The Vice President and Cabinet." *American Historical Review.* Vol. 29 (April 1924): 496-500.

Roosevelt, Theodore. "The Three Vice Presidential Candidates and What They Represent." *The Review of Reviews.* Vol. 14 (September 1896): 289-97.

Ross, Earl D. "The National Spare Tire." *The North American Review.* Vol. 239 (March 1935): 275-79.

Rossiter, Clinton. "The Reform of the Vice Presidency." *Political Science Quarterly.* Vol. 63 (September 1948): 383-403.

Schlesinger, Arthur M., Jr. "On the Presidential Succession." *Political Science Quarterly.* Vol. 89 (Fall 1974): 475-505.

_____. "Is the Vice Presidency Necessary?" *Atlantic.* Vol. 233 (May 1974): 37-44.

Tolchin, Martin. "The Mondales: Making the Most of Being Number 2." *New York Times Magazine.* February 26, 1978.

Tubbessing, Carl D. "Vice Presidential Candidates and the Home State Advantage: Or 'Tom Who?' Was Tom Eagleton in Missouri." *Western Political Quarterly.* Vol. 26 (December 1973): 702-16.

Turner, Michael. "Reagan and the Vice Presidency." *Politics.* Vol. 1, no. 1 (April 1981): 29-35.

Waldman, Raymond J. "The Domestic Council: Innovation in Presidential Government." *Public Administration Review.* May/June 1976: 260-68.

Wallace, Henry A. "How a Vice President Is Picked." *U.S. News & World Report.* Vol. 40 (April 6, 1956): 86-89.

Williams, Irving G. "Senators, Rules, and Vice Presidents." *Thought Patterns.* New York: St. John's University, 1957, pp. 21-35.

Wildermung, Lucius, Jr. "The Vice Presidency." *Political Science Quarterly.* Vol. 68 (March 1953): 17-41.

Worshop, Richard L. "Vice Presidency." *Editorial Research Reports.* Vol. 2, no. 18 (November 11, 1970): 835-56.

UNPUBLISHED

Personal Archive of Nelson A. Rockefeller, Rockefeller Center, New York City, New York. Nelson A. Rockefeller's Vice Presidential Papers.

INTERVIEWS

Rockefeller, Nelson A. Vice President of the United States. Interview, December 21, 1977, Rockefeller Center, New York.

Vice President Rockefeller's Staff

Allison, G. Richard. Assistant to the Vice President. Interview, December 17, 1976, Washington, D.C.

Herter, Susan C. Chief of Staff to the Vice President. Interview, January 5, 1977, Washington, D.C.

Means, Grady. Special Assistant to the Vice President. Interview, January 10, 1977, Washington, D.C.

Morrow, Hugh. Press Secretary to the Vice President. Interviews, March 15, 1978, and December 21, 1977, Rockefeller Center, New York.

Mulliken, John H., Jr. Deputy Press Secretary to the Vice President. Interview, September 29, 1977, McLean, Virginia.

Overman, Dean. White House Fellow attached to the Vice President's Office. Interview, January 17, 1977, Washington, D.C.

Shafer, Raymond P. Counselor to the Vice President. Interview, January 17, 1977, Washington, D.C.

Veneman, John G. Counselor to the Vice President. Interviews, August 17, 1977, and November 4, 1976, Washington, D.C.

Wallison, Peter J. Counsel to the Vice President. Interview, August 17, 1977, Washington, D.C.

Domestic Council Staff

Cannon, James M. Executive Director and Assistant to the President. Interviews, February 23, 1978, and July 25, 1977, Washington, D.C.

Dunham, Richard L. Deputy Director. Interview, February 21, 1978, Washington, D.C.

Hanzlick, Rayburn D. Associate Director. Interview, January 5, 1977, Washington, D.C.

Hope, Judith R. Associate Director. Interview, January 13, 1977, Washington, D.C.

Humphreys, George. Associate Director. Interview, January 3, 1977, Washington, D.C.

Johnson, Spencer. Associate Director. Interview, January 13, 1977, Washington, D.C.

Lissy, David H. Associate Director. Interview, January 3, 1977, Washington, D.C.

May, Lynn. Associate Director. Interview, January 17, 1977, Washington, D.C.

Myer, Paul. Associate Director. Interview, December 28, 1976, Washington, D.C.

Parsons, Richard D. Counsel and Associate Director. Interview, July 15, 1977, Rockefeller Center, New York.

Quern, Arthur F. Deputy Director and Associate Director. Interview, December 15, 1976, Washington, D.C.

President Ford's Staff

Buchen, Philip W. Counsel to the President. Interview, February 8, 1978, Washington, D.C.

Cheney, Richard B. Assistant to the President. Interview, July 27, 1977, Washington D.C.

Hartmann, Robert T. Counselor to the President. Interviews, April 20 and April 11, 1978, Washington, D.C.

Lynn, James T. Director, Office of Management and Budget. Interview, July 29, 1977, Washington, D.C.

Marsh, John O., Jr. Counselor to the President. Interview, March 10 and February 8, 1978, Washington, D.C.

Seidman, L. William. Assistant to the President and Executive Director of the Economic Policy Board. Interview, August 29, 1977, Washington, D.C.

Zarb, Frank. Executive Director of the Energy Resources Council and Administrator of the Federal Energy Administration. Interview, July 29, 1977, Washington, D.C.

Other

Laird, Melvin R. Sometime adviser to Gerald R. Ford. Interview, February 1, 1978, Washington, D.C.

INDEX

About the Author

MICHAEL TURNER, presently Lecturer in Politics at Paisley College in Scotland, received his Ph.D. from the State University of New York at Binghamton. From 1974 to 1978 he was Associate Director of State University of New York's Internship Program in Washington, D.C. His articles have appeared in the *Journal of American Studies*, *Politics*, and *American Politics Group Work Papers*.